The Living
Organization

The Living Organization

SYSTEMS OF BEHAVIOR

Lane Tracy

PRAEGER

New York
Westport, Connecticut
London

Library of Congress Cataloging-in-Publication Data

Tracy, Lane, 1934–
    The living organization : systems of behavior / Lane Tracy.
      p. cm.
    Bibliography: p.
    Includes index.
    ISBN 0–275–93084–X (alk. paper)
    1. Organizational behavior. I. Title.
HD58.7.T73 1989
302.3′5—dc19   88–39746

Library of Congress Catalog Card Number: 88–39746
ISBN: 0–275–93084–X

First published in 1989

Praeger Publishers, One Madison Avenue, New York, NY 10010
A division of Greenwood Press, Inc.

Printed in the United States of America

The paper used in this book complies with the Permanent
Paper Standard issued by the National Information Standards
Organization (Z39.48—1984).

10 9 8 7 6 5 4 3 2 1

Contents

Figures and Tables

Preface

This book is a disciplined excursion through the world of organizations. It is also about the major components of organizations—individual people and groups—as well as their societal environment. The discipline is provided by living systems theory, as developed and expounded by James G. Miller (1978). From the viewpoint of this theory, organizations are alive; that is, they display the same basic functions, structures, and processes as other life forms such as amoeba, plants, and animals. Hence the title of this book, *The Living Organization*.

The subject matter of the book falls under the rubric of organizational behavior (OB), including both its micro and macro (or organization theory) aspects. Organizational behavior is a loosely defined field of study, encompassing various aspects of individual and group behavior within organizations and drawing upon the literature of psychology, sociology, cultural anthropology, and political science for many of its insights. As a field of study, OB lacks a theoretical backbone. The aim of this book is to provide one.

You will find some interesting juxtapositions of topics in this book. Topics that are normally not related, such as structure and role, value and goal, need and stress, perception and decision making, and exchange and conflict, are found together in the same chapters. These unusual combinations reflect the basic theme of the book: that all of the topics of OB are more closely linked than is usually realized.

The book tells more than is known about organizational behavior. In other words it speculates and is, undoubtedly, sometimes wrong. In this respect it is no different from any other OB book. Organizational behavior is a dynamic, rapidly changing field. What we don't know about it exceeds what we do know, and what we think we know is often proven wrong. Before the ink is dry in any OB book, many of its seeming verities will have been supplanted by new ones.

Even as I wrote this book, I found errors and inconsistencies in some of my earlier work and the published work of others. Somehow the corrections never quite catch up with the errors. Consequently, major errors have been perpetuated for decades in the OB literature, even after they were detected and proven wrong.

Wherever living systems theory highlights these errors, I have tried to make (or repeat) the necessary corrections.

Nevertheless, there is still much to be learned from some of the older literature in the field. You will find a number of references in this book to works from the 1930s to the 1960s whose ideas have withstood the test of time. They should not be ignored just because they are not currently fashionable, any more than a physicist would ignore Sir Isaac Newton's work because Newton wasn't aware of quantum mechanics. Indeed, some of these older works are more in tune with the systems approach than much of the current literature, which often deals with very narrow, specific issues.

This book is not a substitute for, or popularization of, Miller's *Living Systems*. I use various parts of living systems theory as a framework, but do not attempt to present the theory in full. The focus here is not on development of living systems theory per se. For that I can only recommend Miller's book, which is several times as long as this one.

The reader of this book is assumed to have at least a basic knowledge of general systems theory. Such concepts as concrete and abstract systems, open and closed systems, entropy and negentropy, environment and boundary, subsystem and component should be familiar to you. If they are not, you may wish to consult Chapter 2 of Miller's book or another systems text.

I acknowledge a considerable debt to James G. Miller, although I have met him only once in person. This book could not have been written without his seminal work in developing living systems theory. Takashi Hiroi, who studied and discussed *Living Systems* with me, helped me to gain a better understanding of that work. I am also beholden to James A. Lee, who reviewed the manuscript and offered many helpful comments, and to several anonymous reviewers of my papers on role conflict, need, motivation, power, and leadership, from which I drew liberally in the respective chapters of this book. Todd Brokaw assisted me in checking the references. The figures in the book were drawn by the staff of the Graphic Arts Department in Ohio University's Learning Resource Center. Diane Bennett assisted in proofreading the book.

The Living
Organization

Systems Concepts and Organizational Behavior

Organizational behavior is the study of organizations, their structure and processes, the functioning of their components, and their relationship to the physical and societal environment. The field of OB is broad, encompassing knowledge about the behavior of individuals, groups, and organizations themselves. It draws upon concepts, theories, and research findings from several other disciplines, notably psychology, sociology, cultural anthropology, and political science.

Developed from such eclectic origins, OB lacks a theoretical framework of its own. Various attempts have been made to draw together and integrate the bits and pieces of OB by means of systems theory, particularly the theory of open systems (Katz and Kahn 1978; Scott 1981). Although people, groups, and organizations are clearly open systems, that theory is very general and has little to say about the usual topics of OB.

This book employs Miller's (1978) living systems theory as a framework. As Ashmos and Huber (1987) pointed out, living systems theory holds much potential for the study of OB and management. The theory treats individuals, groups, organizations, and societies as levels of living systems possessing many characteristics in common—namely, the essential characteristics of life itself.

Within this theoretical framework various aspects of behavior that are usually treated as separate and distinct, using terminology that makes it difficult to see connections between them, become part of a whole. For instance, needs become a basic link between values, goals, communication, decision making, conflict, power, leadership, and all of the other usual OB topics. Together, these topics add up to different perspectives on a single entity, a living system.

The necessities of life are the driving force behind all aspects of behavior. Furthermore, the essential attributes of life are found at the level of the individual, group, organization, and society. Similarities in behavior across these levels are normally obscured by different terminologies and theoretical frameworks. Living systems theory provides a common framework and set of terms that allow us to see the forces of life at work in all of these levels of behavior.

DEFINING ORGANIZATIONAL BEHAVIOR

Organizations are, first of all, *open systems*. That is, an organization maintains a relatively stable structure and boundary while receiving inputs from the environment, processing them, and extruding outputs. The human components of organizations—individuals and groups—are also open systems. Furthermore, these open systems are composed primarily of living entities—cells, organs, and organisms. Miller (1978) characterized such systems as *living systems*, and developed a body of theory concerning their common characteristics. His theory of living systems goes beyond general and open systems theories in describing the vital subsystems and processes inherent in cells, organs, organisms, groups, organizations, and societies. It is natural, therefore, that living systems theory should be applied to the understanding of organizations and their behavior.

Succinctly, *organizational behavior* consists of the acts and thoughts of people in groups and organizations. This definition includes all individual behavior that is influenced by a group or organization. Likewise, the behavior of two people together—the smallest group—is included in organizational behavior. In a broad sense the definition also encompasses the "behavior" of groups and organizations; such behavior is an interactive combination of the acts and thoughts of the people in those social systems.

An *act* is a dynamic event involving processes of movement and/or change. When a person acts upon something, it is either to cause change or to prevent change that would otherwise occur (i.e., maintain a steady state). A person may act to obtain a new job or to protect the job he or she already has. The members of a work group may act to expel a deviant or to save the job of a member who is being fired. A business firm may act to gain new customers or to retain old ones. A nation may act to acquire new territory or to defend its borders.

An act may be directed at change within the system (internal change) or in its environment (external change). For example, in order to change an internal state of hunger a person must first cause change to occur in some article of food. This involves external acts such as gathering, cleaning, cutting, and cooking as well as internal acts of chewing and digesting. Members of a business organization act externally to gain new customers and internally to induce the system to process customers' orders.

The behavior of living systems is considered to be purposeful. Living systems fit the definition of purposeful systems proposed by Ackoff and Emery (1972). Their behavior is directed by a hierarchy of values that determines the purposes and goals of the system. All behavior serves the purposes of the system. Purposes lead to goals, which refer specifically to externally directed behavior.

Note that the definition of organizational behavior includes thoughts as well as acts. You might not have considered thoughts to be behavior at all. From a living systems point of view, however, behavior includes processing (i.e., movement or change) of information as well as matter and energy. External information processing is called *communication*. Thoughts are internal information processes.

The definition of organizational behavior given above is a broad one. Some authors confine the term to individual and group behavior in organizations (the micro level), reserving the term *organization theory* for the study of behavior at the organizational (or macro) level. This book encompasses both micro- and macro-level topics. The behavior of individuals, groups, and organizations is treated equally and concurrently. Such treatment is both necessitated and facilitated by the living systems approach, because a common set of concepts and models is applied to all three levels.

The value of other approaches is not denied. Indeed, living systems theory subsumes many of them, including open systems theory and exchange theory (Ekeh 1974; Pfeffer and Salancik 1978). However, living systems theory goes beyond these approaches and, in the process, reveals gaps and flaws in some of the earlier models of organizational behavior.

LEVELS OF ANALYSIS

Organizational behavior can be studied at several levels of analysis. Psychologists approach social behavior from the individual level by studying such topics as attitudes, needs, learning, and motivation. Social psychologists and sociologists focus instead on interactions between people and within groups. Power, influence, communication, norms, and group cohesiveness are some of the variables that are important at this level. Organization theorists view behavior from the organizational level. They are concerned with such matters as chain of command, roles and role conflict, commitment to organizational goals, organizational design and change, climate, and culture. Some of these organizational concepts are borrowed from political science and cultural anthropology, disciplines that focus on the societal level.

Is there a best way to view organizational behavior? Is the organization more important than the individual, or do organizations exist only to serve the needs of individuals? There are no universally accepted answers to these questions. Obviously, organizations cannot exist without individual members, but it seems equally true that human individuals cannot survive without groups and organizations. At a minimum the protection and nurturance provided by a family are essential for development to adulthood. In modern society it would also be difficult to survive without the infrastructure of organizations that provide us with food, water, clothing, shelter, electric power, communication facilities, and knowledge. The tendency to form, join, and interact with organizations, groups, and other collectivities of people appears to be an integral part of human nature (Wilson 1975: pt. 1; Hayek 1978: ch. 1).

Western culture tends to emphasize the importance of the individual. Organizations and institutions are seen as existing to provide for individual needs. Personal happiness, either individually or in the aggregate, is the most common measure of good in Western societies. As an example, we seem to believe that every adult should have an automobile, even though this is a very inefficient use of scarce resources. Reliance on public transportation would be more efficient but would limit an individual's freedom of movement.

Non-Western cultures are much more apt to emphasize the importance of the family, clan, group, organization, or society. It is considered a duty and an honor for the individual to serve the family, firm, or nation. An individual life may mean little in the greater scheme of things. Under some Eastern philosophies an individual is merely the current receptacle for a soul that has passed through many reincarnations. Thus people from non-Western cultures often find it difficult to understand the Western cult of individualism.

It is not my purpose here to discuss the merits of these views. The point is simply that different views exist and can be defended. It is possible to study organizational behavior from the point of view of the individual, the group, or the organization. Living systems theory allows us to treat all three levels equally and simultaneously.

LIVING SYSTEMS—A BROADER PERSPECTIVE

Living systems are concrete, open systems possessing the characteristics of life. Among other things, that means they are composed primarily of organic compounds and are generated by genetic and/or memetic templates. They actively regulate themselves to maintain steady states of negentropy, as well as to grow, develop, and propagate. In other words, living systems strive purposefully to preserve their own system or structure against entropy, the universal tendency toward disintegration (Miller 1978: 18).

As open systems, living systems must regularly acquire resources to replace those that are consumed by the transformation processes of the system or lost through dissipation and extrusion. Some resources are derived from the nonliving part of the environment, but much of the input comes from other living systems. The products or "wastes" extruded by one system may be valuable inputs to another.

Much of organizational behavior is involved with the exchange of resources between living systems. Such exchanges will be a major theme of this book. To portray them we will employ a simple model called the *systems dyad*, shown in Figure 1-1. This model emphasizes the fact that the typical exchange is two-way, and that other sources and receivers may exist. In some cases the links between the systems become so strong that the dyad itself becomes a living system.

Living systems include all forms of animal and plant life as well as organized groupings (social systems) of organisms. Miller identified seven levels of living systems: cell, organ, organism, group, organization, society, and supranational. In this book we will be concerned primarily with the subset of human systems and with the middle levels—individuals, groups, and organizations.

Figure 1–1
Systems Dyad

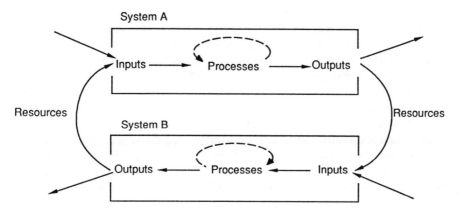

Origins of Life

No one knows for certain how life began on Earth. Some biologists paint a scenario in which the building blocks of life, such as amino acids, emerged from a primordial "soup" of chemicals (Oparin 1957; Rush 1957). Under the right conditions of temperature and pressure and with the aid of external sources of energy such as sunlight, cosmic rays, and lightning, atoms combined to form larger and larger molecules. Growth was directed by the structure of atoms and molecules that permitted some combinations and inhibited others. In this scenario we see at the most elemental level two prerequisites of life: available matter-energy, and information that provides a pattern or template for growth.

At some point in Earth's history certain molecules became so large and complex that they took on characteristics of life. That is, they became capable of acquiring resources from their environment and building replicas of themselves. The information aspect of the molecule was then able to reproduce itself with another collection of atoms, adding structure where it did not exist before. The molecule became a template for building new molecules in its own image. The ability to obtain resources from the environment meant that the molecule could add to its store of matter-energy in order to grow or to replace losses. The molecule, or at least its information aspect, became potentially immortal, limited only by continued availability of resources and existence of favorable conditions in the environment.

These living, reproducing molecules eventually developed ways of surrounding themselves with a captive environment and evolved into the first cells. Single-celled organisms developed into multicelled organisms. Specialization among certain groups of cells evolved into specialized organs, permitting more elaborate organisms to develop. Cells, organs, and organisms formed three levels of living systems, each having the basic characteristics of life.

Dawkins (1976) depicts the development of living systems from the unique viewpoint of genes. Genes have the ability to replicate themselves and to serve as a template for the growth of surrounding systems. This ability allows genes to proliferate structures that enhance the potential for genetic survival. Thus cells, organs, and organisms may be seen as "survival machines" built by genes to cope with such environmental changes as the thinning of the primordial soup and the development of predators.

Even social systems such as the family and the hunting pack can be linked to the struggle of genes for survival and propagation. Barash (1979) describes some of the curious ways in which social behavior can be traced to genetic survival. At the social level, however, a new element, the meme, is encountered. *Memes* are self-replicating ideas (Dawkins 1976: ch. 11; Hofstadter 1985: ch. 3; Drexler 1986: 35-38). For instance, such concepts as democracy and monogamy are memes, because they tend to generate social systems that pass the concept from generation to generation. But a meme can be something as simple as a song or a new fashion in clothing, so long as it induces living systems to propagate it.

Memes have some of the same characteristics as genes. The essence of memes, as with genes, is information (i.e., structure or pattern) that is capable of replicating itself. Memes require survival machines for their maintenance, actualization, and propagation. Memes are potentially immortal, although subject to mutation. As genes generate various patterns of life at the cellular, organic, and organismic levels, memes generate a variety of cultural patterns among individuals, groups, organizations, and societies.

Genes and memes form the *template* or *charter* of a living system. The template/charter is a set of instructions outlining the basic structure and processes of the system. This blueprint must exist from the moment of origin of the system, although it may subsequently be modified. Genes provide the basic template for cells, organs, and organisms, and may also influence groups, organizations, and societies. Memes and genes together provide the charters for social systems.

Living systems theory is the study of the basic structures and processes found in the survival machines that are generated by genes and memes. To the extent that common structures and functions can be identified at all levels among these living carriers of genetic and memetic information, these common features may be regarded as basic requisites of a living system.

Imperatives of Life

Genes, memes, and their host living systems display several broad purposes or imperatives. The first is immediate survival through *maintenance of steady states*. In the short term a living system consists of a large number of relationships or variables that must be held at or near steady states. For example, the human body must maintain a fairly constant heartbeat, metabolism, temperature, flow of oxygen, level of iron in the blood, and so on. Likewise, a business firm must maintain reasonably steady cash flow, level of inventory, supplies of materials and energy, employees, and so forth. In order to maintain such steady states under entropic conditions, the system must regularly take in fresh resources such as food or sales orders. For memes the system must also maintain memory and/or social order.

Living systems can exist only in an environment that stays within narrow ranges of temperature, air pressure, and other variables. Thus a living system may act to try to maintain steady states in the environment as well as within itself. Astronauts and deep-sea divers, for example, take their normal environment with them when they enter environmental conditions that would not support life. In a subtler way the quest for world peace is an attempt to maintain an environment conducive to human life.

When the environment does change or the system itself gains or loses capabilities, maintenance of certain steady states may require deliberate change in others. Adaptation to change, when the basic aim is to maintain the health and integrity of the system, falls within the maintenance imperative.

The second imperative is *actualization of the system's potential*. Actualization generally requires both growth (i.e., incorporation of additional elements into the system) and development (i.e., elaboration of the system to cope with greater complexity in the environment). The aim of this sort of change is purposeful expansion of the system's capabilities, not simply adaptation to maintain the existing system.

Growth and development are long-term survival strategies built into the templates of living systems. Larger and more elaborate systems tend to be better able to control their environment; they feed on smaller and simpler systems. Furthermore, memes may demand actualization. Ideas such as capitalism, communism, superconductivity, thermonuclear reaction, and Velcro cannot simply remain on the drawing board; they must be tried. Some memes seem inevitably to spawn decades, even centuries, of investigation, analysis, elaboration, and development into practice or hardware.

The third imperative is *propagation of the system* through reproduction and/or dissemination. Each gene strives to perpetuate its peculiar pattern. The current survival machine cannot be maintained forever, but in theory the gene or meme can. Reproduction is the ultimate mechanism for genetic survival. For memes, dissemination serves a similar function. The more widespread an idea is, the more likely it will survive.

Levels of Living Systems

Miller (1978: 1) observed that social systems exhibit many of the same basic characteristics as cells, organs, and organisms. He identified four higher levels of living systems: groups, organizations, societies, and supranationals. The seven levels of living systems and their relationships to each other and to the nonliving environment are shown in Figure 1–2.

Figure 1–2
Levels of Living Systems and Nonliving Environment

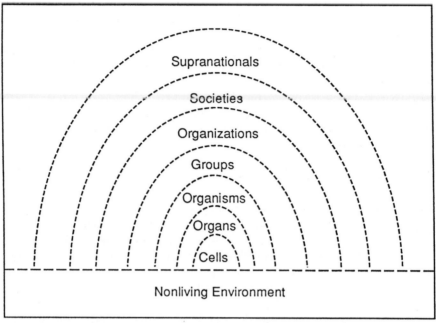

Systems at each level serve as suprasystems for systems at the next lower level. Thus the United Nations (a supranational) is a suprasystem, albeit a weak one, for the nations (societies) of the Earth. General Motors Corporation (an organization) is a suprasystem for its employees as well as a component of its suprasystems, the United States and other nations in which it operates.

Suprasystems provide a certain amount of guidance and training for their component systems. For example, the family (a group) provides training for its member organisms in language, customs, morals, survival techniques, and many other matters. Thus there is a passing downward of memetic heritage just as there is an upward flow of genetic heritage.

SYSTEMS CHARACTERISTICS OF LIFE

Living systems theory applies to people, groups, and organizations because they all share certain characteristics of life. By means of an exhaustive review of literature in the life and social sciences—biology, botany, microbiology, physiology, zoology, psychology, sociology, anthropology, and political science—Miller (1978: 18) was able to extract a set of general characteristics of all living systems. These characteristics are listed in Table 1-1.

Table 1–1
General Characteristics of Living Systems

1. They are concrete systems largely composed of organic compounds, although they may include nonliving components (e.g. dental fillings, clothes, weapons, tools, buildings).

2. They are open systems, receiving inputs, processing them, and releasing outputs.

3. They maintain steady states of negentropy, but at the same time they tend to grow in size and complexity and to reproduce themselves or disseminate parts of their structure.

4. They possess a template from the moment of origin. The template may be encoded in genetic material, written documents, or oral culture and custom. The template provides primary instructions for the development and functioning of the system's structures and processes. Additional instructions may come from the templates of subsystems and suprasystems.

5. They each possess a decider subsystem that controls the interactions of all other subsystems and components of the system. The decider also mediates conflicting instructions from various subsystems and suprasystems.

6. They also possess or have access to 18 other critical subsystems having functions of reproduction, matter–energy processing, or information processing. The subsystems are integrated by template and decider into an actively self–regulating, developing system with purposes and goals.

7. They can exist only in an environment that stays within narrow ranges of temperature, air pressure, and other variables. They monitor and act upon the environment to try to maintain these necessary conditions.

Source: Miller (1978: 18).

We have already discussed several of these characteristics, including the fact that living systems are concrete, open systems; that they display imperatives of maintenance, actualization, and propagation (a characteristic not listed by Miller); and that they possess a genetic and/or memetic template. The subsystem structure of living systems will be discussed in detail in Chapter 2. The decider subsystem, because of its importance, will receive further attention in Chapter 6.

Perhaps the only characteristic that requires elaboration at this point is the need for a supportive environment. Life was created originally out of an environment that provided the necessary matter and energy to sustain certain chemical reactions. Cells developed some ability to store needed resources and protect themselves from adverse conditions, and each successive level of living systems expanded these capabilities. The scientific literature on plans for deep-sea and space exploration provides an interesting glimpse of how living systems continue to extend the range of environments within which life can exist. Nevertheless, there are still limits to the ability of living systems to sustain themselves. As open systems, they require a continued flow of new resources. Boundary and supporter subsystems break down when there is too great a differential of temperature or pressure between a system and its environment.

Considering the characteristics of living systems as a whole, everything seems aimed at preservation and extension of the system. Living systems act to stem, and in a limited way reverse, the universal tide of entropy. They do so by maintaining, actualizing, and propagating their own particular brand of order. These are their primary imperatives, as mandated by their templates.

SUMMARY AND IMPLICATIONS

This chapter has laid the framework for discussion of many facets of human behavior in organizations. Organizational behavior occurs within and between human individuals, groups, and organizations, all of which by definition are living systems. Thus we have examined some of the characteristics of living systems. This chapter has also defined a number of concepts that will be needed in subsequent chapters.

At this point you may think that we are taking an unusually roundabout route to get at how and why people behave as they do in organizations. Why can't we start with actual behavior and bring in the systems concepts later, if necessary? The answer lies in the fragmented nature of what is known about organizational behavior. There are considerable bodies of theory and research about such aspects of human behavior as needs, perception, motivation, communication, learning, roles, decision making, power, leadership, and conflict, but each aspect tends to have its own set of concepts. It becomes difficult to relate needs to motivation or decision making to leadership if we do not first establish a common set of concepts and a framework within which to view each aspect as part of a whole. Living systems theory supplies the concepts and framework.

The living systems framework also helps us to remember that the basic purpose of this book is to understand, predict, and, if possible, influence the behavior of people, groups, and organizations. When examining a particular topic such as learning, we are apt to focus so narrowly on that aspect of behavior that we forget how it relates to other aspects. A living systems approach requires that we consider the interrelationships of all subsystems, structures, and processes. In other words, we must constantly keep in mind the whole system as we examine its parts. Needs and perceptions don't live; people and organizations live. We study leadership because of its importance to groups and organizations, not for its own sake. Living systems theory puts each separate topic in its proper perspective.

The greatest advantage of the living systems approach to organizational behavior is that the theory provides a way of treating individuals, groups, and organizations simultaneously. If we wish to examine the process of communication, for instance, living systems theory treats it in terms that apply equally to the human nervous system, the "grapevine," or a management information system. This makes it easier to deal with the interaction between levels when we examine a situation such as communication between an individual and an organization.

Living systems theory does have limitations. Human beings possess unique characteristics that are not shared by other living systems. Likewise individuals, groups, and organizations each have unique facets (called *emergents*) in addition to those that they share with each other. Life forms generated by memes differ from those that are generated by genes. This book will not ignore the uniqueness of each level of human systems as it attempts to put together an integrated picture of organizational behavior. Nevertheless, it is the commonality of characteristics across levels that will provide the focus for the book.

2

Structure and Process

Concrete systems such as organisms and organizations may be viewed statically or dynamically. A holographic X-ray photograph of a living system would reveal its *structure*, which Miller (1978: 22) defines as "the arrangement of its subsystems and components in three-dimensional space at a given moment of time." A series of such photos would show *process*, defined as "all change over time of matter-energy or information in a system" (Miller 1978: 23).

Processes may be reversible or irreversible. All processes involve expenditure of energy, and such expenditure is irreversible. If sufficient energy is available, however, most other processes can be reversed. That is, in a chronological series of photos, structure would be seen to change and then return to its former state. Life would be impossible without this reversibility of process, because life is largely a matter of returning over and over again to certain steady states after they have been disturbed. Such reversible processes are considered to be the *function* of a living system (Miller 1978: 23).

Of primary concern in living systems theory are the structures designated by Miller as critical subsystems which, as will be described in detail below, perform certain processes that "are necessary for life and must be carried out by all living systems that survive or be performed for them by some other system" (Miller 1978: 32). Typically, critical subsystems are not associated with any single component of the system and are not easily identified by their structure. Rather, they are defined by the functional system requirements that they fulfill, that is, the vital processes they carry out.

Physiology and organizational design focus on structure, whereas psychology and organizational behavior concentrate on process. Living systems theory tries to keep both structure and process in perspective, reminding us of the functional logic underlying structure. When we examine the structure of an organization from a living systems perspective, we do not see the traditional arrangement of departments and divisions linked by a hierarchy of authority. Instead, we are confronted with a set of critical subsystems linked in complex ways and governed largely by a decider subsystem. These subsystems share components in such a way that it is difficult to assign any given component exclusively to a particular subsystem. The "structure" suggested by such a picture is necessarily fluid and overlapping. Nevertheless, we will find that the concept of role can be used as a link between process and structure.

In this chapter nineteen critical subsystems will be defined and their processes and structures will be described as they manifest themselves in human individuals and organizations. This picture of subsystem structure and process will then be compared with the traditional organization theory view of organizational design. The concepts of specialization, differentiation, integration, and centralization will be discussed. Role will be developed as a general concept linking components to the structure and processes of the systems to which they belong. Finally, implications for theory and practice will be drawn from the discussion of structure and process.

CRITICAL SUBSYSTEMS

The survival and health of individuals, groups, organizations, and societies depend on performance and coordination of a set of essential processes. In all, Miller identified nineteen critical subsystems carrying out these processes at every level.[1] For example, a channel and net subsystem to convey information from one part of the system to another was found to be necessary in cells as well as societies. The nature of that subsystem might vary, but the function remained the same.

Note that Miller was not drawing analogies between system levels. He did not say that the human nervous system serves as an analogy to help us understand the data transmission process within an organization. Rather, he induced that the same data transmission processes are necessary at both levels and that each system must have a channel and net subsystem to provide these functions. The similarity between levels derives from the intrinsic nature of living systems, of which human individuals and organizations are examples.

Some critical subsystems process matter-energy, some process information, and some process both. As these subsystems have much to do with organizational behavior, we will now examine them in detail. The nineteen critical subsystems are listed in Table 2–1 and arranged to show a rough correspondence between matter-energy and information processing subsystems.

Subsystems Processing Matter-Energy and Information

The name of each subsystem indicates its basic function. Names will be amplified with brief definitions. To illustrate how each subsystem may manifest itself in terms of structure and process, a human individual and a manufacturing organization will be used as comparative examples.

Reproducer. The reproducer subsystem provides the template and the matter-energy processes necessary to produce other systems similar to the one it is

Table 2–1
The Nineteen Critical Subsystems of a Living System

A. SUBSYSTEMS WHICH PROCESS BOTH MATTER-ENERGY AND INFORMATION

                              1. Reproducer

                              2. Boundary

B. SUBSYSTEMS WHICH PROCESS   C. SUBSYSTEMS WHICH PROCESS
    MATTER-ENERGY   INFORMATION

     3. Ingestor   11. Input transducer

                                           12. Internal transducer

     4. Distributor   13. Channel and net

     5. Converter   14. Decoder

     6. Producer   15. Associator

     7. Matter-energy storage   16. Memory

                                           17. Decider

                                           18. Encoder

     8. Extruder ⎫
                    ⎬   19. Output transducer
     9. Motor   ⎭

     10. Supporter

Source: Adapted from Miller (1978: 54).

in. For individuals the reproducer subsystem obviously includes the male and female reproductive organs. They reproduce not only bone and flesh, but also the genetic information of the parents. Less obviously, the reproductive subsystem includes certain hormones, ova and sperm, lactating breasts, and the structures and processes required by training and caring for children.

The reproducer subsystem of an organization is any individual, group, or department that produces a new organization with an implicit or explicit charter similar to the whole or some part of the original organization's charter. The charter programs the new organization by specifying such parameters as purposes and goals, functions and subsystems to carry them out, policies and procedures, products and processes, capital and ownership.

The reproducer may assemble the new organization with components taken from the original or may simply spin off part of the original. For instance, the Bell System was required to divide into several independent firms in settlement of an antitrust suit; the result was several "Baby Bells." The new organization may also include components, and even ideas, that were not part of the original. When a firm decides to launch into an entirely new line of business, it typically copies some ideas from successful firms in that line and incorporates them into the charter. In the case of a franchise or manufacturing license agreement, the copying is done with the approval of the prototype organization. A firm may also hire people away from another firm in order to start a new organization.

Boundary. The boundary is "the subsystem at the perimeter of a system that holds together the components which make up the system, protects them from environmental stresses, and excludes or permits entry to various sorts of matter-energy and information" (Miller 1978: 56). The boundary of human beings consists of their skin, hair, nails, and membranes such as the cornea of the eye, the eardrum, and the mucous membrane lining the digestive tract. It may also include artifacts such as clothing or suntan oil.

The boundary selectively permits matter-energy and information to enter and leave the system. For instance, skin permits heat to enter the body, but keeps out harmful bacteria. Skin also permits the intake of information through touch receptors and the extrusion of heat and waste products through sweat glands. Closing the eyelids keeps out unwanted light energy and information.

The boundary of a manufacturing firm consists of people in many specialized positions: guards and security personnel, receiving-room and mail-room clerks, receptionists and secretaries, purchasing agents, quality control inspectors, janitorial staff, personnel interviewers, and credit departments. Buildings and fences are boundary artifacts.

Although Miller regards the decider as the most critical and distinguishing subsystem, other theorists distinguish systems by their boundaries. According to Kaufman (1985: 12–16), a system is alive so long as it is able to maintain its boundary. A dead body or a moribund organization quickly loses this ability.

Matter-Energy Processing Subsystems

Ingestor. The ingestor is the subsystem that brings matter-energy into the system across its boundary. The hands, mouth, and nostrils are components of the human ingestor system. A fork or a syringe would be an artifact of that subsystem.

Many components of an organization's boundary are also components of its ingestor subsystem. Purchasers and receiving-dock and mail-room personnel bring in materials; receptionists and personnel departments process inputs of people. Water and gas mains, electric lines and outlets, and windows and fans are artifacts in the ingestor subsystem.

Distributor. The distributor subsystem carries matter-energy throughout the system wherever it is needed. The matter-energy may come from the environment through the ingestor, from another internal process, or from storage. In humans the distributor subsystem consists of the blood vascular system, including the heart, and the lymph vascular system. Blood carries oxygen, carbohydrates, and other substances from the gastrointestinal tract and lungs to cells throughout the body. Blood also picks up carbon dioxide and other waste materials from the cells and carries them to a place where they can be extruded from the system.

A manufacturer's distributor subsystem encompasses components such as material handlers, truck and fork-lift drivers, mail distributors, clerks, and "go-fers." A business firm usually relies heavily on artifacts to carry out distributor processes. Pipes, conveyor belts, fork-lifts, moving bins, and elevators are some of the artifacts commonly found in the distributor subsystem. Part of the distributor may also be dispersed to other organizations. The movement of parts and subassemblies from one company plant to another is often handled by an independent trucking firm, express package delivery, or parcel post.

Converter. As its name implies, the converter subsystem converts or changes inputs into forms that are more useful to the system. The human converter consists of the gastrointestinal tract plus the liver, pancreas and gall bladder. The mouth and teeth grind food into small particles, saliva and other juices soften and dissolve it, and enzymes break it down into simpler molecules. Humans often use artifacts such as cutlery and cooking utensils to aid the conversion process.

The converter subsystem of a manufacturing firm usually changes matter into energy or more useful forms of matter. For instance, the boiler room converts coal, oil, or natural gas into steam or electrical power, which is then used in manufacturing processes. Chemical processes may convert raw chemicals into plastics to be molded.

Converter processes are often dispersed to other organizations. The manufacturing firm may depend on an electric utility to supply electrical power instead of doing the conversion itself. Raw materials often enter the firm in a preprocessed state. An automobile manufacturer, for instance, receives inputs of steel and aluminum, not iron ore and bauxite. Machinery artifacts are often more prominent and numerous than people in a manufacturer's converter subsystem.

Producer. The producer subsystem takes matter-energy inputs directly or from the converter and synthesizes them into new materials. These new materials may be used by the system to provide energy, repair damage, or grow. They may also be extruded as trade goods or waste. Cells are the basic producers. Cells process oxygen and carbohydrates to produce heat and carbon dioxide. Muscle cells produce movement of the limbs, which may in turn produce trade goods or services. Cells in certain organs produce enzymes, hormones, or electrochemical discharges.

The manufacturer's producer subsystem synthesizes materials that become outputs of products or services to the firm's environment, as well as wastes and materials for growth and maintenance of the firm itself. A tire manufacturer, for example, produces tires for sale and scrap rubber, but it also may produce tire molds for its own use.

Production is often considered the primary function of a manufacturing firm. Nevertheless, some parts of the producer subsystem may be supplied by other firms through subcontracting or purchasing. Machinery artifacts are heavily used in production.

Matter-energy storage. The human body ingests and produces more of many substances than it can immediately use. The excess may be held in the matter-energy storage subsystem for future use. Fats and sugars are stored in various tissues, calcium is stored in the bones, wastes are stored in the bladder and bowels.

The matter-energy storage subsystem in a manufacturing firm includes warehouse attendants, inventory clerks, and file clerks (for the physical files). They use artifacts such as warehouses, garages, pallets, shelves, tanks, bins, and file cabinets. Some storage is dispersed to other systems, as when a firm depends on the city for water storage. We could also say that employees are "stored" in their homes when not at work.

Extruder. The extruder subsystem transmits products and wastes across the boundary and out of the system. Extrusion occurs through the nose, mouth, urethra, anus, birth canal, breasts, and sweat glands. The lungs and kidneys are also part of the extruder subsystem.

A manufacturing firm's products are extruded by employees in packaging, shipping, mail room, and delivery with the help of artifacts such as loading platforms, trucks, and railway cars. Waste is extruded by janitors and by artifacts such as sewers, smokestacks, and trash containers.

Motor. The motor subsystem moves the system itself or parts of it, as well as components of the environment. In humans this subsystem consists primarily of striated skeletal muscles and the bones to which they are attached. The motor subsystem is comparable to the extruder because the motor puts out energy and the extruder puts out matter. Humans use many artifacts as adjuncts to their motor subsystem—for example, automobiles, wheelchairs, bicycles, and all kinds of tools.

The motor subsystem of a manufacturing firm would act upon the environment, rather than moving the firm itself. (The motor subsystem of an ocean-going fishing and fish-processing vessel or a traveling theatrical company would move the organization, however.) The motor might include earth movers or cranes and their drivers. Some motor functions are likely to be dispersed to other firms, such as mining and lumbering, that use tools to extract and transport resources.

Supporter. The supporter subsystem separates the various components of the system and maintains the proper spatial relationship between them so that they do not crowd each other. In humans this subsystem consists of the skeleton and muscles, together with artifacts such as chairs, beds, and braces.

The firm's supporter subsystem consists of land and artifacts such as buildings and platforms. The physical arrangement of machinery in a manufacturing firm tends to be fixed, but not the positioning of people.

Information Processing Subsystems

Input transducer. The input transducer subsystem serves the same function with respect to information that the ingestor serves for matter-energy. That is, the input transducer brings information-bearing markers across the boundary and into the system. (A *marker* is a physical representation of information in the form of a structure, pattern, relationship, or interaction of matter-energy.)

The input transducer also converts markers into other forms of matter-energy more suitable for transmission within the system. Eyes receive light markers, ears sense motion and sound markers, the nose and tongue sense chemically coded data, and nerve fibers in the skin sense temperature and pressure. Each of these transducers changes the original markers into electrochemical impulses for transmission to the brain. Artifacts such as hearing aids, eyeglasses, radios, and telephones may be included in the input transducer subsystem.

A manufacturing firm's input transducer consists of people in such departments as marketing research, sales, purchasing, personnel, legal, accounts receivable, and product research. These people obtain information from the environment. In some cases they also transfer the information to different markers, as when a secretary receives a message by phone and notes it on a memo pad. The firm may disperse parts of this subsystem to consultants or research firms.

Internal transducer. The internal transducer subsystem receives information-bearing markers from other subsystems or components of the system and converts the markers into nerve impulses. The receptors are nerve endings similar to those found in the input transducer. Internal transducers receive data about significant changes in subsystems or components. For example, a toothache signals development of a cavity.

The internal transducer subsystem of a firm includes any employee who makes internal reports on the status of, or changes in, variables of the system's components or subsystems. A machine operator reporting a machine malfunction, a union steward transmitting a grievance, a supervisor reporting that the department is running on schedule, and an accountant signaling that a department is running over its budget are all performing internal transducer functions. Individuals may also transduce their own information inputs, as when an employee puts an idea in the suggestion box. Computerized management information systems have become an important artifact of the internal transducer, either collecting data directly or having it fed in by terminal operators.

Channel and net. The channel and net subsystem carries information-bearing markers to and from all parts of the body. It serves the same function for information that the distributor serves for matter-energy. There are two basic networks, the nervous system and the endocrine net, that are interconnected at several points.

Everyone in an organization is connected to the channel and net subsystem, either at the end of a channel or at a node. People at nodes, such as switchboard operators, secretaries, and managers at all levels, may act simply as transmitters of information or as deciders. That is, they may choose to transmit all, part, or none of a message, or they may distort it. They may decide who should receive the message. They may act as input transducers and add their own information to the message. Channels include word-of-mouth in person or by phone, memos, letters, and electronic mail, with their attendant artifacts. Part of the subsystem may be dispersed to other firms such as a telephone company or messenger service.

Decoder. Each living system has its own private internal code for information. Data obtained through the input and internal transducers must be decoded and recoded into this private code by the decoder subsystem. Much of this decoding and recoding occurs as soon as the information is brought into the system, that is, in the sense organs and nerve endings. There are several echelons in the human decoder subsystem. Information may be recoded several times before it reaches the central nervous system.

Much of the information collected by the input and internal transducers of a manufacturing firm is already in a code that is readable by the system. Some decoding is necessary, however. Orders are processed into special codes that specify part numbers and quantities. Computers decode information directly gathered from sensors into digital form and thence into numbers and words. A manager decodes the angry countenance and belligerent stance of an employee into thoughts about the employee's attitude. The people who do such decoding and the machines they use for the purpose make up the decoder subsystem.

Associator. The associator subsystem carries out a learning process of forming links or associations among various items of information. In humans the associator is located chiefly in the cerebral cortex. The associator is analogous to the producer in the sense that an association between two or more bits of information is a new bit of information. That is, putting bits of data together is like combining elements such as carbon and oxygen; the result is something more than the sum of the parts.

The firm's associator subsystem is downwardly dispersed to its members. A machine operator associates a new method with its output and learns that the method is faster. A supervisor learns that one operator is better than another at a particular task. A salesperson associates a successful sale with a new approach. Every employee of the firm is a component of the associator. Through communication, one person's association can spread throughout the system. Computers can also be programmed to do some associating.

Memory. The memory subsystem completes the learning process. It stores original bits of information and associations so that the total information in the system can grow over time. Memory processes involve input (recording or memorizing), maintenance (retention and rerecording as well as forgetting), and output (retrieval or remembering). Humans use artifacts such as books, memos, diaries, files, and recordings to aid the memory subsystem.

Many individuals, groups, and departments are involved in the memory subsystem of a manufacturing firm. The accounting department keeps financial records; clerks and secretaries in various departments maintain files of correspondence and record appointments on calendars; computer librarians store tapes and disks. Blueprints are filed and archives of the history of the business are kept. Much business information is also stored in the memories of individual employees. Memory artifacts include books, microfilms, magnetic tapes and disks, and filing cabinets.

Decider. The decider subsystem is the most essential of all, according to Miller (1978: 32). It is the executive center that receives data from various sources through the channel and net and sends control information (orders) to all parts of the system. Decision making involves four stages: (1) establishing purposes and goals; (2) analyzing discrepancies between the current state of variables and their desired state, (3) synthesizing and choosing a plan of action to attain the desired state, and (4) implementing the plan by issuing appropriate commands. Human artifacts of this subsystem include handbooks, algorithms, and computers.

The decider is the executive subsystem of the firm. The top echelon of the decider may be the board of directors as a group or an individual such as the chairman of the board or chief executive officer. The top echelon determines purposes and goals for the firm and exercises overall control. Organizations differ in the degree of centralization of the decider, but typically some decision making for the firm occurs at all levels of the hierarchy. Computers may be employed as aids to decision making. Because of its importance, this subsystem will receive further attention in Chapter 6.

Encoder. The encoder subsystem reverses the processes of the decoder. The encoder transforms internal information from its private code into one such as a human language or hand signals that can be interpreted by other living systems.

The encoder subsystem of a manufacturing firm includes the billing, advertising, public relations, and legal departments. Letters, bills, speeches, advertising copy, and other messages must be encoded for transmission to other systems. Small firms usually disperse some of these processes to other organizations such as advertising and law firms.

Output transducer. The output transducer transfers information from internal markers to external markers that are suitable for carrying information in the system's environment. In the process of talking, for instance, neural signals are converted into sound waves by means of expelled air acting upon vocal cords, tongue, teeth, and lips. The output transducer and encoder subsystems work together to enable a person to send information to others.

Output transducers in a manufacturing firm include all employees who deal with the public, such as salespeople, secretaries, spokespersons, labor negotiators, and personnel interviewers. The firm may disperse some output transduction processes to other organizations such as newspapers and television stations. Artifacts include duplicating and mailing machines, phone answering devices, and computers (e.g., computerized billing).

Dispersal of Subsystems

All of the nineteen subsystems are required for the survival and proper functioning of a living system, according to Miller. A living system need not include all of these subsystems, however. It is possible to disperse certain functions to other systems. For example, a human fetus in the womb does not process food; the converter subsystem is supplied by the mother. A person may survive for at least a short period attached to a machine that supplies the distributor function of blood circulation. Motor functions lost because of a spinal cord injury may be partially recovered through various prosthetic devices.

The only subsystem that cannot be dispersed to another system is the decider. A living system ceases to exist as an independent entity if it does not have its own decider subsystem. It is the decider that integrates all other functions; without it there is no overall system.

Relationships among Subsystems

From the foregoing description of the nineteen critical subsystems as they manifest themselves in people and organizations it is obvious that there is much interaction among subsystems. They frequently share components. A person's mouth is a component of the boundary, ingestor, extruder, input and output transducer subsystems. A secretary in a firm may be a component of its boundary, ingestor, distributor, matter-energy storage, input and internal transducers, channel and net, decoder, associator, memory, decider, encoder, and output transducer. Furthermore, no subsystem resides totally in a single organ of an individual or a single department of an organization.

There must be a flow of matter-energy and information from one subsystem to another. Matter-energy is brought across the boundary by the ingestor and then carried by the distributor to the converter, producer, or storage. If the flow is to the converter, from there the altered matter-energy may go to the producer or storage. From storage matter-energy may flow to the converter, producer, extruder, or motor, or to any other subsystem to be used for growth and maintenance.

There is a similar flow of information through the boundary, input transducer, channel and net, decoder, associator, memory, decider, encoder, and output transducer. Furthermore, there is substantial interaction between the matter-energy and information processing subsystems. Information is carried by markers of matter-energy; the information and its marker may be processed simultaneously. When a person eats a steak, the eyes, nostrils, and taste buds process the steak as information while the ingestor is processing it as matter-energy. Proper functioning of all matter-energy subsystems depends on the flow of information to the decider, where orders are issued to continue, stop, or alter

Figure 2–1
Relationships among Critical Subsystems: Flow of Matter-Energy and Information

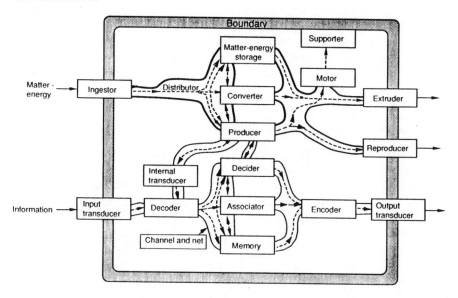

the current processes. Figure 2-1 provides a simplified picture of the relationships among critical subsystems.

If each subsystem decided for itself what it would do, there would inevitably be a great deal of conflict and inefficiency. This is easy to see in the case of an organization. We have probably all been in organizations in which it seemed that every person and every department were operating for themselves. In a business firm we might find that sales cannot cooperate with production and neither of them agrees with accounting. The problem can be traced to a failure of the upper echelons of the decider subsystem, whose function it is to coordinate the operation of all subsystems toward the purposes and goals of the firm. The decider may in turn be hampered by poor information flow from the internal transducer. In short, the firm is a system that is dependent on the proper functioning of all its subsystems and components, both separately and together.

ORGANIZATION DESIGN

A group or a very small organization has little hierarchical structure or division of labor. The owner of a small firm may work alongside the employees, performing many of the same functions. As an organization grows, however, there is usually an attempt to rationalize its structure by separating processes and grouping those that are closely related. A hierarchy of authority develops as the owner/manager distances him- or herself from the employees.

Hierarchy

The development of hierarchical echelons of decision making represents an attempt by the system to cope efficiently with the consequences of growth. The number of potential lines of communication in an organization grows much faster than the number of component members. If all lines were left equally open, members would soon be swamped with messages and would have little time to do anything but exchange information. Establishing a hierarchy of authority closes or constricts many channels and emphasizes the importance of a few. It also helps to maintain centralized coordination and control of the system by its decider, albeit at the cost of some loss and distortion of information.

The loss of information resulting from establishment of a hierarchy would be a more serious problem for organizations were it not for the fact that the individual components are themselves living systems. As independent decision makers, these components are capable of making intelligent, purposeful choices of which information to accept as input and which to ignore. They can detect redundancy in the various channels and filter out unnecessary inputs. They can also choose what to remember and what to forget. Provided that the purposes they use in making these choices are consonant with organizational goals, there may be little loss of useful information.

Differentiation

Efficient processing requires minimization of the distance that matter-energy and information must travel as they flow through the system. At the component level this principle may be translated into specialization, so that a component does not have to switch back and forth from one process to another. The basic organizational component, the employee, may operate most efficiently when stationed at one place and performing one function or a small number of processes. In such a setup employees and tools do not have to move at all, there is little need for new information, and the flow of materials from one station to another can be planned to minimize distance.

A similar rationale holds at the department level. Each department specializes in a related group of processes. The structure of each department reflects its role. Departments are arranged so that those that must frequently exchange matter-energy or information are close to each other. Departments that must interact with the environment are placed on the periphery and close to the doors, docks, telephones, and such.

Lawrence and Lorsch (1969) used the term *differentiation* for the process of departmental specialization. As an organization grows and its environment becomes more complex, it copes with complexity by becoming more differentiated.

How does this differentiation of organizational structure relate to the nineteen critical subsystems? In manufacturing organizations the resulting departments often seem to match closely the matter-energy processing subsystems. There may be separate departments for purchasing and receiving (ingestor), materials handling (distributor), maintenance (converter), production (producer), inventory (matter-energy storage), sales and shipping (extruder), and transport (motor).

This apparent correspondence between traditional departments and critical subsystems should not be overgeneralized, however. First, although a department may be associated with one primary subsystem, it is usually also involved with several others. Production departments typically ingest materials and energy from other departments, handle their own distribution and inventory within the department, process various kinds of information, and extrude products to other departments. Indeed, a department can itself be considered a living system, just as human organs are living systems. Thus the identification of a department with a single subsystem is simply a matter of emphasis.

Second, there are several subsystems that usually have no clear corresponding department or other organizational unit. Subsystems such as the boundary and supporter are primarily associated with artifacts rather than departments, although security might be called a boundary department. Information-processing subsystems tend to be dispersed throughout a manufacturing firm, although they may be concentrated in such departments as accounting, finance, marketing, engineering, and quality control. Information processing becomes less departmentalized at the higher echelons of the decider subsystem, where the various other subsystems must be coordinated.

The number of departments in an organization and the roles assigned to them depend on such factors as the size of the organization, the nature of its business, its technology, and the complexity and turbulence of its environment. Reorganization and the creation of new departments are frequent occurrences in rapidly growing organizations or a turbulent environment. New technology, such as computerized information systems, may generate new departments to deal with it.

Integration

A potential problem resulting from establishment of a hierarchy of authority and the reduction of lateral channels of communication is a failure of coordination between subsystems. As noted above, certain subsystems must work very closely together. Efficiency requires short channels of communication. While the hierarchy might provide coordination two or three echelons above the level at which cooperation is needed, the channels would be too long for regular use.

Increasing differentiation within an organization requires increasing means of *integration* in order to maintain coordination of behavior toward organizational goals (Lawrence and Lorsch 1969). The overlap of subsystems between departments provides one means of integration, because some coordination of subsystems can occur within the department. An example would be the sales department, which must associate the needs of the customer with those of production and shipping in order to make decisions about pricing and date of delivery.

Another method of integration is to incorporate roles from several subsystems into a single department, thereby allowing close, efficient communication between subsystems. For this reason, if no other, departments should not be separated too precisely along subsystem lines.

ROLES

Although individuals function as independent living systems within groups and organizations, their behavior is usually constrained by assignment to specific organizational processes. The set of processes to which an individual is assigned constitutes that person's *role* in the organization. Work groups and departments also have roles. In general, a role is the set of processes assigned by a social system to one or more of its components. Thus role is an emergent property of groups and organizations. Organizational roles are analogous to the specific functions performed by organs within an organism, except that groups and individuals are more versatile and adaptable to a variety of processes.

It is possible that a person may be assigned to carry out a single process, but organizational roles usually involve several processes that may be performed simultaneously, sequentially, or sporadically. These processes may be confined to a single subsystem or they may involve several subsystems. For example, the supervisor of a production department may be required to serve as input transducer for orders, internal transducer for grievances, decoder of budgets, associator and memory for new ideas and processes, decider of schedules, and encoder and output transducer of statistical information on production, not to mention various matter-energy processes. A machinist may develop new processes or train a new employee—processes involving the associator and ingestor subsystems. Certain jobs, such as secretary and maintenance, may require that the holder be a jack-of-all-trades.

A role may also link two or more levels of the hierarchy. A prime example of such vertical linkage is the role of manager. A manager serves as decider for a functional unit and as input and output transducer for the next higher level of the hierarchy. Likert (1961) called this the linking-pin model and stressed its utility in improving communication and coordination between units.

The linkage of two or more subsystems within a person's role provides an auxiliary means for coordinating subsystems. Rather than relying totally upon upper echelons of the hierarchy of authority for coordination, much of it can be delegated to lower echelons where direct links between subsystems occur. This speeds the processing of information and permits tighter control, provided that individuals at the lower echelons understand and accept the goals of the organization. Indeed, organizations often deliberately design boundary-spanning roles for this purpose. An example of such a role would be the product manager whose task is to coordinate the work of several functional departments in order to produce a single product or line of products.

Individuals usually hold roles in more than one social system. A person may play different roles at work, at home, and in various social groups. Even within a single system such as the family a person may play different roles in different subgroups. You may play one role for your parents, another for your children, and a third for your spouse.

Each system is a *role sender*, transmitting instructions on how components are expected to perform their roles within the system. The component may also have its own ideas about how the role should be played. It is obvious that there may be differences of opinion about any given role, as well as competing demands from other roles. These differences of opinion and competing demands lead to *role conflict*.

Several sources of role conflict have been identified. First, there may be more than one sender of role assignments, as when a person has two bosses or a boss whose concept of the role differs from organizational specifications. Second, there may be conflict between the sent role and the role as conceived by the holder. These two types of role conflict involve disagreement about what the role is.

A third type of conflict involves disagreement about what the role should be. In this case the sent role conflicts with the values of the holder. A special case of this third type is called role overload (or underload), in which the amount of time and effort required by the sent role is greater (or less) than the holder thinks it ought to be.

Beginning with the work of Kahn et al. (1964), considerable research has been done on role conflict. Unfortunately, much of this research suffers from measurement problems. Scales commonly used to measure role conflict have been poorly validated and generally fail to distinguish between the types of role conflict, although they do seem to capture generalized role stress (Rizzo, House, and Lirtzman 1970; Johnson and Stinson 1975; MacKinnon 1978; Tracy and Johnson 1981, 1983; House, Schuler, and Levanoni 1983).

SUMMARY AND IMPLICATIONS

Structure provides a static picture of the arrangement of subsystems and components in a system, whereas process has to do with dynamic changes in the matter-energy and information contained in the system. The primary structures of living systems are associated with the critical subsystems, each of which performs a function or set of vital processes for the system. Miller defined nineteen such critical subsystems, governed by the decider subsystem.

Although functionally distinct, these subsystems share components and interact closely.

The specialization of function, departmentation, and hierarchy of authority found in traditional organization design have their roots in the structure and processes of living systems. The principle that efficient systems are the ones that survive requires that, as systems grow, they must find ways to reduce the amount of energy expended in processes. The right amounts of specialization, departmentation, and hierarchization permit growing organizations to limit the energy spent on training, communication, and movement of people and materials.

Departments tend to correspond somewhat to critical subsystems. Specialization leads to the assignment of specific roles (sets of processes) to the individual and group components of the system. Both roles and departments tend to exceed the bounds of any single subsystem, however. This is fortunate, because the conjunction of subsystems within a particular department or role provides a means of aiding the hierarchy in coordinating processes. Some firms have found that despecialization of employees and work groups improves efficiency by shortening channels of communication, reducing storage, and increasing the performance motivation of employees.

One implication is that broad roles and broad departments are apt to be more efficient than narrow ones. Broad individual roles take advantage of the inherently close integration of subsystems within the person. Although there is some trade-off against the advantages of specialization, a well-trained individual performing a role that encompasses processes in several subsystems of the organization is able to provide close coordination of those subsystems and relieve strain on the decision-making hierarchy. Departments that encompass multiple processes likewise provide some inherent coordination. The information-processing capabilities of individuals and departments, as well as their commitment to organizational goals, define the limits of breadth.

An implication for organizational research is that attention should be paid to what subsystems are involved in departments and roles. Is there an optimal amount of overlap of subsystems within a department or role? Do some particular combinations of subsystems work better than others? How do highly successful organizations differ from moderately successful or unsuccessful ones in the ways that they provide coordination of critical subsystems?

It would also be instructive to look at questions such as how the coordination of subsystems changes as organizations grow, and which subsystems can be safely dispersed to other systems. For instance, does growth through vertical integration improve efficiency by reducing the amount of input and output transduction and bringing certain conversion and production processes within the system?

Another area for research has to do with the development of improved information systems. Computers increase the capability of the organization to maintain centralized control over all processes, but at the same time they make it possible to decentralize and to broaden departments and roles. Which is the better way to go? This is an issue that has been debated extensively by computer specialists, but consideration of critical subsystems and their need for coordination might help the debate.

NOTE

1. Some controversy exists over the precise number and arrangement of subsystems (see Merker 1983), but there seems to be no compelling reason to depart from Miller's formulation of them.

3

Values, Purposes, Goals, and Attitudes

Living systems are, above all, choosers. They must choose behavior that is effective in obtaining the resource inputs they need. They must choose effective means of extruding excesses. They must choose how to adapt to changes in the environment. They must choose between the demands of multiple stimuli. Survival and growth of the gene/meme pool rest on making good choices. Poor choosers become extinct.

In choosing behavior, individuals and organizations are ruled by values. Every living system has a hierarchy of values that represents the relative urgency of reducing various strains within the system (Miller 1978: 34). The hierarchy of values thus sets priorities in choosing behavior. A system's set of values is the totality of strains within the system (Miller 1978: 34). These strains are deviations from preferred steady states (called purposes). Values are usually expressed in terms of a preferred state, but a range of values corresponding to deviations from that state is implied.

A strain may be caused by too little or too much input or output of some resource. At any given moment there may be many strains clamoring for attention. Behavior is motivated to reduce such strains and bring the system closer to its preferred states. The hierarchy of values governs which strains will be attacked first.

From this statement it is obvious that values play a key role in organizational behavior. Many OB textbooks contain little or no mention of values in general, though group norms are often discussed. Norms are expressions of some of the values of a group, just as morals and ethics express some of a person's values. Organizational values are often stated in the form of policies, procedures, and rules. Constitutions, laws, and religious texts express many of the values of a society. Individual behavior is influenced by all of these expressed values, as well as by some that are unstated.

This chapter will define values and discuss their sources. Hierarchies of values will be examined, as well as conflict among values. Purposes and goals will be defined in terms of values and related to the maintenance of steady states. Attitudes will be treated as categorical values that influence information processing and behavior. Finally, there will be a brief discussion of implications.

VALUES

The term *value* is used in many different ways. Some meanings are subjective, others objective. In economics, for instance, value refers to the utility or usefulness of something to a person, group, organization, or society. In this sense value is a subjective judgment of the worth of a resource to a particular system.

Value is also given a subjective meaning in philosophy, but here the meaning is broader. Philosophical values are judgments about whole classes of objects or phenomena. For instance, philosophers debate whether the value of truthfulness is absolute or situational. In general it is good to be truthful, but there are situations in which the truth might do more harm than good. There is also debate over whether value lies in the end state or in the process of working toward it.

Objectively, a value is something of worth. Food is a value; so is peace. The worth of food or peace is not absolute, however. Beef has no value to a devout Hindu, nor pork to a Muslim. Peace may have no value to a professional soldier of fortune.

One definition of the objective value of something is its worth as matter-energy and information. Some things hold more energy value or information value than others. Even so, it is difficult to conceive of energy and information as values without some system to make use of them. Is the energy in a lump of coal of value to the coal itself? Siciński (1978) argued that an objective systems concept of value can be derived from the usefulness of something. That is, the worth of a resource can be objectively measured in terms of what it contributes to the well-being of a system.

There is a common core to these various uses of the term *value*. Value refers to *worth to a system*. Value is not absolute; there must be a system of reference. Beyond that, the meaning of value diverges to refer to the worth of (1) an external object or condition, (2) an internal state of the system, or (3) working toward that state. The first is basically the economic meaning of value; the second and third are philosophical meanings. It is the third meaning that will be favored here, because living systems use values as guides for action. Note that the value of working toward a preferred state *increases* as the deviation from that state increases.

When we speak of a person's moral values, we are usually referring to the worth that the person attributes to maintaining certain internal steady states, such as virginity, piety, strength against temptation, freedom from hatred, and so forth. Personal ethical values refer to pursuit of worthy states of orientation toward other people, such as trustworthiness and fairness. When the system of reference shifts to society, ethical values refer to maintenance of worthy states of relationship between people, groups, and organizations. The ethical values of any given system refer to the worth of acting to attain certain ideal states within that system.

In Chapter 1 we noted that living systems act within themselves and upon their environment in order to survive, maintain steady states of order, grow, develop, and reproduce. An internal state has worth for a living system to the degree that it contributes to the imperatives of maintenance, actualization, and propagation. In other words, the usefulness of an internal state and the value of working toward it are determined by these imperatives.

Value may now be defined for living systems. A *value* is the worth that a living system assigns, in accordance with the imperatives of life, to acting toward attainment of a preferred internal steady state. In other words, given that a strain is a deviation from the preferred state, a value represents the urgency of reducing a particular strain. This definition fits one philosophical meaning of value, although not all philosophies would agree with it. It does not correspond to the economic meaning, but the concept of utility can be derived from it.

Value inheres in internal states, not external objects. A bar of gold has value only through attribution of its usefulness in attaining a preferred internal state. For an individual, gold, might be of value in providing a state of security. A business firm might value gold as an asset in maintaining a steady flow of production. For a nation, gold might be useful in preserving the worth of its currency.

The value corresponding to a preferred or optimal steady state is zero, because there is no strain and no urgency in attaining that state. When a variable is not in its optimal state, its value is determined by (1) the *importance* of the variable in accordance with the imperatives of the system and (2) the *degree of deviation* from its optimal state. That is, reduction of a particular strain may be urgent because even a small deviation from the optimal state of the variable is extremely vital or because its current state is extremely far from optimal. Importance changes slowly, if at all, but the degree of deviation may vary rapidly.

Valued internal states are supported by external resources (i.e., matter-energy and information) or relationships (e.g., security, love). Technically, relationships are information, but it may be useful to preserve the distinction. For any given internal variable there is a range of values corresponding to the degree of strain, that is, to the amount of change in resource(s) or relationship(s) required to attain its optimal state.

The range of values of any particular variable may be pictured as a U-shaped curve. The lowest point of the curve, representing the optimal state, rests on a value of zero. Around that point there is a small *range of stability* "within which the rate of correction of deviations is minimal or zero" (Miller 1978: 34). Beyond the range of stability the curve rises on both sides as the urgency of reducing strain increases. The more important the variable is, the more steeply does the curve rise. Figure 3-1 shows value curves for three different variables.

Figure 3–1
Value Curves and Hierarchy of Current Values

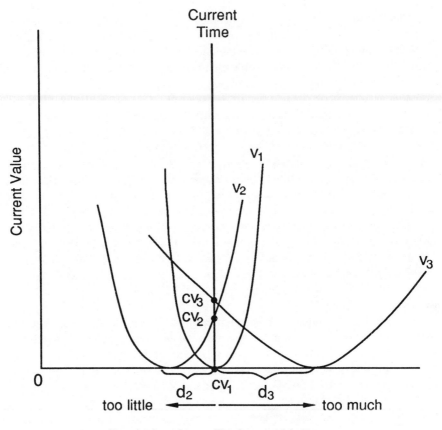

Deviation from Preferred Value

Hierarchy of Values

The hierarchy of values is very difficult to describe or measure, because it is both dynamic and extremely complex. It is a hierarchy of *current* strains within the system. New strains are constantly being created and old strains are increasing or decreasing as action is taken on them. Any given event may affect many different strains. Furthermore, new values are constantly being learned and old values are being modified by experience. Steady states are only relatively stable. Preferred (optimal) states may shift in accordance with the imperatives of actualization and propagation, as well as through learning.

One way to picture the hierarchy of values in action is to think of a large set of

U-shaped curves superimposed over one another. Figure 3-1 presents a simplified set of three curves. Each curve represents a different system variable for which an optimal state exists. Although the shape of each curve remains relatively stable, the curves shift laterally as degree of deviation from the optimal state varies. The hierarchy of values is formed by the current value of each variable.

Both the importance of each variable and its degree of deviation from optimal must be weighed in the balance when making choices. The current value, CV_n, of any given variable, V_n, in the hierarchy of values is a function of the slope of its curve and the current degree of deviation, d_n, from its optimal state. Although the steep slope of V_1 in Figure 3-1 shows that it is more important than the other two variables, it is already at its optimal point. Its current value is zero, as d_1 is zero. V_2 is more important (i.e., it has a steeper slope) than V_3 but the latter is under the greater strain, as represented by its greater distance, d_3, along the X-axis from its optimal point to its current value. Thus, V_3 is currently more urgent than V_2 or V_1.

A relatively simple example illustrates how the hierarchy of values works. A person has a range of values associated with various degrees of hunger or satiation and another range of values with respect to the taste of steak. In most cases hunger values are likely to be more important than taste values, because hunger values are more innate than taste values and hunger is more closely linked to survival and maintenance of the system. Yet a person who has not tasted steak for a long time might be induced to eat some even when satiated with food. Conversely, after a steady diet of steak every meal for a month, even a hungry person might refuse it. Between these extremes we could measure the degrees of hunger that are equal in value to various degrees of taste deprivation. The structure of a value hierarchy can be mapped by measuring such comparative preferences (Winterfeldt and Edwards 1986).

This example deals with conflict between two values that relate to the same object. Values may conflict even when they do not directly relate to an object, however. Hunger values may conflict with the values that a person holds for various degrees of personal honesty. In general, the values of honesty may rank higher (i.e., have steeper slope) than hunger values. One person may endure considerable hunger before even considering the idea of stealing food or obtaining it dishonestly. There comes a point for most people, however, when hunger becomes more important. In fact, some people value honesty so lightly that they will steal food even when they are not hungry.

The hierarchy of values differs in general from person to person, from group to group, from organization to organization, and from society to society. One work group may tend to value incentive wages above job security, whereas another group chooses to ignore incentives and restricts production in order to preserve jobs. One firm may value quality products above maximum production, whereas another firm shoves the product out the door regardless of quality. An industrialized society puts a high value on gross national product (GNP), perhaps higher than on spiritual values. Other societies may be unwilling to violate spiritual values in order to increase GNP.

The hierarchy of values varies not only from system to system, but also with time and experience. A child learns not to take food from another person's plate even when hungry. The child thereby learns to set the values of politeness and property above the innate value of a full stomach, at least in most instances. A society may gradually modify some of its spiritual values and allow the value of some degree of industrialization to predominate. More rapid change occurs as resources are consumed or extruded, thereby creating strain. In spite of constant change in the hierarchy of values, however, at any given moment there exists a hierarchy that permits the system to resolve value conflicts and make choices.

Sources of Values

A basic source of values is the template of a living system. A person's genes determine the values of many internal states. For example, maintenance of a steady body temperature within a given range is important for survival. Thus maintenance of that temperature has great worth to a person. That is not the sort of worth we normally associate with the term *value,* but it fits the definition.

The values we usually talk about are learned. Moral and ethical values may have some remote basis in our genetic structure, but we generally acquire these values from the teachings of parents, teachers, clergy, and peers. The lessons may be formal, as in school, or informal, such as a child being taunted by a peer for lying. From these lessons we learn the worth of a particular code of conduct.

Reward and punishment are often used to reinforce the learning of a set of values. Once learned, these values become as much a part of a person as the innate values set by one's genes. Moreover, even innate values are sometimes subject to change through learning. For example, we learn to accept immunization shots as being good for us, even though our inborn tendency is to prefer an unpunctured skin.

Value Conflicts

Conflict among values is inevitable. Even innate values may conflict with one another. For example, the values associated with pregnancy are apt to upset certain steady states and draw resources away from other uses in the mother's system. When learned values are added, such as the importance of continuing a career, the potential for conflict is increased. A person who is ill may put a high value on obtaining rest, which conflicts with a learned value of showing up for work every day. The value of facilities expansion to a business firm may be in conflict with the value of maintaining a particular debt/equity ratio.

There is also great potential for value conflict from the fact that the subsystems and components of a living system generally have their own sets of values. Certain values of an environmentalist group are likely to conflict with the economic values of the nation. The value of increasing sales may cause a business firm to instruct a salesperson to make promises that the salesperson regards as unethical.

The value of competing may cause an athlete to make demands on the body that violate the preferred states of various organs.

In order to resolve value conflicts, a living system applies its hierarchy of values. This hierarchy reflects the intrinsic urgency of returning each system variable to its range of stability when a deviation from that range occurs. Thus it prioritizes the variables.

PURPOSES

Miller (1978: 39) defined a *purpose* as a preferred steady state. It is the optimal state of a variable, that is, the low point on the value curve. Information feedback is compared against a purpose in order to determine whether a strain has been reduced or eliminated. For example, the purpose of the temperature-maintenance processes of the human body is a temperature that, when measured orally, is approximately 98.6° F. The purpose with respect to hunger may be a particular blood sugar level or an absence of hunger signals from the stomach. A person may have a purpose of absolute honesty or some intermediate degree (e.g., honest enough not to get caught). A business firm might set as a purpose a 10 percent growth rate or a 15 percent return on investment. A population growth rate of zero might be a national purpose.

Note that a purpose may be dynamic (e.g., a steady rate of change) as well as static. Even steady states are only relatively stable; they may change with learning or to enable the system to adapt to change. Purposes also interact. A person's preferred pulse rate varies according to the amount of physical activity generated by other purposes. A firm may alter its preferred debt/equity ratio in accordance with its preferred growth rate.

Miller's definition may not reflect what we normally mean by "purpose," but it fits well with the concept of values and other aspects of living systems theory. What I have called "imperatives" provide the broader purposes of living systems behavior. Specific purposes as defined by Miller operationalize these imperatives. That is, there are preferred steady states associated with the maintenance, actualization, and propagation of the system.

Miller's definition of purpose seeks to avoid any discussion of ultimate origin. Purposes flow from the hierarchy of values, which in turn is determined by the template of the system and the teachings of other systems. Yet we must recognize that living systems have some "ultimate" tendencies that fit the usual meaning of purpose. Living systems are purposeful systems (Ackoff and Emery 1972).

Whether we take a broad or narrow view of purpose, the concept is useful in discussing needs, motivation, and decision making. We have already talked of values in terms of "usefulness to the system." Usefulness can be determined only with respect to purpose. The question, "Useful for what purpose?" must be answered. Needs likewise will be defined in terms of usefulness. Motivation and choice of behavior are directed by usefulness. Thus a concept of purpose is vital to the study of organizational behavior.

Purposes are complex. Purposes may exist within purposes. The purpose of honesty may lead to subpurposes of (1) no involvement in theft and (2) full faithfulness to one's word. Maintenance of body temperature at its purposed level involves maintenance of many subpurpose temperatures in various organs and components. A group's purpose of maintaining its current level of membership may be accompanied by a subpurpose of holding a social event once a month and another subpurpose of monthly dues to cover the cost.

Purposes, like the hierarchy of values from which they are derived, are influenced by suprasystems. An individual purpose of honesty is learned from parents, a peer group, or a religious institution. If a group has a purpose of monthly dues, loyal members may have a corresponding purpose of paying them on time and in full.

Conflicting Purposes

Like values, purposes are often in conflict. The purposes associated with maintenance of steady states may conflict with purposes for growth and development. People may have to take risks with their physical safety in order to develop their abilities. Learning to swim threatens to cut off your air supply until the skill is mastered, yet knowing how to swim might some day save your life.

The fact that purposes are influenced by suprasystems suggests other sources of conflict. The purposes of the family or nation might require that you risk your life. You must then decide whether to accept these purposes as your own or to pursue a purpose of personal safety. In less dramatic fashion a suprasystem may assign you to a role that stunts your development. For example, you might work for an organization that requires you to perform only routine tasks and gives you no scope for advancement. The purpose of such a work assignment might be efficiency for the organization or security for the manager. Your purpose in accepting the job might be your family's monthly budget requirements. Implicit in your choice is the fact that taking the job serves a purpose or set of purposes that is currently higher on your hierarchy than development of your abilities.

Another source of conflict in purposes is the loose coordination of some higher-level systems. A family does not always speak with one voice. A mother may want her son to study medicine whereas his father wants him to be a football player (or vice versa). A shop supervisor may tell employees to do a job one way and work group norms may instruct them to do it another way. The conflict stems from the fact that individual human beings must serve as the deciders both for themselves and for higher-level systems. Leaders must lead themselves as well as the organization. Often the purposes of one become confused with the purposes of the other. This problem will receive further attention in Chapter 9.

Conflict between the purposes of self and suprasystem may be mixed with conflict among one's own purposes. National and state budgets are purposes for taxation. Taxes take away money that a person might prefer to use for other purposes. Yet the individual may agree with at least some of the purposes to which the tax money is put, such as high-quality education or modernized defense capabilities. For the individual the balance may be tipped by the purpose of avoiding trouble with the Internal Revenue Service. In any case, it is evident that a given choice of behavior may serve several purposes to varying degrees while ignoring or going counter to other purposes.

When conflict of purposes occurs, if it is not automatically resolved by the hierarchy of values, it must be mediated by the decider subsystem. For example, each individual must decide whether to obey the dictates of self, family, firm, or society when those dictates are in conflict. We choose one career over another. We may choose to go to a party instead of reading a good book. We may choose to flee rather than fight. In each case we are choosing between behaviors both of which serve purposes. Some purposes are left unmet, at least temporarily.

Purposes of Higher Level Systems

If higher level systems are the source of so much conflict, why do people form them? We could avoid many conflicts of values and purposes simply by acting always as individuals. The fact that we persist in forming families, schools, businesses, churches, and nations and accepting their influence indicates that these institutions also serve our purposes. They do so in two ways.

First, and most obvious, these higher level systems serve purposes of protection, nurturance, sustenance, education, opportunity to develop, and so forth. Human reproduction requires cooperation. In sparse environments the cooperation of a group may be required in order to survive. The full development of our mental abilities requires educational institutions. Protection from enemies may require an army or militia. One person might be able to build a house for shelter, but it is easier and more efficient to build it with a group. Efficiency is a very basic purpose of all living systems. Other things being equal, the more efficient systems are the ones that survive.

Second, the development of social systems is mandated by our genetic templates. We contain the seeds of higher level systems in our ability to manipulate symbols and communicate, our capacity to learn, our long period of dependence in infancy, our ability to use tools, our physical differentiation between the sexes, and perhaps an innate capacity to love. Presumably these characteristics have become part of our genetic heritage through natural selection, indicating that they have survival potential.

The imperatives of our social systems are the same as our own; namely, to preserve and extend the human system. For social systems, however, the "system" includes such facets as law, knowledge, artifacts, culture, government, and other products of human ingenuity. For the nation the preservation of the memes of government and law may be more important than the preservation of individual lives or gene pools. A business firm may place profits and the preservation of jobs ahead of the quality of work life. These systems serve human purposes, but they also come to serve purposes of their own.

GOALS

In order to attain a given purpose, a living system must often act upon its environment. For instance, a person seeks shelter in a rainstorm in order to maintain a dry skin. In this case dry skin is the purpose and shelter is the goal. A *goal* is a preferred external state that is useful for one or more purposes of a living system. The preferred state may refer to a resource or relationship.

The association between goals and purposes is not one to one. Some purposes are attained internally and involve no goal directly. An example would be maintenance of a steady pulse rate. Other purposes involve multiple goals. Eliminating hunger may lead to such goals as finding food, buying or gathering it, and cooking it. Other purposes may be added to make the goal more specific. A taste purpose may specify that the goal be raw carrots, sliced and dipped in a sauce. Thus a single goal may be associated with multiple purposes.

Goals may be stable and long lasting or they may change rapidly. A nation may have a long-term goal of maintaining a stable alliance with several other nations, in pursuance of a security purpose. A shorter term goal might be deployment of a new missile system. A momentary goal might be destruction of an incoming enemy missile.

Long-term goals usually involve subgoals of shorter duration. A long-term goal tends to form an envelope of choices that must be made in order to attain that end. Thus a firm's long-term goal of attaining a 20 percent market share may generate a whole series of subgoals involving new-product development, training of salespeople, improved market research, and development of a new advertising campaign. At the same time that long-term goal may tend to exclude the possibility of other choices, such as diversification into new markets.

Goals tend to change as purposes are attained. When a person is thirsty, water (or milk or lemonade, depending on taste purposes) may become a goal. As soon as the thirst is quenched, the goal shifts to something else. The purpose (i.e., a preferred steady-state value of water in the system) remains basically unchanged, however.

A living system tends to have many goals at one time. These goals may be pursued simultaneously, sequentially, or intermittently. For instance, a person pursuing a degree in business administration does not spend twenty-four hours a day at it, but returns to the goal over and over again, while interspersing the pursuit of goals for sustenance, recreation, rest, and so forth. In some cases the individual may be able to combine pursuits, as when having lunch with friends.

Some goals may be closely linked, as in the example of the subgoals involved in a business firm's pursuit of a long-term market share goal. But the firm may also simultaneously pursue goals with respect to purchasing raw materials, hiring labor, obtaining capital, complying with (or evading) government regulations, and satisfying stockholders. Some of these goals may conflict. Certain stockholders, for instance, may be unhappy with the firm's compliance (or lack of it) with clean air regulations.

Goal conflicts may occur because of conflicts in underlying purposes or because of the system's inability to pursue certain goals simultaneously. A person wanting to buy a compact disk and see a movie may be able to pursue only one of these goals because of limited funds. A group may have to choose between one activity and another because there is not time enough to do both. In these cases there does not seem to be any conflict of purposes. The conflict is simply over allocation of resources to different goals serving the same purpose.

Whatever the source of goal conflicts, they must be resolved by the decider subsystem in light of the system's hierarchy of values. The decider may choose the goal associated with the most urgent purpose, or it may employ a more complex decision rule. Since a goal can contribute toward multiple purposes, the decider may weight these contributions and sum them up. The decider may also consider the cost of pursuing each goal and the likelihood of failure to attain it. We will examine these factors more fully in Chapters 6 and 7.

ATTITUDES

Living systems frequently encounter new items or relationships to which some value must be assigned. Is this new brand of corn flakes a worthy food item? A new employee is trying to join our lunch group; do we want to encourage this relationship? A new supplier is courting our business; do we want additional suppliers?

Instead of evaluating new items from scratch, systems usually begin with attitudes that color the process. An *attitude* is "an individual's *predisposition* to *evaluate* a stimulus (object, person, and so on) in a favorable or an unfavorable manner" (Hamner and Organ 1978: 107). This definition will serve with one modification—namely, it applies to living systems in general, not just individuals.

A system's attitudes are associated with its hierarchy of values. The worth of any resource or relationship to a system is established by the values of the system. If ingesting an object moves one or more values closer to their purposes and does not increase deviations from other purposes, the object has worth to the system. That worth is greater if the values are greater and if the purposes can be more nearly attained. But how does the system assess the worth of something before it has tried it?

We are not concerned with measuring the actual worth of a resource or relationship. The problem is to estimate its worth to the system if it becomes a goal. For instance, a person may want to know the expected worth of trying to form a close relationship with a new neighbor. The actual value of the goal cannot be known in advance, but it can be estimated on the basis of experience with similar situations and objects. Attitudes come into play in making the estimate.

From past experience the person has learned the worth of having a good relationship with one's neighbor. That worth may be generalized as a predisposition to value good neighbors highly. The person may also have attitudes toward racial and ethnic groups that apply in this instance. Neighbors with young children may engender a different attitude than those without children. The observed fact that the new neighbor immediately plants a garden may engender a new attitude. The person has attitudes toward many *categories* of objects or behavior. The person's evaluation of the expected worth of the relationship depends on how the new neighbor is classified and related to the general attitudes.

The use of attitudes to establish the worth of new resources or relationships is efficient. The system does not have to go through a trial-and-error process before assigning worth to each new thing. Of course, attitudes can become a source of inefficiency if categorization is inaccurate or if attitudes are substituted for evaluation from actual experience. Therefore, systems must strive to avoid overgeneralization and hardening of attitudes.

Like individuals, groups and organizations have attitudes. Based on past experience a business firm may prefer to deal with one supplier rather than several. In evaluating new product ideas it may assign greater estimated worth to those that are oriented toward young people or women. Such attitudes are apt to be built right into the decider subsystem of the firm and passed from one employee to another, so that they are not simply the attitudes of individual decision makers.

Attitudes help not only to establish some uniformity of value judgments within groups and organizations, but also to avoid conflicts. Without common organizational attitudes toward certain matters, every new potential resource or relationship would become the source of great discussion and controversy. Conflict would arise between the members as they tried to agree on its worth or to make a decision in the absence of such agreement.

From the foregoing discussion we may summarize the following points about attitudes. Attitudes are judgments about the worth of classes or categories of stimuli. Attitudes are learned from experience with stimuli in those categories or from acceptance of the judgments of others. Attitudes toward stimuli in any given category are predispositions to expect the same worth in any new stimulus placed in that category. For complex stimuli several different attitudes may apply and must somehow be combined to produce an overall judgment. Attitudes provide an efficient means to evaluate new goals. Thus attitudes influence the choice of goals and of behavior toward those goals. In groups and organizations attitudes help to establish uniform evaluation of new goals and to avoid conflict.

SUMMARY AND IMPLICATIONS

In this chapter value has been defined as the worth ascribed by a living system to reaching a preferred steady state or purpose. The value of any given variable is a function of its importance to the system and its current degree of deviation from the preferred state. Every living system has a hierarchy of values that reflects the relative urgency of attaining various purposes.

Goals are directed toward the environment and are formulated in accordance with purposes. Attitudes toward categories of stimuli are used in estimating the value of new goals. Conflict often occurs among purposes, goals, and attitudes. Such conflict is mediated by the decider subsystem and is ultimately resolved in accordance with the hierarchy of values.

One implication of this chapter is that the behavior of living systems is purposeful. Values, purposes, goals, and attitudes influence the choice of behavior. If we know something about the values by which behavior is directed, we should be better able to predict that behavior.

All attitudes as well as many values, purposes, and goals are learned. That means they can be modified. In some cases behavior can be influenced by changing the underlying attitudes or values. Conversely, by modifying behavior one may be able to provide new experience that will cause a change in attitudes.

Values, purposes, goals, and attitudes are common to all living systems, not just individuals. If you want to modify the attitudes of one individual in an organization, you should understand that some of them may actually be the attitudes of the organization or a work group. Other members of the organization may work against you to keep the individual's attitudes in place. Training programs such as T-grouping often fail to produce the desired results even though there is an apparent change of attitudes during the training. When the trainees return to their organizational units, the organization quickly dispels the changes that occurred during training. If *organizational* attitudes are to be changed, the entire membership may have to be trained at once or by moving from the top downward.

A similar point can be made about the values of a work group. These values, particularly the purposes, are often expressed as norms. The group sets up a control system to enforce its norms. If group norms are at odds with the purposes of the organization, some modifications will be needed. Directing the modification effort at individuals probably will not succeed, because it is group values rather than individual values that you are trying to change.

The worth of anything differs from one system to another. Differences in value often are the key to a worthwhile and lasting relationship between systems. A person who has several blankets but no food can probably make a mutually beneficial exchange with someone who has excess food but no blanket. Likewise, a person who has excess energy for labor but no money should be able to establish a worthwhile relationship with an organization that has money and lacks labor.

Conflict occurs when two or more systems put a high value on the same scarce resource. In the money markets when everyone wants to sell Swiss francs and buy U.S. dollars, the worth of dollars rises and the worth of francs falls. In their own nations, however, these currencies may continue to have much the same worth in terms of what they can buy in local goods. Money markets reflect subjective value, not objective value. The same is true of many other commodities that may become goals of people or institutions.

This chapter, and the book as a whole, takes the position that all behavior is motivated and purposeful, directed by values, goals, and attitudes. This position is somewhat controversial. Some people believe that behavior can occur randomly, without purpose.

It is certainly true that a lot of seemingly senseless behavior occurs. That does not mean that the behavior is without purpose, however. A system chooses behavior on the basis of the information it receives. If that information is incomplete or distorted, the chosen behavior may be ineffective even though directed at a purpose.

Furthermore, in order to say that a given act is purposeless we would have to show that it serves no purpose of any system. Individuals learn and accept values from other systems. When they do something that seems to serve no purpose for them, it may nevertheless serve the purposes of their cerebellum, family, peer group, firm, or nation. If all of these different sources of purpose are taken into account, it becomes difficult to show that behavior can occur without purpose.

4

The Need Concept

The concept of need plays a prominent role in the literature of psychology, organizational behavior, and management. A need concept is implicitly or explicitly incorporated in many popular theories of motivation, learning, compensation, job performance, job satisfaction, attitude change, perception, decision making, conflict, and communication. Thus a well-grounded need concept would serve as a solid base for much of this book.

Several theories of human needs are currently in vogue. Foremost, perhaps, are the need hierarchy theories of Maslow (1943, 1970) and Alderfer (1972). Related to these is the two-factor theory of Herzberg, Mausner, and Snyderman (1959; Herzberg 1966). Atkinson (1958, 1964) and McClelland (1961) developed a theory of needs for achievement, affiliation, and power that, although not a "complete" theory of human needs, is quite popular. Less prominent, but linked to living systems theory, is Murray's (1938) drive theory.

Unfortunately, none of these need theories serves as a solid foundation for models of perception, motivation, learning, and the like. In these theories need is defined (1) poorly or not at all, (2) in conflicting ways by different authors, or (3) in ways that confuse need with motivation. Descriptions of human needs and need categories are ambiguous, and the lists of needs and categories are demonstrably incomplete. The origin of needs is disputed. Furthermore, there is little empirical evidence for most of these theories and they are formulated in ways that make them difficult to test.[1]

Collectively, current need theories were criticized by Salancik and Pfeffer (1977: 441) as being "potentially misleading and unnecessary for the development of theories of human behavior." The authors went on to say that

from a scientific point of view. . . the fact that the concept of need is ambiguous on the points of the origins of needs, the development of needs, and even the meaning and measurement of needs makes the possibility of empirical refutation remote and the concept, in its present stage of development, of limited utility (443).

More specific criticism will follow, as we examine these theories in detail. One particular shortcoming should be mentioned now, however. All of the theories named above refer specifically to individual human behavior. They are not designed to be applicable to groups and organizations, even though it is common parlance to refer to the needs of a group (e.g., for new members) or of an organization (e.g., for capital). In this book we seek a concept of need that is applicable to all levels of living systems, or at least to human individuals, groups, and organizations.

This chapter will begin with a discussion of the meaning of "need," followed by a review and critique of the need theories named above. After showing why these theories are inadequate, I will present a need concept based on living systems theory that is designed to answer the criticisms, insofar as possible. The theoretical and practical implications of this concept will be examined.

THE MEANINGS OF "NEED"

A major weakness of some currently popular need theories is that they do not bother to define "need." Maslow, for instance, proceeds in his later writings as if the term required no definition. To put need theory on a solid foundation, we must begin with a good definition, preferably one that accords with everyday meanings of the word.

Need is used both as a noun and as a verb. As a noun it has at least three major meanings: (1) a lack of something useful or required; (2) the something useful or required that is lacking; and (3) a compulsion to act.

In living systems theory Miller (1978: 457) adopted Murray's (1938) concept of need, which Miller saw as synonymous with his own concept of strain. A *strain* in a living system is a deviation of some variable from its range of stability within the system. Strains are produced by *stresses* on the system, which are lacks or excesses of input or output. The concept of strain is similar to the first meaning of need cited above, except that a strain may be an excess as well as a deficiency. To refer specifically to a deficiency, Miller (1978: 34–35) used the terms *lack* or *underload*.

Other need theories, such as those of Maslow (1970), Alderfer (1972), and McClelland (1961), list needs primarily in the sense of the second meaning. They speak of safety or affiliation or recognition as something that is required but lacking. To avoid confusion, Lederer (1980) recommended the term *need satisfier* to designate this meaning.

A problem with this second meaning of need is that it tempts us to refer to things as needs whether they are currently lacking or not. That is the trap that Maslow and Alderfer fell into, listing broad categories of needs simply because they are things that *may* be useful and *may* be lacking. But food is not a need to a person who has just eaten a full meal. It is neither lacking nor useful. In this book I will use the term *resource* for things that are capable of satisfying a need. When a lack exists, a resource becomes a need satisfier.

The third meaning has sometimes been employed in the literature of psychology, for instance by Murray (1938) and Hull (1943), who listed needs for specific acts such as aggression or deference. But there is another term, *drive*, that is more often employed for this meaning.

Unfortunately, the distinction between meanings is often blurred. "Need *to achieve*," a drive (meaning 3), tends to be used interchangeably with "need *for achievement*," a resource or satisfier (meaning 2). "Need *of achievement*," a lack (meaning 1), is less common. Maslow (1970) listed needs in all three senses, without any apparent recognition of the difference. Confusion of drives, satisfiers, and lacks contributes to the failure to distinguish between need and other concepts such as desire and motivation. The confusion of need satisfaction with motivation and performance was cited by Salancik and Pfeffer (1977: 432–33) as an argument against the usefulness of need as a separate construct.

In order to avoid confusion and establish need as a distinct construct, in this book need will be defined in accordance with meaning 1, a lack of something useful or required. The choice of meaning 1 is arrived at by a process of elimination. Drive (meaning 3) is virtually synonymous with motivation; thus it is not a usefully distinct construct. Need satisfier (meaning 2) has no meaning without lack (meaning 1); that is, lack defines what is required for satisfaction. Need as lack is the most basic and useful meaning of the term.

Need is defined here as "a lack of a specific resource which is useful for or required by the purposes of [a living] system" (Tracy 1986: 212). Purpose was defined in Chapter 3 and resource was defined above. Thus the definition of need is clear and unambiguous. Its implications will be examined in detail later in this chapter. In Chapter 7 we will see how needs direct the choice of behavior that is expected to be optimal for the system.

Need is one kind of strain in a system, the other kind being an *excess*, that is, more of a specific resource than suits the purposes of the system. The concept of excess will later be developed more fully.

Two other terms should also be defined at this point, in order to distinguish them from needs. A *want* is a felt or perceived lack. Needs may or may not be consciously perceived. The concept of need may be applied to all levels of living systems, whereas want applies only to those with cognitive abilities.

A *desire* is a want of something that is not demonstrably useful to or required by the system. In other words, a lack of something is perceived even though there is no objective requirement or use for it. Desires may stem from the values of subsystems, particularly the decider subsystem, that are not in accord with the values of the system as a whole. For example, a manager may desire a larger share of organizational rewards even though the organization would be better off if rewards were more evenly dispersed.

Living systems act upon desires as well as needs and excesses. For instance, people may desire and seek something such as cocaine that is clearly bad for them. Cocaine may be perceived by the user's decider subsystem as being useful for producing altered states of consciousness, but it is harmful to the system as a whole. An act directed toward fulfillment of a desire is suboptimal, if not harmful, for the system.

CURRENT THEORIES OF HUMAN NEEDS

This section will review five well-known theories of human needs. The first is the drive theory developed by Henry Murray in the 1930s. Although no longer in vogue, it is presented here because Miller adopted it into living systems theory. A modern form of drive theory formulated by Atkinson and McClelland will be discussed second. Third, we will look at Maslow's need hierarchy, probably the best-known theory of needs. Fourth will be Alderfer's ERG theory, a revision of the need hierarchy. Finally we will look at the dual-factor theory of Herzberg.

In reviewing each of these theories particular attention will be paid to how need is defined or described. The clarity and specificity of categories of needs will be examined. Empirical verification or the lack of it will be carefully noted.

Murray's Drive Theory

Murray (1938) defined a need as a force in the brain. This force is also called a drive. According to Murray, needs (drives) organize thought and behavior to deal with an unsatisfying situation. A need may be provoked by an internal or external stimulus. Need is usually accompanied by a particular feeling or emotion. Need leads to behavior that changes the situation so as to quiet that feeling. Thus the existence of a need can be inferred from (1) the feeling or expression of a particular emotion, (2) selective attention to a particular stimulus, (3) a particular pattern of behavior, (4) the end result of the behavior (presumed to be the goal), or (5) the feeling or expression of satisfaction when the result is obtained (Murray 1938: 124).

In 1938 Murray published a list of twenty needs. Part of this list is shown in Table 4–1; it was subsequently modified and expanded, but Table 4–1 provides a good sample. From the list we can see that, in spite of his definition of need as a force in the brain, Murray named needs according to the behavioral process that is elicited. Moreover, the listed processes all involve interaction with the environment. Purely internal needs are not recorded, even though Murray acknowledged that a need can arise from within.

There is ample evidence that drives of a simple nature do exist. Hunger, for instance, elicits quite specific responses from a wide variety of animal life. Sexual drive, a good example of an excess, is likewise well established. At the level of human behavior, however, even these rather basic drives are expressed in socially influenced ways rather than in raw forms. Is the cooking of food or the use of utensils to eat it part of the driven behavior? A drive for a complex form of behavior such as aggression or deference is even more difficult to define or establish.

Table 4–1

A Sample of Needs (Drives) Listed by Murray

Need	Brief definition
n Achievement	To accomplish something difficult. To master, manipulate, or organize physical objects, human beings, or ideas. To do this as rapidly and as independently as possible. To overcome obstacles and attain a high standard. To excel oneself. To rival and surpass others. To increase self-regard by the successful exercise of talent.
n Affiliation	To draw near and enjoyably cooperate and reciprocate with an allied other (an other who resembles the subject or who likes the subject). To please and win affection of a cathected object. To adhere and remain loyal to a friend.
n Aggression	To overcome opposition forcefully. To fight. To revenge an injury. To attack, injure, or kill another. To oppose forcefully or punish another.
n Defendance	To defend the self against assault, criticism, and blame. To conceal or justify a misdeed, failure, or humiliation. To vindicate the ego.
n Deference	To admire and support a superior. To praise, honor, or eulogize. To yield eagerly to the influence of an allied other. To emulate an exemplar. To conform to custom.
n Dominance	To control one's human environment. To influence or direct the behavior of others by suggestion, seduction, persuasion, or command. To dissuade, restrain, or prohibit.
n Play	To act for "fun" without further purpose. To like to laugh and make jokes. To seek enjoyable relaxation of stress. To participate in games, sports, dancing, drinking parties, cards.
n Understanding	To ask or answer general questions. To be interested in theory. To speculate, formulate, analyze, and generalize.

Source: Excerpted from C. S. Hall and G. Lindzey, *Theories in Personality* (New York: Wiley, 1957), 173–74.

Miller (1978) adopted Murray's theory for living systems, but applied it only to organisms. When expressed in the more general "strain" terminology of Miller, it is also applicable to groups and organizations. Murray's emphasis on feeling and emotion, which lacks any clear analogue at the level of social systems, limits the applicability of his theory per se.

Another problem with drive theory is that it focuses on need for processes rather than for resources. Why do we need processes such as aggression, achievement, or understanding if not for their end products? Is there something in the human system that requires these processes?

Presumably such needs are listed because we feel them or perceive them in behavior. If we occasionally feel aggressive and if other people are seen to display aggressive behavior, the argument goes that people must possess a need for aggression. With this line of reasoning we don't even have to identify what this need contributes to the system. All we require is a vague impression that aggression has survival value.

There are several problems with this line of reasoning. It seems to imply that aggression is valued for its own sake, rather than for what may be gained by it. Yet if we examine a specific act of aggression, we are likely to find that its purpose was to obtain a specific resource from another system. It is the resource that was required, not the process of aggression. Probably the resource could have been obtained by several other means as well, such as dominance, affiliation, or barter. The process used to obtain the resource is at least one step removed from the actual requirements of the system.

Suppose that a person "feels" aggressive or engages in aggression even when there is no apparent resource to be gained by it. Are these evidences of n Aggression? Not necessarily. The feeling may represent a desire rather than a need. The desired (or required) end product may be a feeling of exhilaration or a relationship of power over others. The "kick" that one gets or the relationship that is established is information. Aggression is simply a means of fulfilling the need or desire for that information.

Drives such as Murray postulated cannot be directly observed. Furthermore, we cannot point to any specific organ or subsystem and say: "The function of that subsystem is aggression." We do possess organs with specific functions and processes that are required, however. Clearly we need a heart and a brain. We could link these organs to their processes and talk about a need of blood circulation or a need of decision making. We could even link external processes to these organs. The brain needs accurate data in order to do its work properly; thus we could assert a need of such processes as data gathering and education. But Murray and other drive theorists ignored such mundane process needs, presumably because they are not felt. Instead, drive theorists focused on needs that can be linked to perceived emotions and observed behavior patterns.

When we observe behavior such as one child hitting another, we might classify this behavior as aggression and present it as evidence of n Aggression; but we are making inferences that cannot be tested. There is no way we can be sure that the behavior was motivated by n Aggression rather than some other drive. Even the child will not know for sure what his or her motives were. The same behavior might be explained by n Defendance or n Dominance or by need of an apology from the other child.

The most serious problem with the drive concept is that it confuses need with motivation. Several theories of motivation treat need as an independent concept. Needs are seen as a starting point for several steps in the arousal, energizing, and direction of behavior. Yet drive theory makes need and motivation synonymous; a drive provides both the energy and the direction for behavior. For instance, n Dominance supposedly motivates people to act to control their environment. This is like saying that a need to eat motivates people to eat. Such a statement is tautological. On the other hand it may be quite meaningful to say that people are motivated to eat by a need of calories, vitamins, minerals, and so on. The meaning of this statement will be explored further in Chapter 7. Meanwhile, in order to preserve the distinction between need and motivation, we must avoid defining need in terms of process.

Please note that I am not rejecting drive theory in toto. The functioning of drives for specific behavior is well documented, particularly for lower order animals. Even for human individuals there are certain involuntary responses such as the eye blink that could certainly be classified as drives. At the group and organizational levels as well there may be "knee jerk" responses to certain strains. The firing or expulsion of a member for disloyalty or insubordination might be an example of an organizational drive.

Although drives exist and determine some behavior, they are not the same as needs. Much of the behavior of human individuals, groups, and organizations is too complex to be attributed to drives. Need theory, in the form developed in this chapter, can help to explain the more complex instances of living systems behavior.

Needs for Achievement, Affiliation, and Power

Atkinson (1958) and McClelland (1961) focused on three drives in particular: need to achieve (nAch), to affiliate (nAff), and to hold power (nPow). These drives, especially nAch, seem to have considerable importance for managerial effectiveness and economic development. The theory is that the need to achieve drives people to set higher goals and strive for better performance than they otherwise would.

McClelland (1961: 82–103) tested and confirmed the hypothesis that economic growth of a nation is preceded by the cultural development of high nAch in a generation of that nation's youth. This finding fits well with the living systems notion that some important individual needs are learned from higher level systems such as the family or society.

Given that nAch, nAff, and nPow are learned drives, the question arises as to how they are related to human purposes. Is achievement required or useful, or is it simply desired? Is there a minimal amount of achievement necessary for the health of any human being, even though a preference for greater amounts can be learned? Or are achievement, affiliation, and power entirely learned needs?

Neither McClelland nor Atkinson has attempted to present a comprehensive picture of human needs. They have simply focused on specific drives that might be instrumental to performance in an organizational context. They did not measure nAch, nAff, or nPow directly, but inferred these drives from content analysis of responses to the Thematic Apperception Test (TAT).[2] If these drives do indeed exist, they are obviously complex rather than simple. That is, the drive to achieve or to hold power can only be expressed through learned, socially defined behavior. Thus these drives are far from providing the basic concept of need that we are seeking. Nevertheless, according to Lee (1980: 74–90) the documentation of these drives is much firmer than for most other need theories.

Maslow's Need Hierarchy

Few students escape a course in management or organizational behavior without hearing about Maslow's need hierarchy. Although it has defied attempts to confirm it empirically, Maslow's (1943, 1970) theory remains popular. The theory consists of two basic parts: The first part classifies needs into five categories; the second part explains the dominance of a particular category of needs at any given time and the shifting of dominance over time.

Maslow postulated five categories of needs, which he labeled (1) physiological, (2) safety, (3) belongingness and love, (4) esteem, and (5) self-actualization. He described these categories as follows:

The *physiological needs* for food, water, sleep, and so forth are the most basic, in the sense that they will dominate a person's attention if unfulfilled. This category includes strong levels of need associated with survival, such as hunger stemming from starvation. But it also includes mild levels associated with maintenance of a steady physiological state, such as the appetite that leads us to eat at regular intervals. The physiological category also includes the needs for sensory stimulation (e.g., taste, odors, tickling) and for physical exercise. When these needs are reasonably well met, higher order needs emerge or become dominant.

The next higher order needs are the *safety needs*, which include "security; stability; dependency; protection; freedom from fear, from anxiety and chaos; . . . structure, order, law, limits; strength in the protector . . ." (Maslow 1970: 39). This seems to be a broad category merging with the next lower and higher categories. That is, needs for stability and freedom from anxiety are related to maintenance of steady states, whereas dependency and strength in the protector touch the next higher category, the belongingness and love needs.

Belongingness and love needs are grouped in a single category, although they represent somewhat different aspects of interpersonal relationships. Belongingness seems to encompass the human requirement of a place in a family or group. This need surely is related to the needs for dependency and protection. Love, on the other hand, is used as a general term for friendship, acceptance, empathy, and so forth. The acceptance aspect extends into the next higher category, esteem.

Curiously, Maslow does not identify the central core of the belongingness and love needs, which is a basic need of human contact. A need of interpersonal contact seems to be built into the human template. Spitz (1945) found that infants in foundling homes, if not given some personal attention and handling (stroking), did not develop properly even though their physiological needs were met. According to the theory of transactional analysis, this need for "stroking" or interpersonal recognition of existence remains strong throughout life (Berne 1964).

Maslow indicates that *esteem needs* may be classified into two subsidiary sets.

These are, first, the desire for strength, for achievement, for adequacy, for mastery and competence, for confidence in the face of the world, and for independence and freedom. Second, we have what we may call the desire for reputation or prestige (defining it as respect or esteem from other people), status, fame and glory, dominance, recognition, attention, importance, dignity, or appreciation (Maslow 1970: 45).

The first subset might be called self-esteem. It is closely related to the highest category, the need for self-actualization. The second subset could be called interpersonal esteem, which is certainly akin to love.

Self-actualization means "to become everything that one is capable of becoming" (Maslow 1970: 46). It appears to differ from achievement or self-esteem in that it involves discovering one's unique talents and developing them. If a person has the potential to be a great machinist or a mediocre manager, presumably it would be more self-actualizing to develop skills as a machinist. It is often overlooked that self-actualization implies development of physical as well as mental abilities.

Maslow looked at self-actualization in terms of a person's ultimate potential rather than current abilities. This led Maslow (1970: xx) to assert that no one under the age of forty could hope to fulfill the self-actualization needs. Yet infants and children probably spend more time than any other age group on activities designed to discover and develop their abilities. Children in a good home are easily able to fulfill most of their physiological, safety, and belongingness and love needs. It is not surprising, therefore, that esteem and self-actualization needs should be dominant in such children. They cannot fulfill their ultimate potential at this stage of life, but they can certainly gain esteem and realize their current abilities.

Although Maslow did not define need, for the most part he described his need categories in terms of required material and informational resources (i.e., need satisfiers, the second meaning of need). Yet he was not consistent about it; he also employed the third meaning, mixing in such processes as protection, acceptance, appreciation, and the entire category of self-actualization. Mixing needs for resources and for processes in this fashion results in double counting and confusion.

Maslow's need categories are far from complete. He did recognize needs to know and to understand, as well as esthetic needs, although these needs are not integrated into the hierarchy. However, his list ignores internal needs for matter and energy (e.g., enzymes, pulse) and for certain kinds of information (e.g., pain, limb position), although he does include self-assessment needs. Certain needs for external information are recognized (e.g., information relating to safety, belongingness, love, and esteem), but information concerning the environment and opportunities for self-actualization is ignored. Maslow correctly recognized the impossibility of listing all needs, yet these are omissions of large, important areas of need.

The *need hierarchy* is arranged in order of dominance. At any given moment the lowest order or category that remains relatively unfulfilled is dominant. That is, primary attention is given toward behavior that will fulfill needs in this category. The lowest order in the hierarchy, namely physiological needs, is dominant until these needs are reasonably well fulfilled. Then attention shifts to needs in the next higher category, the safety needs, and so on. In a nutshell that is the hierarchy concept.

Unfortunately, the basis of dominance is not clear. In some cases dominance appears to be based on urgency, as when it is argued that people must have food before they can afford to worry about shelter, and safety before they can concern themselves with love. In other cases the hierarchy of dominance seems to be built on a logical order of development. Maslow argues that a firm base of love is necessary for the development of self-esteem, and that self-esteem is a prerequisite for self-actualization.

A hierarchy based on relative urgency of broad categories of needs is on shaky ground. Granted that a specific physiological need such as a lack of food or water is likely to be more urgent than a safety need such as lack of shelter, the same cannot be said of other physiological needs such as of vitamins and minerals. In time of war or in a cold climate many safety needs may be more urgent than most physiological needs. The hierarchy seems to be based on comparison of a few of the most prominent needs in each category under the assumption of average environmental conditions.

The hierarchy could be based on nothing more than the breadth of the categories, which is arbitrary. If there are *more* different needs falling within the physiological category than the safety category, then the physiological needs will appear to be dominant. When most of these needs are fulfilled, so that they are no longer perceived as lacks, then it may appear that there are more safety needs, and so on. If this is the case, then the rationale for the need hierarchy is trivial.

Even if the basis for the hierarchy is not trivial, there is no clear indication of how much fulfillment is necessary at one level before the next level becomes dominant. It seems that, if we find a particular level to be dominant, we must

Table 4–2
Correspondence of Alderfer's and Maslow's Need Categories

Alderfer categories	Maslow categories
	Physiological
Existence	
	Safety--material
	Safety--interpersonal
Relatedness	Belongingness and love
	Esteem--interpersonal
	Esteem--self-confirmed
Growth	
	Self-actualization

Source: Adapted from Alderfer (1972: 25).

assume the lower levels are sufficiently fulfilled. For purposes of testing the theory this is an unsatisfactory state of affairs.

Maslow's need hierarchy seems plausible, but it is based on nothing more than introspection and observation of behavior. The theory is difficult to operationalize and test, partly because the categories overlap. Movement from one category to another occurs slowly, requiring a longitudinal study. The small amount of research that has been done has generally failed to confirm the theory (Wahba and Bridwell 1976; Wanous and Zwany 1977). Nevertheless, the need hierarchy remains popular because it seems to make sense when not examined too closely.

Alderfer's ERG Theory

Alderfer (1972) proposed an alternative research-based theory of needs. He listed three basic categories of needs—Existence, Relatedness, and Growth (hence, ERG)—that are related to Maslow's categories as shown in Table 4–2 (Alderfer 1972: 25).

Alderfer divided safety into two categories, material and interpersonal. Clothing, shelter, weapons, financial security, and medical treatment fall under the material category and are included in Existence needs. Law, protection by the group or clan, social structure and order, and nurturance by parents are interpersonal, to be included in the Relatedness category.

It was already noted that Maslow (1970) divided esteem needs into two subsets, although counting them in one category. Utilizing the same division, Alderfer put needs for recognition, dominance, status, and the like in the Relatedness category. Needs for achievement, confidence, and autonomy belong in the Growth category. These divisions and categorizations seem reasonable, just as Maslow's did.

Alderfer's three categories, like Maslow's five, are arbitrary and form a hierarchy. Alderfer (1972: 13–17), however, specified three mechanisms that tend to shift dominance from one category to another. Whereas Maslow indicated only that attention will shift to the next higher category when the needs in all lower categories are reasonably well fulfilled, Alderfer added that a need category may become dominant because of deprivation of needs in that category or the next higher category. For example, a severe lack of fulfillment of some of our Relatedness needs may cause us to focus on those needs even though our Existence needs are only partially fulfilled. Prolonged failure to fulfill those Relatedness needs, however, will tend to force us to shift our attention to Existence needs. That is, we substitute fulfillment in the lower category for the unattainable fulfillment in the higher category.

Alderfer's theory is better supported by research than Maslow's. Some evidence has been found for the three hierarchical mechanisms. People also seem to be able to perceive Alderfer's three categories more easily than Maslow's five, lending greater reliability to measurements (Alderfer 1969; Wahba and Bridwell 1976; Wanous and Zwany 1977).

Nevertheless, Alderfer's theory suffers from some of the same deficiencies as Maslow's. The categories of needs still contain many gaps, and process needs are mixed with resource needs. The basis of hierarchical dominance is still undefined. Existence needs seem to be dominant on the basis of urgency, whereas Relatedness needs are prerequisites for Growth. Meanwhile, Alderfer's added mechanisms of movement focus on intensity of need as a basis of dominance, but intensity may vary rapidly.

Herzberg's Dual-Factor Theory

Herzberg, Mausner, and Snyderman (1959) developed an empirically based theory of need satisfiers. By asking subjects to describe instances in which they felt happy with their jobs and other instances in which they felt unhappy, and coding the content of the stories thus generated, Herzberg et al. developed two categories of resource items. The first category, which they called dissatisfiers or hygiene factors, consisted of items that seemed to generate unhappiness when not present but that produced no great happiness when present. The

Table 4–3
Satisfiers and Dissatisfiers Listed by Herzberg

Dissatisfiers or hygiene factors

1. Company policy and administration
2. Technical supervision
3. Interpersonal relations with supervisor
4. Interpersonal relations with peers
5. Interpersonal relations with subordinates
6. Salary
7. Job security
8. Personal life
9. Working conditions
10. Status

Satisfiers or motivator factors

1. Achievement
2. Recognition
3. Advancement
4. The work itself
5. Opportunity for personal growth
6. Responsibility

Source: Herzberg (1966).

second category, called satisfiers or motivators, consisted of items seldom mentioned as producing unhappiness when absent, but often associated with periods of happiness. Herzberg et al. concluded that these results reflected two basic categories of needs (i.e., need satisfiers).

Table 4-3 lists the dissatisfiers and satisfiers identified by Herzberg (1966). Note that dissatisfiers fall primarily into the first three categories of Maslow's need hierarchy, whereas satisfiers correspond primarily to the esteem and self-actualization needs.

Because they are based on research, the two categories of the dual-factor theory seem less arbitrary than those of Maslow and Alderfer. Yet it is possible that the two categories result from coder bias. Other researchers have failed to detect these two categories when using different methodology. Consequently, House and Wigdor (1967) criticized the dual-factor theory as being an artifact of the methodology used by Herzberg et al. (1959).

Another explanation of the source of the two categories can be derived from social exchange theory (Homans 1958). It may be that hygiene factors are need satisfiers that are *expected* from work as part of the unwritten social contract between employee and employer, whereas the motivators are unexpected. There is some evidence to suggest that the motivator factors tend to lose their power if they are overused, perhaps because they come to be expected.

Subsequent research on other samples of workers and in different cultures, but using the same methodology, have partially confirmed the two-factor structure. Yet, there are important differences from sample to sample. Furthermore, criticism has been directed at the way in which Herzberg aggregated his data. Secondary analysis of Herzberg's data indicates that for most respondents achievement was more often a dissatisfier than were relations with supervisors or working conditions. Similarly, although salary is mentioned more often as a source of unhappiness rather than happiness, salary is nevertheless cited in conjunction with happiness more often than some of the so-called motivators. In other words, achievement and salary are so important as need satisfiers that they might reasonably be placed in both categories (House and Wigdor 1967).

Yet another criticism of the dual-factor theory is the linkage it assumes between satisfaction and work performance. Reviews of research on the satisfaction-productivity relationship found, at best, only a small correlation (Brayfield and Crockett 1955; Herzberg, et al. 1957). Thus there is little justification for proceeding from the satisfier-dissatisfier terminology of the research to the motivator-hygiene terminology. In any case the dual-factor theory is inadequate for purposes of this book because it (1) is confined to human needs in a work context and (2) defines need in terms of satisfiers.

Table 4-4 compares the five theories reviewed above with respect to the meaning of need, the sorts of needs listed, and the basis of the theory. Having reviewed five current need theories, we now return to an exploration of the living systems view of need.

LIVING SYSTEMS MODEL OF NEEDS

Need was defined earlier as a lack of something that is required or useful. This definition does not specify the degree of lack. The deficit might be slight or total. A need for food could mean that the person is starving or simply that it has been several hours since the last meal. A firm may be a bit short of cash or bankrupt.

Range of Stability

The idea that something is lacking implies that some specific amount or degree of it would be enough to remove the deficit. The point at which the lack is

Table 4-4
Summary of Need Theories

Author	Meaning of need	Need listed in terms of	Source of needs	Derivation of theory
Murray	drive	process	innate	intuition
Atkinson, McClelland	drive	end state	learned	empiricism
Maslow	satisfier	resource, process, end state	mostly innate	intuition, observation
Alderfer	satisfier	resource, process, end state	innate, learned	intuition, empiricism
Herzberg	satisfier	resource	learned	empiricism
Tracy	lack	resource	innate, learned	deduction

removed and strain is relieved is called the *level of fulfillment*. When the level of fulfillment of a need is attained, the need is said to be fulfilled.

Living systems suffer strain not only from lacks of required resources, but also from excesses. Excess is similar to lack in the sense that both tend to motivate behavior. For instance, too much heat motivates people to seek shade just as too little heat motivates them to seek the sun. In order to get a complete picture of system requirements we must consider excesses as well as lacks.

Below a given level an excess becomes acceptable. This acceptable degree of excess is called the *level of acceptance*. Between the level of fulfillment and level of acceptance for each resource there is a *range of stability* in which the requirements of the system are met. This range centers around the specific purpose value for the resource. Figure 4-1 models the relationship between lack, purpose, and excess.

Since lack and excess are on a continuum, it is often convenient to use the term *need* for both. When used in this sense, need has the general meaning of being beyond the range of stability for a specific resource. Lack and excess both represent a system imbalance or strain.

Intensity of Need

Various theories have been proposed for predicting the intensity of a need, and thus the likelihood that it will arouse behavior. First, there is a natural cycle of lack and fulfillment. Living systems constantly consume, lose, and extrude

Figure 4–1
The Resource Need Continuum

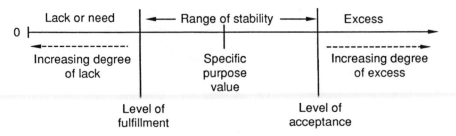

Source: From Tracy (1986: 211).

resources, which must then be replenished. An act of replenishment is aroused by need.

The *frequency* of the replenishment cycle is one measure of likelihood of need. Frequency of replenishment depends on how much of a resource is available at one time, the storage capacity for that resource, and its rate of decay, loss, consumption and/or extrusion, as well as its intrinsic importance. An important resource that is consumed rapidly and for which the system has little storage capacity would produce an urgent need, one that must be acted upon quickly. Some resources, such as oxygen for the human organism or cash for a large firm, are replenished on such a rapid cycle that the process appears to be almost constant and the need is hardly recognized. A rationed resource may have to be replenished frequently because it can only be obtained in small amounts. A resource such as the latest stock market quotations may require frequent replenishment because its worth decays rapidly. Other resources, such as shelter for a family or machinery for a manufacturing firm, may have a cycle of twenty years or longer.

Another measure of likelihood is the probability that, at any given moment, a resource will be lacking. Some needs are seldom, if ever, fulfilled; there is always some degree of lack. The need hierarchies of Maslow and Alderfer and the dual-factor theory of Herzberg seem to reflect this measure of likelihood. As one moves up the hierarchy, or from hygienes to motivators, it becomes more probable that a lack will be found and that behavior aimed at fulfilling it will be aroused.

In addition to the probability of lack there is the question of intensity. The *intensity* of a need is a function of degree of lack and intrinsic importance of the resource. An intense need is more likely to arouse behavior than a weak one. Indeed, one of the reasons that some needs may remain perpetually unfulfilled is that other, more intense needs require attention first. Maslow's need hierarchy seems to be based in part on the notion that more important (i.e., lower order) needs must be served first, regardless of degree of lack in other needs.

The intensity of a need is related to the hierarchy of values discussed in Chapter 3. The importance of a need is directly related to the importance of the variable, and the degree of lack corresponds to the degree of deviation of the variable from its preferred state. As the position of a variable in the hierarchy is a function of its importance and degree of deviation, so the intensity of a need is a function of its importance and degree of lack. In Chapter 5 we will reexamine the concept of a need hierarchy that is based on the importance of categories of needs, and in Chapter 7 need intensity will be related to motivation.

SUMMARY AND IMPLICATIONS

This chapter examined the need concept and found it generally wanting. Theories of needs as presented by Murray, Maslow, Alderfer, McClelland, Atkinson, and Herzberg et al. were reviewed. Because these theories are derived from introspection and observation of behavior, they are limited to human needs that can be consciously felt or observed. Excesses and needs for information from nonhuman sources, for purposes of physiological and material growth, and for reproduction and dissemination are ignored, as are the needs of groups and organizations. Furthermore, these theories confuse needs with resources and motivation. The theories of Maslow, Alderfer, and Herzberg divide needs into arbitrary or ad hoc categories and erect unsupported and insupportable hierarchies among them.

To avoid these problems with the concept, need was defined as the lack of a resource that is useful or required by a purpose of a living system. This definition of need allows it to be applied to groups and organizations as well as individuals. We will thus be able to treat these three levels of living systems in parallel fashion as we deal with such topics as motivation, power and influence, decision making, and leadership. By broadening the concept of human needs to include the needs of human social institutions, we also improve our understanding of individual needs. The broader concept weans us from the notion that needs are indicated by emotion or feeling, and forces us to identify needs by examining the nature of living systems, their purposes and objective requirements. It also allows us to consider unconscious needs that are not accessible to introspection or direct observation.

A model of human needs based on the nature of living systems was presented. Around each purpose is a range of stability, bounded on the lower end by its level of fulfillment and on the upper end by its level of acceptance. Below the level of fulfillment a lack or need exists; above the level of acceptance there is a condition of excess.

What is the practical value of a sound need concept? First, from a personal point of view the knowledge gives us a better understanding of the requirements of our own system. It makes us aware of requirements that we ordinarily might not notice because we don't feel them, or the behavior aimed at fulfilling them is internal, or a lack seldom occurs. It is important, for instance, to understand that we sometimes need pain as an indicator that something is wrong, and that we may need something like vitamins without being aware of it. It is also important to realize that excess can be as much of a problem as lack. Too much cholesterol, for example, can clog the arteries, but too little may cause a deterioration of the lining protecting the spinal cord. Needs are about maintaining a proper balance of things.

Several popular approaches to motivation, such as job enrichment and Herzberg's dual-factor theory, are based on or supported by Maslow's need hierarchy. On the basis of the critique of Maslow's theory, you are forewarned that his need hierarchy is not supported by evidence or logic. Thus you should be wary of the motivation approaches based on it. They may be sound, but they must stand on their own evidence.

This chapter has presented a homeostatic model of needs. Some critics reject homeostatic models as being simplistic and unable to explain behavior directed at change. The model presented here is not simplistic, however; it is dynamic. Needs may change because purposes change or new purposes are learned. The intensity of needs varies with change in the rate of input, consumption, loss, and extrusion of resources. The frequency of recurrence of needs varies with availability of resources, storage capacity, and rate of consumption, loss, and extrusion. Dynamic homeostasis results not only in maintenance of steady states, but also in growth and development, retrenchment, reproduction, and dissemination.

A research implication of this model is that more study ought to be directed at establishing ranges of stability for various resources. Some research has been done in this direction. Minimum daily requirements have been developed for human intake of calories, vitamins, and minerals. Maximum acceptable levels have been established for cholesterols, radiation, alcohol, certain minerals, and poisonous substances. Sociologists have studied the effect of membership size on group cohesiveness. Economists and business researchers have attempted to specify organizational limits for information input, capital formation, cash flow, market share, new product development, employee turnover, and the like. The living systems model of needs emphasizes the importance of these lines of research and shows how much is yet to be learned.

Another line of research that ought to receive more attention is the investigation of excesses as motivators. There is a tendency to focus on needs and need satisfiers to the exclusion of excesses and processes for their reduction. Yet once the importance of excesses is realized, it is easy to think of examples of their motivating properties. For instance, excess inventory motivates manufacturers and retailers to cut prices and offer special incentives to consumers. This behavior is often explained in terms of a need of cash, but there are other ways to fulfill that need. Excesses of energy and ideas may cause employees to engage in dysfunctional behavior if a proper outlet is not provided. Investigation of excesses would likely uncover many unrecognized sources of motivation.

NOTES

1. These and other criticisms are examined in Tracy (1986). See also Turner and Lawrence (1965), Hall and Nougaim (1968), Hulin and Blood (1968), Wahba and Bridwell (1976), Salancik and Pfeffer (1977), Mitchell (1979), and Rist (1980).

2. For a description of the development and use of the TAT, see J. Veroff, J. W. Atkinson, S. C. Field, and G. Gurin, "The use of thematic apperception to assess motivation in a nationwide interview study," *Psychological Monographs*, 74(12), No. 499.

5

Need Fulfillment
and Stress

Having established what need is and how it is related to purpose, we may now return to the question of how needs are fulfilled; that is, how are strains reduced? There are several related questions. Given that a need is a lack of a required resource, what sorts of resources are needed and how are they obtained? What is the nature of an organization's needs? How is a lack determined, and how does it vary in degree? If needs cannot all be fulfilled at once, how does a system choose which ones to act upon first?

Another question we will seek to answer in this chapter is: What happens to a system when a need cannot be fulfilled? The answer to this question leads us to the topic that is commonly referred to as stress.

FULFILLMENT

What does it mean to fulfill a need? In Chapter 4 the lower end of the range of stability was designated as the level of fulfillment. Technically, fulfillment of a need should mean attainment of the purpose for that variable. Given the imprecision of measurement and the variability of purposes, however, it is sufficient that the range of stability is attained.

Fulfillment of a need is rarely, if ever, permanent. The same lack occurs over and over again, or else it is continuous and never completely fulfilled. A manufacturing firm may fulfill its need for raw materials for a few days or weeks, but eventually the need will arise again. The need for human labor is continuous when the factory is in operation. Recurrence of lack is a function of storage capacity and rate of consumption, loss, or obsolescence.

We often speak of need satisfaction as well as fulfillment. In this book a distinction will be made between these two terms. The term *satisfaction* indicates a feeling or awareness of fulfillment. People are often unaware of their needs and may not feel any satisfaction when a need is fulfilled. Furthermore, the term *satisfaction* is usually applied only to people, not to groups or organizations. Fulfillment of needs, on the other hand, has meaning for all living systems.

According to Porter (1962), satisfaction is associated with aspirations. A person's *level of aspiration* for something is defined as the minimum that would produce a feeling of satisfaction. Is level of aspiration the same as level of fulfillment? Not necessarily, although it could be. An aspiration may be related to a desire rather than a need. Furthermore, a person may aspire to more or less than is really required. Thus a person may feel satisfied even though the need is not completely fulfilled, or may feel dissatisfied in spite of fulfillment of the need in an objective sense. For instance, people often feel dissatisfied with their income even though it is sufficient for their requirements. Their aspirations for wealth are based on desire as well as need. Indeed, too much money may be bad for people. Many a story has been written on that theme.

EXCESSES

Living systems are very active in ingesting resources. Often they ingest a lot of chaff with the wheat, cinders with the coal, packing material with the product. Useless materials must be extruded or else they will tend to accumulate and poison the system. For instance, a family or a restaurant must regularly get rid of garbage before it produces noxious odors, attracts vermin, and breeds disease organisms.

Excesses of useful materials are also possible. The human body needs calories, but many people fight a lifelong battle against ingesting too many of them. Groups often seek new members, but too many members can spoil a group's cohesiveness. A brokerage firm needs orders, yet too many orders in a short period of time can flood the firm in paperwork.

Excesses may also be generated internally. Certain human illnesses are caused by excessive production of hormones. A work group may generate so much gossip or horseplay that it fails to get its work done. A business firm may produce excess inventory. In fact, all inventoried products are excess in the sense that the firm has no direct use for them itself. The firm must extrude its products in exchange for resources that it does require. The firm may also generate pollution, scrap, and stress among its employees, all of which would tend to poison the system if the excess cannot be extruded or its production curtailed.

Note that one system's excess may be just what another system needs. A cow's excrement is a farmer's fertilizer. A firm's excess inventory may be the stock that an individual or another firm requires. Such differences of opinion about the worth of resources are the basis for exchange. A worker trades excess energy and skill for an employer's excess cash. The worker then exchanges the cash for a grocer's excess groceries—the grocer can't eat them all—and so on.

Excesses include energy and information as well as matter. A healthy human body generates more heat and muscle power than it needs. The excess is extruded through work and play. People also accumulate more knowledge and skill than they can use personally. Such excesses often are traded for money, goods, services, or personal relationships. Money may usually be regarded as excess information, in the sense that the system has no direct use for it other than to get rid of it in exchange for needed resources. As we shall see in Chapter 8, however, retention of excess resources is a source of power.

We often say that we need more time or more space. Actually this is a way of saying that we have an excess of information or matter. Sometimes information floods in upon us and we feel we need more time to sort it out and act upon it. We are in the same situation as the university computer facilities at the end of a term when all of the students are trying to run their programs at the same time. The university's need for more computer time is equivalent to an excess of data input.

An apparent need for more space is likewise equivalent to an excess of matter. A family may feel an urge to move to a bigger house when the closets are all full. A nation may assert a need for more territory in which to settle its excess population. But a garage sale and a birth control program would also serve these needs.

Similarly, peace and rest are the absence of energy. When a parent demands peace and quiet in the house, the cause is likely to be an excess of childish energy. A cease-fire in the fighting between groups or nations is a call for reduction in explosive energy output.

Space, peace, and time might be regarded as resources in the same sense as matter, energy, and information. But space, peace, and time are "empty" resources. Their worth lies in their absence of excess.

In a broad sense we could say that excesses fit the definition of needs, because an excess is a lack of space, peace, or time. But lacks and excesses tend to motivate opposite forms of behavior. Lacks are fulfilled by increasing inputs or internal production and by decreasing outputs. Excesses are reduced by decreasing inputs or production and by increasing outputs.

THE NATURE OF NEEDS AND RESOURCES

Obviously, living systems have needs for matter—food, raw materials, tools, and machinery, for example. Energy such as heat, light, muscle power, and electricity is also needed. Information is another class of needs; for example, recognition of good work, knowledge of surroundings, weather forecasts, economic forecasts, sales orders, balance sheets, understanding of capabilities.

These three classes of needs—matter, energy, and information—include everything that exists. In fact matter, energy, and information are three aspects of the same reality. Matter holds potential energy in its mass, its motion, and its chemical and atomic bonds. Energy is stored in matter. Matter is converted into energy in an atomic reaction. Information is carried by markers of matter and energy. That is, information is coded in the pattern of material such as the ink on this page or in the magnetic fields on a computer disk.

The distinction between matter, energy, and information is largely a question of how we process reality. A book is obviously solid matter; you could use it to prop open a door or you could shred it and stuff a pillow with it. It also contains energy, as you would discover if you dropped it on your foot or burned it. Yet we tend to process a book for its information content rather than its matter or energy content.

As we noted in Chapter 2, the critical subsystems of living systems can be divided into two groups, depending on whether they process matter-energy or information. For matter-energy there are the ingestor, distributor, converter, producer, storage, motor, supporter, and extruder subsystems. Information is processed by the input and internal transducers, channel and net, decoder, associator, memory, decider, encoder, and output transducer subsystems.

The two groups of subsystems interact extensively. A given substance may be processed by both groups at once. A factory receives (ingests) a shipment of parts, distributes them to the assembly line, produces a finished product, stores it in inventory, and finally ships (extrudes) it. At the same time receipt of the shipment of parts is noted on an invoice, which is sent through channels and associated with an order that was recorded in memory. A decision is made to pay the invoice, payment is encoded on a check, and the check is extruded through the mail room. In similar fashion the human body processes food as matter (vitamins, minerals, roughage), energy (calories), and information (taste, aroma, texture).

Although many inputs are processed in more than one way, they can usually be categorized as primarily matter, energy, or information. Let us see if needs can be listed nonarbitrarily in these three categories.

Matter

Human individuals need food, water, and air. These are often called physiological needs. To this list we could add vitamins, minerals, medicines, and dental fillings. But people use matter externally as well as internally. Other material needs include clothing and shelter, which are often called safety needs, as well as eye glasses, hearing aids, tools, and vehicles. The latter items are usually not listed as needs at all, though they might be considered adjuncts to safety or self-actualization.

Thus far we have only listed needs that are normally fulfilled from external sources. The human body also produces certain required substances, such as blood and digestive juices. These should be added to the list of physiological needs. Although produced internally, they fit the definition of needs. In fact they can be supplied from external sources (e.g., a blood transfusion), if necessary.

In addition to the material needs of its members, a work group requires tools, machines, transporters, raw materials, and a place to meet and work. Likewise, a restaurant needs inputs of foodstuff (fresh, frozen, canned), spices, oils, water, soap, kitchen equipment, plates, cups, silverware, linen, tables and chairs, and customers. It may produce some of its need satisfiers, such as sauces and menus.

Some kinds of matter are used up rapidly, whereas other matter is retained for long periods. The human body quickly consumes food, air, and water, converting them into energy and waste products. But clothing, shelter, and eyeglasses are consumed very slowly. Likewise, an organization consumes raw materials rapidly, but machinery and plant tend to last a long time.

Rate of use and storage capacity are important variables in determining how often a need must be acted upon. Living systems vary in their storage capacity for various kinds of matter. The human body can store only enough air (oxygen) for a few minutes of life, enough water for a few days, and enough food (in the form of fat) for a few weeks. Some material needs, such as clothing and shelter, are not stored internally at all, but can be retained through external storage. The storage capacity for food, water, and other needs can likewise be expanded through use of artifacts such as boxes and jars.

Organizations also vary in their storage capacity for various material needs. A restaurant retains kitchen equipment, plates and cups, silverware, and tables and chairs for long periods. Canned and frozen foods can be stored for weeks or months. But fresh foods and customers must be replaced daily.

Energy

People need various forms of energy. Some energy is produced internally by processing food and flexing muscle fibers, but we also import energy, particularly warmth, directly from the environment. Electrical energy provides light and heat. Energy is derived from gasoline to power vehicles.

A work group or organization uses the kinetic muscular energy generated by its members, as well as various external sources of energy, to drive machinery, provide heat and light, and transmit information. An organization may obtain energy such as electricity from external sources, or it may produce its own.

Energy is not as easy to store as matter. Heat can be retained for short periods through insulation and by limiting circulation. Kinetic energy can be stored in a flywheel for a short period. Electricity can be stored in a capacitor or battery. But energy is most commonly stored in the form of matter, which is processed when the energy is required. Thus coal and oil are stored to produce heat or electricity on demand. Gasoline is stored to fuel engines; water is stored behind dams to power electrical generators.

As a result of poor storage capacity, energy needs tend to recur frequently, even to appear constant. For instance, human survival requires that the muscle energy of the heart be supplied continuously.

Energy needs tend to be fulfilled so automatically that we are not aware of them as needs. Thus they are often not listed in compilations of human needs. Yet, if you were suddenly deprived of heat or a heartbeat, you would quickly realize that you require it and it is lacking. Likewise, we tend to take electricity for granted until the power fails and we are stuck in an elevator in the dark.

Information

Information is probably the least understood aspect of reality. Foster (1975) pointed out that there is information coded in any physical relationship, although a relationship may not hold meaning for a given observer. Morse code carries very complex information in the form of a string of dots and dashes; computers use a similar string of electrical pulses and gaps. Whether the information contained in Morse or computer code holds any meaning for you rests on whether you understand the code.

There is information contained in the fact that a supervisor silently watches an employee from a distance of fifteen feet. The supervisor does not have to move or say anything in order for the employee to derive meaning from this relationship. Of course, we cannot be sure that the meaning the employee derives is correct. The employee might assume that the supervisor suspects something, whereas the supervisor may actually be admiring the employee's work. But the information is there, whether it is read correctly or not.

People require accurate information about the weather, the placement of objects in their vicinity, the intentions of other people, relationships with other people and groups, the laws and customs of their society, and many other external matters. They also need information about their own identity, internal states of physical and mental health, levels of alertness and energy, emotions, feelings toward others, and so forth.

A work group needs information about what tasks it is supposed to accomplish, whether it is meeting organizational standards, how it will be rewarded, and what its status with other groups is. Internally, the group needs to know about its morale, its plans, and the maintenance of norms. A business organization requires information about the economy, laws, competition, availability of capital and labor, new products and services, customer needs and wants, prices of parts and raw materials, transportation costs, and a host of other external matters. It must also know about its internal inventory, productive capacity, cash flow, efficiency, morale, the status of orders, and many other forms of control data.

Information is used to monitor steady states and changes both internally and in the environment. Another use is to assess the worth of things. People and organizations need money and credit as symbols of their worth and ability to pay for goods and services. Information is also used internally to give direction to acts, as when the brain sends signals to the limbs or a supervisor gives instructions to an employee.

Information is easier to store than matter or energy. People store information in the memory as well as in motor synapses. They also use external storage devices such as books, files, photos, and recordings. Groups and organizations likewise use the memories of their members, but tend to rely more heavily on external devices such as plans, blueprints, charts, books, journals, reports, computers, and filing systems.

A problem with information storage is that some information, such as data on the current status of the environment or of an ongoing process, tends to become quickly outdated. It clogs the memory and influences decisions when it shouldn't. Thus new data must constantly be sought and obsolete information must be removed from the system.

One interesting characteristic of information is that it is not necessarily consumed when it is used. Provided that it is encoded, transmitted, decoded, and recorded faithfully, it can be replicated almost indefinitely, though with some degradation. Human reproduction is a process of replicating in a child some of the genetic information contained in the parents. Education is a process of spreading ideas to an ever-wider audience. Photocopying and tape recording are processes for copying visual and aural information so that it can be disseminated. In each of these cases information is copied without loss of the original. Thus, unlike matter and energy needs, information needs can often be met without taking any information away from the environment or from other systems, though not without consuming matter-energy.

NEED CLASSIFICATION BY PURPOSE

Thus far we have noted that needs vary according to (1) the nature of what is needed (i.e., matter, energy, or information), (2) the immediate source of fulfillment (internal or external), (3) storage capacity, and (4) rate of consumption. Needs may also be classified by the purposes they serve. There are at least two important distinctions that can be made among different purposes. First, a purpose may be primarily innate or learned. Second, we can group purposes in broad categories such as maintenance and actualization.

Innate and Learned Needs

Needs may be classified as innate or learned in accordance with the purposes that define them. That is, an innate need is defined by an innate purpose and a learned need by a learned purpose. This classification cannot be absolute, however. Many purposes are originally innate but modified through learning. In addition, some needs are defined by more than one purpose. A need of money, for example, may result from many purposes, some innate and some learned.

It is often assumed that innate needs are somehow more basic or important than learned needs. One argument for this assumption is that innate needs are based on survival. A related argument is that, when a purpose is really important to the health of a system, it becomes built into the template of the system through natural selection.

There is some truth in each of these arguments, but there are also exceptions. Some innate needs are not based on survival of the individual, and some learned needs are. Innate needs that are based on purposes of reproduction are important for the survival of the genes or the species, but not the individual. Indeed, reproductive processes may take away resources that are needed for the parents' survival. Childbirth can be hazardous to the mother's health, and child rearing entails sharing resources. On the other hand, the learned purpose of obeying traffic signals is very important for survival in a modern city.

This latter point also illustrates a fallacy in the argument that the most important purposes become built into a system's template. The template adapts slowly, but survival may require more rapid adjustment to environmental changes. Consequently, some of the values specified by the template may be obsolete. People don't need an appendix and it can be dangerous to have one, but the genetic template still instructs the human body to form one. Certain innate aggressive purposes may be similarly out of place in modern society. In their stead we must learn new purposes that are appropriate to life in an industrialized, overpopulated society.

The same point can be made with respect to the purposes of groups, organizations, and societies. The charter of a business organization may specify that a major purpose of the firm is to manufacture cash registers. As technology changes, however, the firm may find it has an opportunity to survive and prosper by producing small computers. The original purpose is modified; it is now partly innate, partly learned. Eventually the charter may be rewritten to reflect the new purpose, but this process only ratifies the importance of the learned purpose.

Learned purposes and learned needs are important because they represent the adaptability of living systems to changes in their environment. They may also represent purposes that are important to suprasystems. A system may learn or modify some purposes simply through its own experience, but often purposes are deliberately taught by a suprasystem. For instance, people are taught by the family or school to obey traffic lights. These same suprasystems teach children the values of reading, writing, and arithmetic. These are not innate values, but they are certainly important for survival in modern society. They are also important to the survival of the society itself. Commerce and warfare alike require that individuals in the society have these skills.

Learned purposes and needs sometimes conflict with innate ones. People are taught to make sacrifices for the good of the family, church, or nation. In some circumstances these sacrifices may involve substantial risk to life and limb. Obviously, such purposes conflict with the innate purposes of individual survival and maintenance. Yet people often accept the purposes of family and nation as their own, and act upon them. Likewise, a business firm may willingly accept a national purpose such as clean air, even if it reduces corporate profit.

Categories of Needs

It is an impossible task to list all the needs of living systems, or even of one such system. We may be able to suggest the extent of these needs, however, by developing general categories for them. For instance, groups of specific purposes are associated with each of the three imperatives of living systems. These groups of purposes can be used to classify needs.

Let us define three broad categories of needs. The first category is called *Maintenance needs* and is defined by purposes of maintaining the health of the system. *Actualization needs*, the second category, consist of needs defined by purposes of growth and elaboration. Growth and elaboration differ from one another, but both involve purposeful change in order to actualize the potential inherent in the system. Other purposeful change, such as retrenchment or simplification in order to adapt to a changing environment or an aging system, belongs in the Maintenance category. The third category, called *Propagation needs*, consists of needs defined by purposes of reproduction and dissemination.

These three categories may be subdivided according to the nature of what is needed. Thus there are material (matter-energy) and informational Maintenance needs. With respect to human individuals, we might call them physiological and psychological Maintenance needs, respectively. The former category includes food, water, and air, but also blood and a steady pulse as well as shelter and protection from physical harm. Devices such as eyeglasses, dentures, a hearing aid, crutches, a wheelchair, and a heart pacemaker are included in this category. Informational (psychological) Maintenance needs have to do with maintaining orientation, identity, self-esteem, and secure interpersonal relationships.

Material Actualization needs are those required for physical growth and elaboration of the system. For individuals this includes maturation and development of strength, agility, and beauty, as well as acquisition of various devices, such as tools and vehicles, that increase human physical capabilities. Informational Actualization needs include accumulation of knowledge as well as elaboration of the system itself and its relationships to the environment. At the individual level this means growth of knowledge and skill, elaboration of personality, moral and ethical development, and extension of interpersonal relationships.

Material Propagation needs are the requirements for physical replication of all or part of the system or its artifacts. Human biological reproduction would generate such needs, as would painting a portrait or printing a book. Informational Propagation needs include the template for reproduction as well as anything required for dissemination of the information content of the system. The human genetic code, but also human knowledge, languages, laws, customs, beliefs, roles, and ideas fall in this category.

At the organizational level material Maintenance needs might include plant, machinery, labor, and a steady supply of electrical power and raw materials. Informational Maintenance needs would be such as sales orders, credit, cash, inventory records, payroll, production orders, budgets, expense vouchers, machine maintenance manuals, and blueprints of existing facilities. Actualization needs of a business firm might include materials such as enlarged plant, new employees, improved machinery and raw materials, research laboratory equipment, and prototypes of new products, as well as information such as fresh capital, mergers, economic projections, market research, new patents, employee suggestions, and training programs.

Material Propagation needs of an organization might consist of new stores or plants as well as product inventory (in the sense that products represent part of the system that is reproduced and disseminated). Informational Propagation needs might include franchises, patents, reputation, operating instructions, and cash. Propagation needs of a university would consist of materials such as graduates, books, and inventions, plus information such as current knowledge, new ideas, art, music, literature, patents, attitudes, and skills. For a religious organization Propagation needs would probably include converts, places of worship, books and tracts, and beliefs.

By focusing on the imperatives of living systems, these categories help us to identify requirements without having to list every need. With a little imagination we could use the categories to generate representative lists of needs for a family, a work group, a city government, or a nation. What these categories do not tell us, however, is which needs are most important or most salient at any given moment.

HIERARCHY OF NEEDS

A living system ordinarily cannot reduce all of its strains. The system is limited by time (that is, by the fact that there are more needs demanding attention than can be acted upon at once) and by resources. For practical purposes we would like to be able to identify which needs and excesses are most likely to lead to action. Which strains are the most intense or urgent or important? The answer to this question is far from simple.

The answer begins with the hierarchy of values that was discussed in Chapter 3. According to Miller (1978: 4), this hierarchy indicates "the relative urgency of reducing each of [the] specific strains" in a living system. Strains, in turn, are produced by lacks or excesses of required resources or by the threat of such lacks or excesses. A system acts to reduce strains in accordance with their relative urgency (i.e., the hierarchy of values) and its resources and capabilities. Unfortunately, this doesn't help us much. The hierarchy of values varies constantly, as we noted in Chapter 3. At best we may be able to identify some general tendencies of dominance.

It would help if we could establish a basis for dominance of one need over another. Dominance of a need has many possible meanings. Are we looking for differences in intensity, the degree of lack or excess? Or is it urgency, the immediacy of threat to the system? Perhaps it is simply frequency or likelihood of a lack occurring. Or is it importance, the centrality of the need to the purposes of the system? From a practical point of view it appears we must focus on importance. Intensity, urgency, and frequency of lack tend to vary rapidly, depending on such variables as storage capacity, rate of consumption, and the specific purposes to be served. Thus intensity, urgency, and frequency would not be good bases for establishing general, long-term dominance tendencies. Importance, on the other hand, changes slowly if at all.

How might needs vary in importance? We have already noted that innate needs are not necessarily more important than learned needs. Likewise, external needs such as food and water may be as important as internal needs such as blood and hormones.

Is there any basis for proclaiming greater importance for matter or energy or information? In one sense it could be argued that information comes first. A living system cannot exist without a template, and the template is information. Furthermore, a system cannot act upon any of its needs without data input to the decider indicating the degree of lack or excess as well as data output indicating the chosen action. However, although information needs may assume primacy, we must not forget that information is stored and conveyed in markers of matter or energy.

We might suspect that the imperatives—Maintenance, Actualization, and Propagation—are not equally important. Is not maintenance of steady states most central to the vitality of a living system? After all, a sick system is in no shape for growth or reproduction. Even though growth and reproduction usually require alteration of some steady states, a degree of stability must be maintained during the change process lest the system collapse. A certain amount of growth and development, in turn, is necessary before the system is ready for reproduction or dissemination of ideas. Thus one could argue that Maintenance, Actualization, and Propagation needs form a hierarchy of importance in that order.

The trouble with this assertion is that we can think of many exceptions to it. Often a system must grow and develop or else fall easy prey to other systems. People must mature and gain knowledge or else become dependent on the charity of others for their livelihood. Business firms that remain small are very vulnerable to changes in the economy or customer preferences. Large, complex organizations such as General Motors or the Roman Catholic Church, on the other hand, seem to be able to survive great upheavals. If survival is the criterion, we cannot always assert the primacy of Maintenance over Actualization.

In Chapter 1 we noted Dawkins' (1976: ch. 2) argument that living systems are "survival machines" for the genes. From that point of view long-term genetic survival is more dependent on reproduction than on maintenance of the current system. Dawkins also suggested that ideas may be similar to genes, possessing potential immortality through dissemination. People who know they are dying often choose to spend their last months or moments trying to communicate some final words of wisdom distilled from their experience of life.

Whether Maintenance, Actualization, or Propagation is most important seems to depend on at least three factors: environmental conditions, stage of life, and viewpoint. When the environment is harsh or threatening, maintenance tends to assume dominance. If the system perceives that maintenance is likely to fail, however, it may turn to growth and development as a means of meeting the challenge or to propagation as a way of preserving something of itself.

Assuming that the environmental niche is capable of supporting the system, its stage of life becomes a factor in determining the dominant purposes. In youth both people and organizations tend to emphasize growth and elaboration of the system. Middle age is devoted to reproduction and dissemination with a modicum of maintenance. In old age maintenance tends to become primary, although some systems continue to develop and to disseminate ideas. This picture is drawn from the viewpoint of the system, itself. From the viewpoint of the genes or template, however, Propagation comes first. The template is already well developed and stable, although its carrier systems might not be.

Henceforth we will consider the hierarchy of importance of needs from the viewpoint of a given living system. As indicated above, the hierarchy of importance is conditional, depending on the system's environment and stage of life. Under good conditions Actualization needs assume primacy in the early stages and Propagation needs in midlife. Maintenance needs, although always having some importance, tend to take primacy in a harsh environment and during the declining years of the system. Information needs precede matter-energy needs.

Comparison with Other Hierarchies

The living systems need hierarchy described above differs substantially from those proposed by Maslow, Alderfer, and Herzberg. First, the basis of the new hierarchy has been clearly defined as importance or centrality of the need, whereas the basis of the earlier hierarchies was unclear. Second, the categories of needs, although still somewhat arbitrary, are clearly defined in terms of the purposes of the system. Third, the living systems need hierarchy is contingent on environmental conditions and the developmental stage of the system, rather than being fixed. Fourth, this hierarchy applies to groups and organizations as well as human individuals.

The new need hierarchy is less ambitious than its predecessors. It doesn't claim to indicate by itself what needs are likely to be dominant at any instant. It recognizes that other factors such as urgency and intensity must also be taken into account. The new hierarchy may be perceived as a set of weighting factors to be combined with other factors in determining the strength of a need. Other factors being equal, a youthful system is more apt to act upon an Actualization need, whereas a mature system is more likely to choose a Propagation need, and an old or troubled system is likely to focus on Maintenance needs.

There is another practical difficulty in making use of the living systems need hierarchy. It is a hierarchy of lacks based on purposes, rather than a hierarchy of resources. A given resource may serve needs in all three categories. Money, for instance, is useful for purposes of maintenance, growth, and dissemination. Thus the new hierarchy cannot easily predict what resources will have the greatest worth to a system. It is not an automatic guide to the choice of appropriate rewards and punishments, as the hierarchies of Maslow, Alderfer, and Herzberg seem to be. To the extent that the earlier hierarchies are inaccurate and ambiguous, however, their seeming value as predictors is no advantage.

STRESS

Miller (1978: 34) defined stress as a lack or excess of input or output that forces a system variable beyond its range of stability, or the threat of such a lack or excess. In other words, stress is a stimulus that produces a strain or anticipation of strain in the system.

According to Ivancevich and Matteson (1980: 5–9), this is one of three ways in which human stress is generally defined. Stress may also be defined as a set of physiological and psychological responses to pressure (Selye 1956) or as the interaction between the environment and a person's reaction to it. Selye's response definition is most often cited in the literature on human stress, but it is specific to the organism level of systems. Therefore, Miller's definition will be used here.

Stress and strain may be either good or bad for a living system. A moderate amount of stress is almost unavoidable and, in any case, makes life interesting. In Chapter 7 we will see the importance of stress in motivation. Problems for the system occur, however, when sources of stress cannot be controlled and resultant strains cannot be relieved.

The focus of much of the literature on human stress is upon the deleterious effects of excessive strain in the system. Selye (1956) identified a syndrome of innate human responses that occur when strain builds up. Initially, these responses are designed to cope with the strain by marshalling additional resources. If the effort is unsuccessful, however, the result is exhaustion and illness.

Organizations show a similar set of responses to stress. When a sharp drop in sales occurs or is anticipated, for instance, a healthy business firm is able to draw upon and commit additional resources to marketing, new product development, cost reduction, and so on in order to reduce the strain on income. Employees usually pitch in with renewed energy to save the company. If the effort is unsuccessful after many months, however, panic sets in and the components of the organization begin to compete for increasingly scarce resources or to look for ways to abandon the ship. The system loses its ability to fight back.

The degree of strain generated by any given stress varies from system to system, depending on such factors as differing purposes, storage capabilities, and processes for coping or making substitutions. A given amount of work may be excessive for one person and insufficient for another. One firm may weather an oil shortage much better than another because it has greater oil reserves or is better able to conserve energy or convert to other power sources. Although we can objectively measure the amount of stress on a system, we cannot know whether it is harmful until we know the capabilities of the system to cope with it.

The key factors creating a condition of excessive stress and strain are (1) lack of control over the environment and (2) inability to reduce strain to an acceptable level. Although the environment of a living system is largely out of its control, it normally attempts to establish some influence over the flow of inputs and outputs. The possession and use of power for this purpose will be discussed in Chapter 8. When power fails or is inadequate, the system must fall back on its second line of defense, which is the use of processes to reduce strain.

There are several reasons why a system may be unable to reduce a strain. Perhaps the foremost is inadequate resources. The system simply lacks the matter-energy or information required to do the job. Indeed, it may lack information about the nature or causes of the problem, thereby making it difficult to decide on a solution.

Another reason for difficulty in reducing strain is that there are too many stresses occurring at once. Although the system has the resources to cope with any single stress, it cannot handle all of them. It may also waste valuable time trying to choose which strain to deal with first, or switching back and forth among them.

Yet another reason is the lack of a subsystem or process for coping with a particular stress. Nature did not design the human system to cope with certain poisonous substances or with a constant condition of information overload, for instance. Small businesses often have no subsystems designed to cope with labor problems, government regulations, or sudden success. Trying to develop such subsystems when the need arises is likely to fail.

Management of stress may focus on controlling inputs and outputs or on modifying internal processes. Inadequate input or excessive output (*lack stress*) calls for action such as searching for additional resources, conserving stored resources, and curtailing production. Excessive input or lack of output (*excess stress*) requires such acts as moving away from the source of input, filtering inputs, or diversifying production. Stress management also requires awareness of the capabilities of the system and avoidance of stresses for which it lacks coping processes.

People and organizations face both necessary and unnecessary stress. Coping with unnecessary stress caused by ambiguous or conflicting role specifications, excessively rigid structure, unreasonable demands, or the leader's personal agenda consumes resources that might better be devoted to the necessary stress of competition. Good management avoids unnecessary stress and focuses the energy of employees on coping with that which cannot be avoided.

SUMMARY AND IMPLICATIONS

Fulfillment of a need means acquiring sufficient resources to attain its range of stability. Need satisfaction involves feeling or awareness of the fulfillment of a need or desire.

Resources are required for broad purposes of Maintenance, Actualization, and Propagation of the system. Needs form a conditional hierarchy wherein Actualization needs are most important to a young system, Propagation assumes dominance in maturity, and Maintenance becomes most important in the declining years or under threatening conditions. Information generally is required before matter-energy.

Needs are a key to motivation, as we will see in Chapter 7. In order to devise methods for motivating superior work performance, a manager must know how performance can lead to fulfillment of workers' needs. Knowledge of the living systems need hierarchy may enable a manager to predict which needs are likely to be most important at different stages in a worker's life. The manager may then be able to arrange for fulfillment of those needs as a consequence of superior work performance. A manager may also be able to stimulate (and fulfill) needs that the worker isn't even aware of, thereby gaining power and influence. This will be discussed further in Chapter 10.

It is important for managers to realize that groups and organizations have needs in the same sense that people do. Part of a manager's job is to plan for the fulfillment of organizational needs. Furthermore, in trying to motivate superior work performance it may be better to try to arrange for fulfillment of work group needs instead of, or in addition to, individual workers' needs. For example, recognition of the status of a work group based on collective performance may be an important motivator. Under some technologies work performance depends more on cooperation within the work group than on individual effort.

An understanding of organizational needs and the basis of them may aid a manager in planning to meet those needs. For example, the need to plan for managerial succession is often overlooked in small, entrepreneurial organizations. An understanding, first, that the organization must have a strong decider subsystem and, second, that a maturing organization must begin thinking more about maintenance of the system may lead to decisions that will preserve the health of the organization. Managers must also be aware that the needs of the organization and of its members are closely intertwined. Mutual fulfillment of needs is the underlying basis of membership or employment in groups and organizations. This topic will be explored further in Chapter 7.

With respect to stress, managers should be aware that not all stress is bad and, indeed, some stress is to be expected as a condition of life. Stress becomes harmful when it cannot be relieved. Overloading people with work so that they cannot complete one task before another intrudes, making work demands that conflict with each other or with the employee's values, withholding resources needed to complete a task, and continually presenting a bleak picture of the future are ways of creating excessive, unproductive stress. A wise manager attempts to present employees with tasks they can handle, provides sufficient resources, and gives proper rewards for success.

A line of research suggested by this chapter is to test the idea that the hierarchy of needs varies with stage of life. Do Actualization needs dominate in youth, followed by Propagation needs in maturity and Maintenance needs in old age? Do Maintenance needs become dominant under threatening environmental conditions? Is this true for groups and organizations as well as individuals?

Research on stress might fruitfully investigate the relationship between strain in a group or organization and in its members. A family that is struggling to make ends meet may transfer the strain to members of the family. Likewise, a failing business firm seems more likely to produce a stressful environment for its employees than a successful one would. In such circumstances the family members or employees may run into personal problems of coping, thereby increasing the pressures on the family or firm. If this vicious cycle exists, is there any way out of it? Does new leadership or family counseling remove some of the burden of stress, enabling the members to cope with the rest of it?

6

Information Processing and Communication

No aspect of living systems can be ignored in understanding organizational behavior, but the information processing subsystems are particularly important. They are usually discussed in a fragmented fashion in OB books under such headings as perception, decision making, and communication. In this chapter they will be treated together.

Perception is the combination of processes by which an organism receives, decodes, and interprets information from its environment. It involves the input transducer, channel and net, decoder, memory, associator, and decider subsystems. Data are brought across the boundary of the system by the input transducer, decoded into signals suitable for the nervous system, selected by the decider, and interpreted or recognized by the associator in conjunction with memory.

Decision making is the function of the decider subsystem. As we noted in Chapter 2, there are four basic stages in the deciding process. First, a purpose or goal is established. Second, information is obtained and analyzed to determine the current state of the system and its environment with respect to that purpose or goal, and what adjustments are possible. Third, an act or acts are chosen from among the possible adjustments in order to attain the purpose or goal in an efficient manner. Fourth, orders are issued by the decider to other subsystems in order to implement the chosen act(s). The second and fourth stages involve interaction with other information processing subsystems in obtaining information and issuing orders.

Communication is usually regarded as purposeful transmission of information from one system, the sender, to one or more receiving systems. It involves the decider, channel and net, encoder, and output transducer of the sender as well as environmental conditions and the perception processes of the receiver. Communication is often a mutual dyadic process in which both systems alternately send and receive. In that case all of a system's information processing subsystems are engaged at some point in the process.

In contrast to perception and decision making, which are viewed as internal processes of a system, communication is treated as occurring between systems. This is partly a matter of perspective, however. Communication between two organisms constitutes internal information processing for the group, organization, or society to which they belong. From this perspective communication may be defined generally as purposeful transmission of information between systems or components of a system.

Although perception, deciding, and communication are purposeful, it should not be assumed that they are necessarily conscious processes. Living systems process much information without self-awareness. A system may also be unaware of biases that distort its perceptions. It may communicate unconsciously through body language or choice of medium. The vast majority of choices (e.g., where to place the next footstep, which order to process next) are normally made below the level of consciousness, using patterned responses.

The concepts of perception, decision making, and communication apply to groups and organizations as well as individuals. From a living systems theory viewpoint social systems *do* cognize, contrary to opinion of some experts (James, Joyce, and Slocum 1988). An organization's cognitive processes are downwardly dispersed to individual members but, when they are acting for the organization, their perceptions and decisions are the organization's perceptions and decisions.

In this chapter the three topics of perception, decision making, and communication will be discussed from a living systems point of view. Their relationships to values, needs, and motivation will be examined. Implications of the discussion for practice and research will be drawn.

PERCEPTION

Perception is the means by which new information becomes available to the decider subsystem. Living systems need many kinds of information, both for its intrinsic value and as a means to achievement of other purposes. A wealth of information is present in the environment as well as within the system, but it must be perceived in order to become useful.

In human individuals the five senses constantly receive information from the environment, and internal sensors monitor subsystem processes. Only in sleep are some of these sensors turned off or their input ignored. During waking hours the total amount of information impinging upon a person is much greater than can be processed. The information must be selected or filtered in some way.

One method of filtering is simply to shut down some of the sensors. The eyes may be closed, the ears covered, and internal sensors numbed with drugs. This method carries dangers for the system if practiced for long periods, because it eliminates whole classes of information. Pain may be unpleasant, for instance, but it provides valuable information about the state of the organism. Complaints serve a similar purpose in an organization. Numbing the pain or ignoring the complaint does not solve the basic problem, which may harm the system if uncorrected.

Lower echelons of the decider subsystem filter out much of the incoming information on the basis of relatively simple criteria such as the intensity or persistence of the signal. That is, signals below a certain threshold of length, volume, brightness, and such are ignored. A slightly more complex filter might employ characteristics such as pitch, hue, or taste in selecting signals for attention (or action without attention). At higher echelons of the decider such criteria as the source of the signal, frequency of repetition, number of different channels carrying a similar message, and medium or topic of the message may be used to select information. Of course, the meaning of the information itself can be used for selection, but in that case the decider must give it full attention, thereby losing much of the benefit of filtering.

The effectiveness of the system depends greatly on the filtering process. If filtering cuts out too much useful information, the system will make poor decisions. If too much information is allowed to reach the decider, however, it may become overloaded and have little time to make decisions. Thus the quality of the decision rules used to select information becomes very important. A bias against a large category of people as sources of information, for instance, may be efficient if information from them is always of poor quality, but it puts the system in jeopardy if information from those people is often useful.

Another problem in perception is that noise and distortion may mar the signal before it reaches the decider. Noise is the addition of random data to a signal, such that the original signal may become obscured. Distortion is a nonrandom alteration of the signal.

Noise may be added at any stage of information processing, as well as in the environment. It is impossible to avoid noise completely, because it is a product of entropy. The effect of noise in the environment can sometimes be reduced, however, by moving away from its source. When you want someone at a party to perceive an important message, it is wise to move into a quiet corner. Noise within the system may be overcome by intensifying the signal before the noise is introduced, and by using multiple channels or redundancy. A manager may try to insure that everyone reads an important memo by issuing it in an unusual color or type style, by following up with an announcement at a meeting, or by sending reminder memos.

Distortion may occur because of a misreading of the signal in the transducer or decoder, or through misclassification in the associator or memory. Distortion may also occur deliberately through conscious or unconscious application of a decision rule by the decider. For example, a person may have the attitude that all information from a certain source is probably false, and may employ a decision rule that inverts all messages from that source. This is an attempt to correct anticipated distortion, but the rule will itself cause distortion when the source happens to be truthful.

Distortion is difficult to correct, unless the exact nature of the alteration of the signal is known. RCA Victor records used to employ a process of "reverse" distortion that was supposed to compensate for the distortion inherent in the average record player. Unfortunately, their records sounded distorted on good hi-fi systems that lacked such distortion. It is better, whenever possible, to remove the source of distortion (e.g., improve the record player) than to try to compensate for distortion after it has occurred.

Removing sources of distortion once they are in the system can be difficult. Distortion is often self-protecting. The severest forms of distortion simply cancel the signal entirely. Biased attitudes, for instance, tend to cause rejection of information that might correct them. If women as a class are assumed to lack managerial potential, information that a particular woman has such potential is likely to be rejected or interpreted to indicate something else. Only a salient message from a respected source is likely to remove or overcome such a bias.

Bias and selectivity in perception are purposeful. Indeed, perception as a whole is purposeful, motivated behavior. Bias and selectivity are intended to protect the system from the stress of too much information or information that does not meet the needs of the system. Processing useless or harmful data is costly; it is efficient to eliminate such information before it is processed. The problem with bias and selectivity is not that these processes exist, but that they are often wrongly applied. The rules and criteria governing their application are simply inadequate for the complexity of the input.

Perception is usually regarded as an individual phenomenon, but it applies as well to groups and organizations. Most information input processes to social systems are downwardly dispersed to the individual members. For example, sales orders usually enter a business firm via a salesperson, although it is possible for them to enter through a computer link. The salesperson thus becomes part of the input transducer for the firm. If the salesperson distorts the order, for instance by changing the price or specifications, that distortion affects the perception processes of the firm. A firm may display biases, such as a preference for certain suppliers, that automatically cause the organization to reject information about good alternatives.

Distortion and noisy channels are likely to be more of a problem in groups and organizations than for individuals. The reason is that the channels in organizations are longer. Information passes through many individuals, each one adding his or her own alterations to the signal. To counter this, most organizations build redundancy and multiple channels into the system. Management information systems also represent an attempt to ensure that sufficient accurate information is received by the upper echelons of the decider subsystem. Without valid information the decider cannot perform efficiently.

DECISION MAKING

At all levels Miller (1978: 32) found the most vital subsystem to be the decider, because it coordinates the activities of all other subsystems. Some subsystem functions can be supplied by other systems, as in the case of parasites and many small businesses, but a living system must have its own decider in order to be an independent entity.

The brain is the center of the decider subsystem for humans and higher animals. Within the brain there are several hierarchical levels (echelons) of control, ranging from the cerebral cortex down to the medulla. Choices are also made at even lower echelons, such as spinal cord neurons and endocrine glands. Indeed, lower echelon choices may influence upper echelons, as when the adrenal gland acts through the hypothalamus to stimulate emotion and conscious decision-making activity in order to counteract a threatening situation.

The top echelon, the cerebral cortex, serves as coordinator for the subsystem, which in turn controls the entire body as well as artifacts of the system. Without the decider subsystem the body would quickly disintegrate into an uncoordinated collection of cells and organs. Because the organs and many of the cells are interdependent, they would soon die, leaving only a few relatively independent microorganisms.

An organization likewise must have its own decider subsystem. The top echelon resides in the cerebral cortex of the leader(s). As in the human body, however, the top echelon is dependent on many lower echelons for supplying accurate information, carrying out instructions, and making lower level decisions in accordance with policy. These lower echelons are found not only within the leaders but also in the decider subsystems of all other members of the organization. Without a central decider subsystem an organization disintegrates into individuals and groups, each deciding things for themselves.

The decider subsystem is an essential element in system coordination, but it is not the only one. For instance, the channel and net subsystem is required to carry information and orders to and from the decider. Without the channel and net and other subsystems, the decider would be impotent to implement its choices.

Another source of coordination within a system is its template, which specifies certain purposes. Some forms of coordination are built into the subsystems and components of a system. Thus components may act autonomously and yet be serving purposes of the system. An example is your heartbeat, which does not require any coordination from your nervous system. Pulse rate is influenced by higher echelons of the decider, of course, but in the absence of such direction the heart beats anyway, at a rate set by its own purpose.

Structure, whether designed according to a template or directed by a decider, often serves as a means of coordinating the activities of components and subsystems. A healthy heartbeat is built into the structure of the heart. Bureaucratic structure, control systems, standardized forms, policies and procedures, automation, work flow specification, and job design are ways of building coordinative structure into an organization, so that people may act autonomously and still get the organization's tasks done.

Whether coordination is supplied by the decider, the template, or structure, the key element is information. Under conditions of stability or of change within anticipated parameters, a subsystem or component may be able to maintain a

Figure 6–1
A Model of Adaptive, Motivated Decision Making

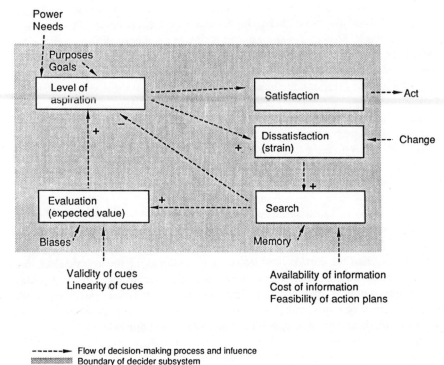

steady state autonomously, using the information contained in its own template or structure. When unexpected change is perceived, however, the decider subsystem is required in order to process new information that permits the system to adapt or respond.

The Decision-Making Process

Ebert and Mitchell (1975) employed March and Simon's (1958) general model of adaptive motivated behavior as a model of the decision-making process. This model, shown in augmented form in Figure 6-1, fits well into the living systems framework. The model reflects the sequential and iterative nature of decision making.

One may start at any point in tracing the model. Let us begin with strain or dissatisfaction. Dissatisfaction causes the decider to search for a plan of behavior that will bring about satisfaction or reduction of strain. This search process involves gathering and analyzing data and synthesizing one or more action plans. Since the success of these plans in bringing about satisfaction cannot be known with certainty in advance, each plan is evaluated in terms of expected value of reward or subjective expected utility (SEU). The SEU of each plan is compared with the level of aspiration, that is, the minimum level of satisfaction. As soon as a plan is found whose SEU meets the level of aspiration, search ceases and the plan is implemented.

The model is dynamic and iterative rather than static. It is influenced by exogenous variables as well as internal relationships, as indicated by the arrows and signs in the model. For instance, strain is often caused by a change in the environment. The search process is affected by many variables, including the availability and cost of information and the feasibility of alternative plans. Judgment of the SEU of each plan depends on such factors as the validity and linearity of environmental cues as well as the biases of the decider. Level of aspiration stems basically from the decider process of setting purposes and goals. Aspirations may be influenced by the length of the search process and the expected values of previously evaluated plans, as well as by power and needs.

Within the context of this model several issues have been raised by decision theorists. How do deciders search for alternatives? How do they limit the search? What do they search for? How is the SEU established? What biases affect the calculation of SEU to be derived from various alternatives? How is the level of aspiration determined?

The number of issues is large and the literature on decision making is extensive. We cannot hope to cover it all. This review will be limited to two areas, search and judgment processes, that have interesting implications for living systems theory. The calculation of SEU and probabilities will be discussed in Chapter 7.

Search Process

A substantial amount of research has been devoted to the search process in human individuals. Among the issues of interest to living systems theory are (1) complexity and the capability of the decider to deal with it and (2) strategies of search.

Complexity. Cyert and March (1963: 121) pointed out that search is simple-minded in the sense that "it proceeds on the basis of a simple model of causality until driven to a more complex one" and that search is biased. The decider's perceptions of alternatives are limited and distorted by training, experience, goals, and organizational rules. Business executives, for instance, usually search for the most proximate cause of a problem and consider solutions that have worked before. Only when these solutions fail do they deepen their search for the cause of the problem or broaden their consideration of possible corrective acts.

One of the better-known concepts regarding individual search behavior is bounded rationality (Simon 1957). The human mind lacks the capacity to deal rationally with complex problems. Instead of searching for the optimal alternative, decision makers tend to stop searching as soon as they find a plan that is satisfactory. Such satisficing behavior is reflected in our model, which indicates that search tends to cease as soon as the level of aspiration is attained. But note that the aspiration level varies even during the decision process. Finding many alternatives tends to raise aspirations; when no satisfactory alternatives are found, aspirations may eventually drop to the level of the best available alternative.

One method of coping with complexity is to separate the decision into several parts and deal with them sequentially. This method is typical of decision making in committees, which may go even further by delegating parts of the problem to different subcommittees. Unfortunately, this process may easily lead to a suboptimal decision.

The sequential process is followed because of the difficulty of juggling many issues and alternatives at once. If the issues interact, however, an early decision on one issue may limit the options on other issues. A decision to solve a financial crisis by means of budget cuts, for example, precludes consideration of strategic budget increases in areas of high profitability.

Cognitive complexity is an important characteristic of individual decision makers. That is, some individuals view the world in terms of black and white, whereas others see many shades in between. Driver and Streufert (1969) proposed a model in which a group's response to environmental complexity is moderated by the integrative complexity of individual members. Studies employing tactical and bargaining games have offered support for the notion that groups composed of cognitively complex individuals make better use of information and search more effectively for information. One may conjecture that greater cognitive complexity permits more appropriate association and more efficient filtering of information.

Search strategy. Limited search may be quite efficient if the problems are familiar and the decision maker is experienced with them. Novel problems, on the other hand, are best served by "deferred judgment" (Parnes 1964), which allows the generation of unique ideas. Unfortunately, there is a bias toward diagnosing a problem as a familiar type when, in fact, it is novel. Decision makers are apt to leap to the stages of synthesis and implementation of an action plan before the problem is fully understood (Kepner and Tregoe 1965; Ackoff 1978). To counteract this bias, several authors have offered frameworks designed to force the decider into careful diagnosis of the problem before looking for solutions (Ackoff 1962; Checkland 1981; Acar 1984).

Assuming that the problem is correctly diagnosed, the next stage is to search for solution ideas. Emory and Niland (1968) recommended that some mechanism be used to separate the generation of ideas from evaluation of them, because these two processes require different and conflicting modes of thought. For individuals the separation of search from evaluation is a matter of self discipline. Techniques have been developed to enhance this separation in group decision making, however. Brainstorming (A. F. Osborn 1957) is a group technique which requires participants to withhold judgment until a wide variety of ideas has been generated. The Delphi and nominal group techniques ensure separation by keeping the participants apart and dividing the process into stages (Delbecq, Van de Ven, and Gustafson 1975).

Research has shown that people are selective about the strategy they employ in making decisions (Beach and Mitchell 1978; McAllister, Mitchell, and Beach 1979; Christensen-Szalanski 1980). For decisions of little consequence people use simple heuristics and very limited search for alternatives. The more significant and irreversible the decision and the more accountable the decision maker, the more complex and analytical is the decision strategy. Deadlines, however, tend to force a curtailment of the preferred strategy.

Judgment Process

Search is followed by evaluation and selection of ideas that have been generated. If the choice among alternatives is to be anything but random, judgment must be exercised by the decider. Judgment involves the use of inferred relationships between cues and expected outcomes. A fair amount of research has been done on how human individuals utilize cues. Among the issues studied are (1) the accuracy with which deciders assess the validity and weight of cues, (2) the comparison of configural and linear models, and (3) the development of judgment.

Assessment of cue validity and weight. A cue is information from which one may infer future outcomes. Seldom do decision makers have any precise notion of the predictive validity of a cue or of the weight it carries in determining the future. In situations of uncertainty Peterson, Hammond, and Summers (1965a, 1965b) found that deciders tended to rank cues correctly but to underutilize highly valid or negative cues and overutilize cues of little or no validity. Nonlinear relationships are also underutilized (Hammond and Summers 1965). Dudycha and Naylor (1966a) found that when cues are presented sequentially, judges tend to overutilize more recent cues that have little validity. It appears that human deciders are poor at assessing the validity of cues, and therefore inefficient in their use of them. A study by Summers (1969) suggested, however, that when people are forewarned about the changing validity of cues, they are able to adjust their judgments accordingly.

Consistency of judgment is another variable that has been studied. It has been found that even decision makers who have developed valid models for the use of cues do not apply their models consistently (Hammond, Hursch, and Todd 1964; Dudycha and Naylor 1966b). Redundancy of information tends to improve consistency of judgment, but a computer programmed with an expert clinician's own decision rules does a better job of diagnosis than the clinician (Kleinmuntz 1968).

Configural versus linear use of cues. Experienced clinicians and stockbrokers often claim that the sorts of decisions they make depend on the interaction or configuration of cues, rather than on a linear model. Research on these groups has confirmed that some clinicians and stockbrokers do use configural models, but there is substantial individual difference and most of the variance in their judgments can be explained by linear, additive models (Wiggins and Hoffman 1968; Slovic, Fleissner, and Bauman 1972; W. F. Wright 1979). The use of configural models is hampered by the fact that such relationships are more difficult to learn through experience (Brehmer 1969).

Development of judgment. Research by Hammond, Hursch, and Todd (1964) on clinical psychologists suggested that experience is important to the development of accurate judgments (i.e., judgments that make good use of valid cues). In order for experience to be effective, however, there must be valid feedback about earlier judgments. Furthermore, the decision maker must develop a valid classification scheme that allows the associator to compare the current situation with memories of appropriate prior judgments and their outcomes.

Perception of cues is biased by such factors as ideology, mental set, motivation, cognitive complexity, propensity toward risk or conservatism, and memory capacity (Ebert and Mitchell 1975). These biases in judgment may cause misclassification of the problem and application of the wrong experience, as well as improper weighting of cues and preference for inefficient, or even harmful, solutions.

The use of group judgment processes tends to dampen or cancel the effects of individual biases. Judgments by groups tend to be more accurate than the average of the judgments of individual group members (Shaw 1971), but the group advantage disappears on very complex judgments (Kaplan and Schwartz 1975). Groups also tend to make better decisions (i.e., find more effective solutions to problems) than do the individual members, although the group solution often is not as good as that of the most competent member.

One aspect of group decision making that has received a lot of attention is the risky shift phenomenon. Stoner (1961) found that, when choosing among alternatives that involve varying degrees of risk, groups tend to choose riskier acts than the individual members would choose alone. This result has been replicated many times (Vinokur 1971). Additional research has shown that after participation in or observation of group discussion of alternatives, individuals make riskier choices than they would have made without the discussion.

Group Decision Procedure

There are several possible procedures for combining individual decisions into a group decision. A group may reach a decision by consensus, majority vote, nominal vote, or acceptance of the leader's decision. In each case the individual members of the group make a decision, but it does not become a group decision until the individual decisions meet some criterion. The criterion for consensus is that all members must reach essentially the same decision. Majority or other proportional rule requires that at least a specified percentage of the members reach the same decision, and that other members have predecided to abide by it. A nominal vote requires acceptance of a formula (such as averaging) for combining individual decisions. Leadership requires that the other members decide to follow the leader.

The strategy of group decision making is affected not only by the group's decision procedure, but also by its channel and net structure. When all communication must flow through a central individual, for instance, that person tends to assume leadership and make decisions for the group. Other members accept these decisions because they lack information to challenge them.

The structure of the network also affects the quality and speed of group decision making. Shaw (1971) found that a centralized network operating on complex problems tends to be slower, communicates less, and makes more errors than a decentralized network. Vroom and Yetton (1974) formulated a normative model of strategy based on characteristics of the problem, the group, and individual members. This model will be discussed in Chapter 10, as it focuses on choices made by the leader.

Centralization versus Decentralization

The issue of organizational centralization versus decentralization deals primarily with the question of the level at which various decisions are to be made. Tied to this question is the structure of the organization's channel and net subsystem. If the network is organized hierarchically, such that there are few or no channels of communication between lower levels of different branches, then decisions involving two or more branches must be made centrally at a level that controls all of the relevant branches. Conversely, if decentralized decision making is desired, provision must be made for a rich network of lateral and diagonal channels.

Theoretically, centralized decision making provides the greatest degree of coordination of the system. This assumes, however, that the top echelon of the decider has the capacity to absorb and process all of the necessary information. It also assumes a relatively full, unbiased flow of information upward, as well as lack of judgmental bias at the top echelon. Further assumptions are that the top echelon is wholly dedicated to the good of the system and that lower echelons are willing and able to follow the directions of the top echelon. These conditions are rarely met. For practical reasons most organizations operate under some degree of decentralization.

Centralized decision making tends to be slow, because of competing demands on the attention of the top echelon. The greater number of nodes through which information must flow upward and downward in order to complete the decision cycle also slows the process, as well as providing more opportunity for the introduction of noise and distortion. Although centralized deciders receive a greater variety of information, it is often of poor quality. When decision making is centralized in a single individual, there is little protection for the system against biased or self-serving choices by the decider.

Decentralized decision making provides greater protection against bias, but at a cost in efficiency. Many more channels must be maintained and more energy must be spent on transmitting, selecting, and processing information. On the other hand, fewer nodes are involved in a typical decision cycle and the decider is less likely to be overloaded. Thus decisions are likely to be made more quickly and on the basis of more accurate, if less varied, information.

A personal element also enters the equation. Upper-echelon deciders are apt to have more experience and, therefore, better judgment than those at the lower echelons. Furthermore, upper-echelon deciders are more likely to be committed to the purposes and goals of the organization as a whole. People at the lower echelons often are the top-echelon deciders for a subsystem or component of the organization. Their commitment to the purposes and goals of their unit may cause them to make suboptimal decisions with respect to the organization. This issue of personal commitment will be explored further in Chapter 9.

COMMUNICATION

As noted at the beginning of the chapter, communication may be regarded as purposeful transmission of information between systems or components of systems. When a manager issues an order to a work group or a child asks a question of a teacher, these acts may be seen equivalently as instances of communication between two living systems or as internal transmission between two components of a business firm or school. Whichever view is taken, clearly communication involves the information processing subsystems of two or more living systems.

Communication may be one-to-one or one-to-many (i.e., broadcast). Furthermore, it may be one-way or two-way. When the manager issues an order, that may be all that is necessary. If the order is understood (or even if it isn't), the work group may respond with action rather than further communication. Of course, action carries information that can be "read" by the manager, but there may be no intent to communicate on the part of the group. The communication becomes two-way when one or more members of the group ask questions to clarify the order or when they show disrespect through gestures and facial expressions. Communication does not have to be coded verbally; the only requirement is that there be a purposeful attempt to transmit information.

In one-way communication the sender's decider, channel and net, encoder, and output transducer subsystems are involved in outputting the information, while the receiver's input transducer, channel and net, decoder, associator, memory, and decider are used to receive it. Thus, one-way communication is a combination of decision making by the sender and perception by the receiver. All of the problems of effective decision making and accurate perception that we discussed previously are combined in the process of communication.

Figure 6–2
Dyadic Exchange of Information

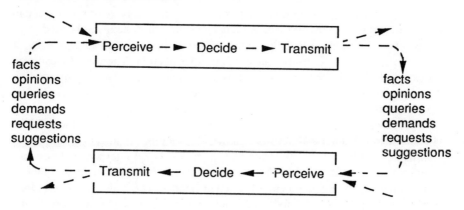

facts
opinions
queries
demands
requests
suggestions

facts
opinions
queries
demands
requests
suggestions

In two-way communication all of the information processing subsystems of both systems are involved. Two-way communication is a special case of dyadic exchange, in which the resources traded between systems are data. Mutual dependence may be established through such exchange. The lawyer-client relationship is an example. Communication may be modeled by the systems dyad, as in Figure 6-2.

One of the difficulties in communication arises from the fact that the message is often unwelcome. The information that is sent may have negative worth for the receiver. Indeed, both systems may be sending unwanted information, such as mutual threats or recriminations. As noted in our earlier discussion of perception, systems tend to reject or distort unwanted information. Thus the message that is received may be quite different from the message that was sent.

Given that communication is purposeful on the part of the sender, it is axiomatic that the sender wants to convey specific information to the receiver. Yet ultimate control of the result rests with the receiver, whose perception processes are also purposeful. Whatever information the receiver perceives is what has been communicated (Redding 1972).

Communication suffers from all of the difficulties mentioned for perception and decision making. Many messages are ignored or discarded before they ever reach their intended target. Others are covered by noise or distorted in decoding or interpretation. Even if the message is correctly perceived, it may be rejected because it does not suit the values, purposes, or attitudes of the receiver. "I don't want to hear it" is a common response to unwanted messages.

To overcome these difficulties it is generally recommended that important messages be sent forcefully and/or repeatedly, on a clear channel or multiple channels. More importantly, as the systems dyad model suggests, the sender can structure the exchange to make it worthwhile for the receiver to accept the message. If the message is likely to have negative worth to the receiver, it can be "sugar coated" by linking it with a positively valued message or reward. It can also be linked to a threat of a worse exchange if the message is not heeded.

Two-way communication helps to resolve errors in communication, making it possible for the receiver to ask questions for clarification. The receiver can also check on whether the message was received and interpreted correctly by sending it back to the source for confirmation. If fairness of exchange is perceived to be a problem, the receiver can ask for (or offer) additional inducements. Bargaining is a special case of two-way communication and decision making (Tracy 1985).

Most of the channel and net subsystem of a group or organization consists of communication links between individual members. Good interpersonal communication is vital to the health of a social system. A blockage or breakdown of communication among members is like a degenerative nerve disease or severance of the spinal cord in an individual. Important information cannot flow to the decider and orders cannot be transmitted to the subsystems.

SUMMARY AND IMPLICATIONS

As open systems, living systems require input, throughput, and output of information. These three stages of information processing correspond roughly to the traditional topics of perception, decision making, and communication. More can be learned from linking these topics than from treating them separately.

The processing of information is purposeful, motivated behavior that serves the needs of a system. Information processing may be conscious or unconscious, and it may occur at all echelons of the decider subsystem. Perception, deciding, and communication apply to groups and organizations as well as individuals. When a person acts for an organization in making a decision, it is the organization's decision.

Perception involves selecting useful information from a welter of data impinging on the system, while protecting the system from excessive, useless, or harmful inputs. Good decision rules and criteria are vital to the efficiency of the system. Pathologies develop when the decision rules used in selecting and interpreting information are inadequate to the task.

Decision making provides the coordination of subsystem processes that is essential to maintenance of the system. The decider makes and implements choices that allow the system to use its resources efficiently. This requires searching for information and action alternatives, analyzing cues, and making reasonably accurate judgments about what behavior will best serve the purposes of the system. Decision making is an iterative process of assessing alternative action plans until one is found that meets the system's level of aspiration. Pathologies include inadequate or biased search, improper weighting of cues or use of invalid cues, inaccurate probability estimation and revision, overloading the decider, and making choices at the wrong echelon.

Communication is purposeful transmission of information by a sending system coupled with purposeful perception of the transmission by one or more receiving systems. Often the roles of sender and receiver are alternated and communication becomes a cyclical two-way process. Any two systems involved in two-way communication become a dyad exchanging resources. A key to effective communication by a sender is understanding the needs of the receiver and shaping the message to those needs. Pathologies of communication include failure to anticipate receiver needs and biases, use of noisy channels, overload of key nodes in the network, missing channels, and buildup of distortion in long networks.

From a living systems viewpoint a key concern about perception is the efficiency of the decision rules used to screen information. The filtering process has a dual role: To protect the decider from excessive or useless information, but to assure that the decider receives information it needs. Energy can be saved by correctly rejecting useless information at an early stage of processing, but complex decision rules may be needed to do this accurately. The trade-offs of simple versus complex rules require further investigation. Cognitive complexity and the learning process must also be considered.

Similar trade-offs exist with respect to the extent of search for additional information or alternative action plans. At what point does it become efficient to end the search, which has its own costs, and make a decision based on the available information or the best known alternative? Another type of trade-off discussed above was between centralization and decentralization of decision making. Some progress has been made in identifying the factors involved in this question, but much more research is needed.

The biases and inadequacies of human judgment pose a major problem for social systems. Our organizations and societies are becoming increasingly complex and interdependent. To remain healthy, these living systems require information processing subsystems that are capable of making good judgments with complex, often nonlinear cues.

Some improvement in human judgment may result from the development of computer programs, based on social judgment theory (Hammond et al. 1975), that externalize the implicit relationships underlying an individual's judgments. In a few seconds on a personal computer the POLICY PC program, for instance, can analyze a series of judgments, calculate the regression weights, and plot the function forms of several cues used by the decision maker, and indicate the consistency of judgment. This process allows the decision maker to examine and improve judgment processes. When two or more individuals make judgments from the same cues, they can compare their judgments and learn from each other or develop better agreement. Several promising applications of social judgment theory are presented by Arkes and Hammond (1985).

The systems dyad model of communication highlights the fact that more attention should be paid to the value aspects of messages. The idea that people tend to see and hear communications that suit their needs is not new; it was well documented by Berelson and Steiner (1964). Yet we know too little about how to assess the receiver's needs, or whether tying an unpleasant message to a desirable stimulus can overcome the defenses of the filtering process.

We also know too little about communication as an *exchange* process. The key to assessing the receiver's needs may lie in listening to the response. What does the receiver offer or demand in return? What is the effect of cutting off the opportunity for response? Viewing communication as an exchange of information resources between living systems opens up new vistas for exploring the process.

7

Motivation

Motivation is a central topic in organizational behavior. Theories of motivation attempt to explain why and how people behave as they do. The concept of motivation is not limited to people, however. All living systems exhibit motivated behavior. Thus the major task of this chapter will be to develop a living systems model of motivation.

Mitchell (1982: 81) defined motivation as "the psychological processes that cause the arousal, direction, and persistence of behavior." Except for the word "psychological," this definition may suitably be applied to all living systems. Mitchell also noted that some social scientists view motivation as voluntary and goal directed. In other words, motivated behavior is purposeful. *Motivation* will thus be defined here as the processes of a living system that cause the arousal, direction, and persistence of its purposeful behavior.

There is no dearth of theories and models of motivation. There are need-based approaches, information processing approaches, and social-environmental approaches; drive theories and reinforcement theories. Need-based approaches to motivation, such as the need hierarchies of Maslow (1970) and Alderfer (1972) and the strain theory of Miller (1978: ch. 8), focus on needs as activators of tensions that influence the choice of behavior, its intensity, and its duration. Information processing approaches, such as Adams' (1963) equity theory, Vroom's (1964) expectancy theory, and Locke's (1968) goal-setting theory, focus instead on the decision processes by which goals or behavior are evaluated, chosen, and maintained. Social-environmental approaches, represented by the work of Salancik and Pfeffer (1978) and Ferris, Beehr, and Gilmore (1978), focus on social facilitation or evaluation apprehension as determinants of motivation. Bandura's (1986) social cognitive theory combines elements of the information processing and social-environmental approaches. Drive theories (e.g., Murray 1938; Hull 1943) posit motives that are built into the system, whereas reinforcement theories (e.g., Thorndike 1911; Skinner 1938), emphasize the role of extrinsic rewards in shaping behavior.

All of these theories contribute something to our understanding of motivation, but each shows only part of the picture. For example, need, expectancy, and social cognitive theories deal with conscious motivation, whereas drive and reinforcement theories ignore cognition and focus on unconscious processes. Further dividing the motivational processes, need theories concentrate on arousal of behavior, while expectancy theory emphasizes the choice of direction and equity theory focuses on persistence of behavior. Drive theory posits that some needs are innate and may trigger relatively automatic responses, but reinforcement theory emphasizes the role of learning in the formation or modification of needs and responses.

Each of these theories treats one particular aspect of motivation as if it were the whole process. Rather than building on one another, each theory is presented as a separate entity, couched in different terms that obscure the possible links between theories. Furthermore, research on motivation tends to investigate one theory at a time. Mitchell (1982: 80) noted that "few studies have been designed to integrate theories, to test them competitively, or to analyze the settings in which different theories work best."

Assuming that each theory has something worthwhile to offer, a model is needed that integrates them. This chapter will present such a model, one that combines aspects of need theory, expectancy theory, reinforcement, goal setting, social cognition and social interaction. The living systems concept of needs (Chapter 4) will be taken as a starting point. Needs will be linked to the valences of outcomes. Goal setting and expectancy theory will be combined to explain the choice of behavior. Reinforcement, social facilitation, and social cognition will be added to form a dynamic model, responding to evaluation of outcomes and self-evaluation. Individual work motivation will then be considered in the context of an organization attempting to influence the individual's choice of goals, define the path to goal attainment, apportion outcomes, and influence the evaluation of those outcomes.

The proposed integrative model is imbedded in the framework of living systems theory. Both individuals and social systems have needs and goals that can be fulfilled by means of cooperation and exchange. Thus the final discussion will develop the idea that motivation processes of individuals, groups, and organizations are parallel behavior systems with many points of interaction.

SINGLE-SYSTEM MOTIVATION

Motivation is a psychological construct used to explain why people and other organisms behave as they do, why they perform one act and not another. Motivation is inferred from behavior; it cannot be observed directly. It consists of three distinct aspects: (1) arousal or energizing, (2) direction, and (3) persistence of behavior. In this chapter the motivation construct is extended beyond the realm of psychology to include the behavior of groups and organizations.

Figure 7–1 provides a broad overview of a model that represents the three

Figure 7–1
Model of Single-System Motivation

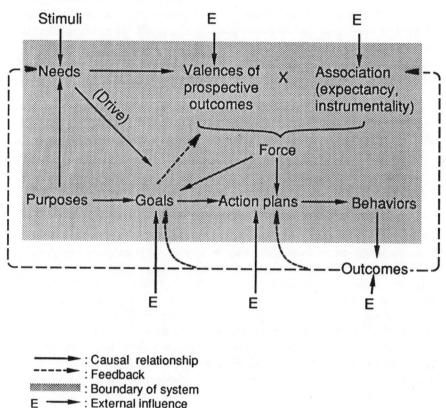

```
                    : Causal relationship
         - - - - ▶  : Feedback
         ▓▓▓▓▓▓▓▓   : Boundary of system
    E ───────▶      : External influence
```

aspects of motivation within a system (Tracy 1984). Arousal begins with a *stimulus*, an information input that changes the degree or intensity of a *need* for something. This in turn changes the *valence* of that resource as a goal for behavior. Current and alternative *goals* and *acts* are evaluated in conjunction with internal *standards* or *purposes*, *expectancies* of outcomes and *feedback* from current *outcomes*. The current direction may be continued or a new direction chosen. A new choice of acts (and sometimes goals) leads to new outcomes. Information from these outcomes is fed back for comparison with needs, goals, and expectancies. Behavior persists so long as feedback indicates that it is on target and no new stimulus causes a new direction to be chosen.

Certain elements of this model, particularly expectancies and goals, may seem to apply only to conscious, voluntary motivation of behavior. It will be shown, however, that all elements can reasonably be defined in terms that apply to all levels of living systems. Thus the model will be called a living-systems model of motivation.

The model possesses four advantages over many other models of motivation. First, it is not specific to animal organisms or human individuals. Second, it encompasses both conscious and unconscious motivational processes. Third, it covers all three aspects of motivation: arousal, direction, and persistence. Fourth, it is dynamic; it provides mechanisms for explaining both how motivation persists and how it changes.

Theories and research exist for all parts of this model, providing some of the details necessary to understand how the model works. But no one theory encompasses all facets. Therefore, the model will have to be built piece by piece.

Arousal of Behavior

Approaches to an explanation of arousal of behavior include need-based theories, drive theories, and social-environmental theories. In broad terms, behavior is seen as an aroused response to an internal or external stimulus.

Stimulus. A stimulus consists of information that changes the degree or intensity of one or more needs, excesses, drives, or desires, thereby initiating, increasing, or decreasing a strain within the system. The information may be generated internally or externally. For instance, either the smell of cooking or a feeling of hunger may provide the stimulus to arouse the need of food. Likewise, feeling full or observing that one's plate is clean would tend to decrease the strain and bring about cessation of eating behavior.

Theories of social facilitation and evaluation apprehension focus on particular kinds of social stimuli that may influence individual human needs. Other systems, especially suprasystems, are seen as providing information that helps a person to interpret other information inputs. For example, a girl may not know how to react to the aggressive behavior of a boy until her parents or peers help her to put his behavior in context. Information inputs from suprasystems may also cause a person to alter existing purposes or adopt new ones, thereby initiating a relatively long-lasting change in needs. For instance, an employer's introduction of a wage incentive may cause an employee to set a new purpose value for money. Likewise, the presence of other people may strengthen the need of achievement in a competitive individual.

To some extent these theories have meaning for groups and organizations as well. A work group may be motivated toward better performance by information that allows the group to compare its achievement with that of similar groups. The existence of competition alters the group's purposes. Similarly, an organization may set a high value on need of new products if it already has a strong reputation for product innovation.

Need. Need was defined in Chapter 4 as lack of a specific resource that is useful for or required by the purposes of a living system. Purposes specify the personal standards required for self-direction, as posited by social cognitive theory. The intensity of a need varies with external stimuli, degree of lack, urgency of fulfillment, and intrinsic importance of the resource to the health of the system. The same can be said with respect to an excess. As a strain (i.e., need or excess) becomes more intense, the likelihood increases that it will arouse behavior aimed at relief. The mechanisms whereby this occurs will be discussed later in this chapter.

At any given moment the intensity of need for a particular resource determines the value of that resource, and hence influences the valence (expected value) of prospective behavioral outcomes involving that resource. It is primarily through this influence mechanism that specific behavior is aroused and energized.

Strains. Miller (1978: 34) explained the arousal of behavior as follows: Living systems act to maintain preferred steady states (i.e., purposes). *Stress* (i.e., too little or too much input or output) or the threat of it produces a *strain* that the system seeks to reduce. Thus motivation is a homeostatic process. At any given moment, however, there may be many strains within the system. The choice of direction in acting upon these strains is governed by the intensity of each strain and by the resources of the system. The relative urgency of reducing each strain is called a system's *hierarchy of values.*

Strains are generated by stresses in several ways. Lack occurs when rates of input or production are inadequate to replace losses caused by consumption, decay, and extrusion. Likewise, excesses are caused by excessive rates of input or production and by inadequate rates of consumption or extrusion. Information indicating that a lack or excess is imminent may also produce a strain.

Strains can be caused by change in purposes or in the environment. The demands of growth and development, or of illness or old age, may cause purposes to change. For example, a firm's requirements for capital may increase as the business grows. The firm may then act to reduce the strain by issuing stock or increasing its debt.

Thus far we have only considered strains that are generated from within the system or by normal processes. Strain can also be caused by external stimuli, such as a sudden change in the environment. For instance, a system may be maintaining a steady state of peace with its neighbors. If one of the neighbors suddenly attacks, a strain is aroused of such intensity that it may override all other strains and immediately initiate choice of a new direction for behavior. What happens in such a case is that the sudden environmental change (stress) creates an immediate and intense lack where none existed before. Of course, a gradual change in the environment may have a similar but less dramatic effect. The failure of one of a firm's suppliers may cause a growing shortage in parts inventory and a gradual increase in strain, until the firm is moved to look for a new supplier.

Attempted influence by suprasystems constitutes another sort of strain-generating external stimulus. For their own purposes suprasystems often seek to implant new values or modify existing values in their component systems.

For instance, a school may try to teach values to children that will make them better citizens. If the school is successful, the children will develop needs for lawful behavior, community service, and the like.

Systems learn new purposes through such processes as reinforcement and commitment to superordinate goals. These new or modified purposes create strains that may change behavior. An example of the effects of commitment might be the changes that occur when a person is "saved" or converted to a new religion. Reinforcement effects can be seen when employees receive monetary incentives for improved performance.

Finally, a change in choice of behavior may be caused by reduction of a strain. Feedback from a completed task may serve as a stimulus reducing the strain that initiated task-directed behavior. Although the process is homeostatic, it does not lead to stasis. Given that not all strains can be reduced at once and that some may never be reduced to zero, and that purposes change over time, the homeostatic process is also a dynamic one. When one strain is reduced, others clamor for attention and a new cycle of behavioral choice is begun.

Thus we see that the stimulus in our living systems model of motivation may be internal or external, sudden or gradual. A stimulus may consist of change in the environment, feedback from outcomes, or internal information about inputs, outputs, production, consumption, or decay. Each stimulus invokes reassessment of the degree of lack or excess of one or more resources and the consequent increase or reduction of various strains. In time the hierarchy of values shifts sufficiently to recommend the choice of new goals or behavior.

Drive. Another mechanism whereby at least simple behavior patterns may be aroused is described by drive theory. As explained in Chapter 4, drive theory postulates a direct, noncognitive link between need and behavior. For example, a stimulus that signifies danger may directly arouse aggression or avoidance behavior (fight or flight). What drive theory does not seem to explain is how the system chooses whether to fight or flee.

In some cases the reaction of the decider subsystem may be automatic (i.e., at a low echelon), as when the human body responds to a lack of heat by shivering and constricting capillaries. Yet the reaction may also be a conscious choice, as when in the same situation the person decides to put on a sweater. In either case, the person is aroused to respond to a lack. The response consists of directing the application of energy (which is already available in the system) to parts of the motor subsystem, causing behavior such as shivering or putting on a sweater. In one case the behavior is directly driven by the need, whereas in the other a conscious choice is made.

Drive theory bypasses the valence and expectancy steps of the living systems model of motivation, proceeding directly from needs to goals and choice of behavior. It accounts well for some instances of motivated behavior, such as simple, reflex behavior that is not consciously chosen. A cognitive theory seems more appropriate for most complex behavior, however. People, groups, organizations, and societies possess the capability of fulfilling a lack in more than one way. Furthermore, they do not always react immediately to a lack. They may defer action indefinitely or until they finish acting upon other stresses. Such behavior seems to require a cognitive model.

Direction of Behavior

Stimuli create or intensify strains, which in turn influence the choice of behavior. It is not yet clear, however, how strains affect choice. Many strains of rapidly varying intensity exist at any moment. How does a system sort out all of these conflicting demands so that a rational, or at least effective, choice can be made?

Choice of behavior is one of the functions of the decider subsystem. As noted in Chapter 6, the deciding process has four distinct stages: (1) setting purposes and goals, (2) analyzing information concerning action alternatives, (3) synthesizing and choosing a plan of action, and (4) implementing the plan.

Expectancy theory is a model of the deciding process. This theory grew out of the work of Tolman (1932), who developed a purposive or goal-directed psychology of behavior. Tolman assumed that a person's behavior is directed by a system of values. His theory indicated that choice of behavior is influenced both by the attractiveness of an outcome and by the perceived likelihood that a given action will lead to that outcome.

Valences. Attractiveness of outcomes and perceived likelihood of attaining them are central elements of Vroom's (1964) expectancy theory. The attractiveness of an anticipated outcome is called its *valence.* Valences are associated with both the direct (first-level) outcome of behavior and the contingent (second-level) consequences. A valence may also be assigned to the behavior required to attain the outcome. For example, an employee may anticipate that working hard at a difficult task will result in first-level (task) outcomes of fatigue and completion of a work quota each day, together with second-level (reward) outcomes of a regular weekly wage, a steady job, and approval from the supervisor or coworkers. Each of these anticipated outcomes may have a positive valence for the employee or some outcomes, such as fatigue, may have a negative valence. The behavior of working hard at the task may also have a positive or negative valence, depending on the employee's behavioral standards (Bandura 1986).

Valences are the link between needs and choice of behavior. The valence of an anticipated outcome varies in accordance with the intensity of the needs it can fulfill. For example, a regular wage can indirectly fulfill various matter-energy needs, as well as a need of feedback about status. The valence of the wage depends on the strength of these needs as well as the degree to which the wage can fulfill them. If an employee is under financial stress, the valence of the wage is higher than when the employee is financially secure. Unless the employee has no need for money, an increase in the wage will increase its valence because the higher wage can better fulfill needs.

Vroom (1964: 23–24) noted that valences may be manipulated by arousing needs, for instance through deprivation. Conversely, as needs are fulfilled by means of a particular act, the valences of outcomes of that act decrease, thereby reducing the force of motivation for that act. At some point, presumably, another act comes to have greater force and a change of behavior occurs.

Outcomes have negative as well as positive valences. One of the outcomes of working to fulfill a quota may be that the employee must forego an opportunity to go fishing with friends. This outcome will have a negative valence to the extent that the fishing expedition would fulfill needs for food, rest, or companionship.

When a reward such as a wage is contingent upon a task outcome such as meeting a work quota, the valence of the reward also contributes to the valence of the task outcome. That is, the task outcome is seen as a path to the reward. The task outcome may also have a positive valence of its own, to the degree that it can fulfill needs such as affirmation of ability and self-worth.

In some cases the valence of the behavior, itself, may be the controlling factor. Bandura (1986: 18) stated that "in the social cognitive view people are neither driven by inner forces nor automatically shaped and controlled by external stimuli." Rather, they develop personal standards of behavior that provide a means of self-regulation and self-direction. These standards and other cognitive factors interact with behavior (acts) and environmental influences, each determining the others to some extent.

Personal standards of behavior are values, much like the purpose values against which needs are measured. Standards are guided by a self-concept that indicates that certain forms of behavior are appropriate and others inappropriate for the system. An individual who puts a high value on personal dignity would tend to avoid behavior such as begging, no matter how high the valence of prospective outcomes might be. Similarly, a firm with a reputation for honest dealings would set a negative valence on any behavior that involves cheating a customer. Other tasks, however, might have high intrinsic valence, if they are seen as enhancing the behavioral standards of the system. Therefore, the high valence of bravery in the face of enemy fire may overcome the negative valence of anticipated outcomes.

Other factors also affect the valence of the behavior. Many tasks have a negative valence because they require expenditure of valuable resources and because they preclude other acts, such as recreation, that have positive valences. Yet a behavioral task may have a positive valence, if it is intrinsically interesting or challenging.

According to Vroom (1964), people assess the net valences of a variety of behavioral alternatives (acts) and choose the alternative having the greatest force or net expected value. Success and reward are not certain, however; goals are not outcomes. In assessing alternatives, the decider must discount the valences of anticipated outcomes according to estimates of the likelihood that they will be attained. Although Vroom did not employ the term *goal*, we will use it here to indicate an anticipated outcome. Discounted outcome valences will be called *goal valences*.

Expectancy theory. Expectancy theory, or VIE (for Valence–Instrumentality–Expectancy) theory as it is sometimes called, has been formulated in several different ways. Clarifications and extensions of the theory were suggested by Galbraith and Cummings (1967), Porter and Lawler (1968), Graen (1969), Campbell et al. (1970), Lawler (1973), and Campbell and Pritchard (1983). Any of these formulations might be inserted into the living systems model of motivation without loss of generality. The following description of expectancy theory includes some of these modifications, as well as some of my own.

The goal valence of each task t, GV_t, is discounted from the valence of the task outcome, OV_t, by multiplying it by the expectancy, E_t, that the outcome can be achieved. That is,

$$GV_t = OV_t \times E_t.$$

Expectancy is defined as the estimated probability that the chosen task behavior will lead to accomplishment of the task goal.

Similarly, rewards are not certain even if the task goal is achieved. The goal valence of each reward r, GV_r, is discounted from the valence of the reward outcome, OV_r, by multiplying it by the expectancy, E_t, and the instrumentality, I_{rt}, of the task goal toward that reward. That is,

$$GV_r = OV_r \times E_t \times I_{rt}.$$

Instrumentality is defined as the estimated correlation between accomplishment of the task goal and receipt of the reward.

Finally, the total goal valence of a given act a, TGV_a, is the algebraic sum of the valences of the task goals and of the reward goals expected to follow from task accomplishment. That is,

$$TGV_a = \Sigma GV_t + \Sigma GV_r.$$

Vroom (1964) calls TGV_a the *force* of motivation toward act a.

At any given moment a person may be considering several alternative acts each having several possible task outcomes, each such outcome leading to several possible rewards. The theory may be pictured as a tree diagram with multiple branches for acts, task outcomes, and rewards. A rational decision maker is expected to choose the alternative act having the greatest (or least negative) force; that is, the act that maximizes expected need fulfillment.

The term *act* might suggest a simple, brief instance of behavior, but expectancy theory permits its interpretation as a complex set of behaviors persisting at a specific level of intensity over a specific time period. For instance, an individual deciding what tasks to work on, how hard to work, and/or for how long would fit the model. Indeed, Vroom (1964) applied the theory to vocational choice.

The theory has also been applied to prediction of the amount of effort a person will put into a task (Galbraith and Cummings 1967; Graen 1969; Campbell and Pritchard 1983). That is, various amounts of effort are considered to be alternative acts. A person chooses to exert greater effort when the total goal valence of the act is greater.

Yet effort is not even represented in total goal valence. For a given goal there is no reason to exert more effort than is necessary to attain it with reasonable certainty. Indeed, if there are two or more ways of obtaining the same or equal outcomes with the same degree of likelihood, a rational decider would choose the one that requires the least effort. For instance, an employee faced with a choice of how to reach a work goal may decide to work more efficiently or more cooperatively rather than with greater effort.

Effort is part of the intrinsic valence of an act. This intrinsic valence may be positive or negative. Effort involves a cost (negative valence) to the system in energy and other resources. An act may also be boring or dangerous (i.e., threatening security needs). On the other hand, an act may be intrinsically meaningful, interesting, challenging, and rewarding. Various job design approaches to work motivation are built on this notion (Herzberg 1966; Porter, Lawler, and Hackman 1975; Hackman and Oldham 1980). The intrinsic valence of act a, V_a, is the sum of its positive and negative characteristics.

In order to use expectancy theory to predict expenditure of effort, the intrinsic valence of each act must be incorporated in the model (Galbraith and Cummings 1967). Adding the intrinsic valence to the total goal valence of act a, we obtain the total valence or motivational force, TV_a. That is,

$$TV_a = V_a + TGV_a.$$

Expectancy theory has received considerable attention because it is intuitively reasonable. Yet there are some unresolved ambiguities that make the theory difficult to test. Reviews of research results have indicated many methodological problems (Heneman and Schwab 1972; Mitchell 1974, 1982; Wahba and House 1974; Connolly 1976; Lee 1980). Until such ambiguities in the theory are resolved, we cannot choose one formulation over another.

One difference of opinion may be useful in a living systems model of motivation. Expectancy and instrumentality have been interpreted as estimates of correlation (Dachler and Mobley 1973) or probability (Mitchell 1974; Wahba and House 1974). The probability interpretation seems best for a cognitive model applying to motivation of complex behavior at upper levels of living systems. For simple, goal-directed behavior at lower levels, however, the correlation interpretation may be used. It assumes only the ability to associate an act with memories of a similar act. Association and memory are not necessarily conscious. All living systems possess or have access to associator and memory subsystems. Thus this interpretation permits the model to represent processes that might operate in reinforcement or operant conditioning.

Expectancy theory models the simultaneous choice of behavior and goals. The choice of an act is inextricably linked by expectancy theory to the choice of preferred outcomes (i.e., goals). The choice of goals may not be a conscious one, and an individual may not be aware of the calculus by which an act is chosen. Nevertheless, some standard must exist by which the decider, consciously or unconsciously, measures outcomes and controls behavior. At the least the decider must have a standard to determine when the preferred outcome has been attained, so that the act can cease. For acts directed toward the environment, that standard is called a goal.

Goal-setting theory. Locke (1968) modeled the motivational effect of goals chosen consciously and prior to a choice of behavior. Locke's model specifies five steps to motivation: (1) an environmental event such as the offer of a reward (i.e., a stimulus), (2) cognition of that event, (3) evaluation of the event (e.g., the valence of the reward), (4) goal setting, and (5) task performance (i.e., task outcomes). The steps appear similar to an expectancy model. The key differences are that in Locke's model goals are chosen before acts and a conscious commitment is made to goals.

Locke emphasized that goal setting directly precedes task performance. Causally, he argued, performance is tied more directly to goal setting than to the stimulus or the cognition and evaluation of the stimulus. Consequently, performance level should be influenced more strongly by goals than by goal valence or an event such as the offer of a reward.

This argument can be questioned. Locke leaves out a step between goal setting and task performance—namely, the choice of acts to implement the goal. The living systems model indicates that outcomes are more closely tied to choice of acts than to goal setting. A poor selection of behavior is likely to result in poor performance no matter how strong the goal is.

Nevertheless, there is substantial empirical support for goal-setting theory. Locke (1968) cites many studies confirming the hypotheses that task outcomes will be greater if a person sets goals that are (1) hard rather than easy to meet, and (2) specific rather than general. Reviews and metaanalytic studies of the research on goal setting likewise indicate considerable support for these propositions (Steers and Porter 1974; Latham and Yukl 1975; Tubbs 1986; Mento, Steele, and Karren 1987).

There is a growing recognition of links between expectancy and goal setting theories. Campbell et al. (1970: 345–347) include an explicit goal-setting stage in their hybrid expectancy model. Locke (1978: 597) notes that expectancies and valences may be viewed as factors influencing the choice of goals. Goals obviously cannot be chosen in isolation from other factors. Goal attainment requires an investment of time, energy, and other resources in the behavior that is chosen. The decider must weigh the value of a goal against the value of the resources required to attain it. If strenuous activity is required, it may create new strains. Furthermore, other goals and their attendant needs are apt to be competing for some of the same resources. The use of expectancy theory in conjunction with goal-setting theory permits us to model these considerations.

Goal-setting theory has also been tied to social cognitive theory (Locke, Latham, and Erez 1988). Commitment to a goal may be seen as a personal standard for behavior, activating the forces of self-regulation to attain the goal and avoid loss in self-concept. Another possible explanation is that commitment activates cognitive dissonance. That is, when a person commits to a goal that is higher than its total goal valence (TGV) would warrant, the person may cognitively increase the TGV by altering outcome valence estimates or expectancies or by perceiving additional outcomes. For example, employees who commit themselves to improved performance may convince themselves that their supervisor is going to help make the task easier or that additional recognition will be given them for meeting the goal.

Persistence of Behavior

Goals influence not only the direction of behavior but also its persistence. Once a goal is set, behavior directed toward it tends to persist until the goal is reached. The goal serves as a standard against which outcomes can be measured. Information from outcomes is fed back and compared with the goal. Behavior is either maintained or modified as necessary in order to continue progress toward the goal. When the goal is reached, the behavior normally is terminated, although it may continue (Tolman 1932).

Feedback. The key element in persistence of behavior is feedback from outcomes to some standard, so that the system can decide whether to maintain the current behavior, modify it, or stop it. Persistence requires a dynamic model of motivation, one that is responsive to change in outcomes. The living systems model includes feedback from outcomes to acts, goals, needs, expectancies, and instrumentalities. By implication there is also feedback to standards of behavior.

A chosen act, itself, may provide a standard for evaluation of outcomes. That is, the act may have specific limits. For example, a person may have a half hour free and may decide to take a walk along a specific route. The act persists until the route has been traversed, then it stops. When a specific goal is chosen, it tends to act in the same way. Behavior persists and may even intensify as the goal is approached, but when the goal is reached the behavior tends to cease. If it is an habitual act, however, it may soon be chosen again.

Feedback and learning influence valences, expectancies, and instrumentalities. Although Vroom did not include feedback as part of his expectancy model, he noted that valences of outcomes may be "affected by communicated information concerning their desirability" and "as a result of being associated contiguously with established rewards and punishments" (Vroom 1964: 23–24). Expectancies can be influenced by "communicated probabilities" and by "the proportion of times a person has received the outcome following the act" (Vroom 1964: 26). Estimates of instrumentality are similarly based on promises and past experience.

Porter and Lawler (1968) made feedback an explicit part of their theoretical model. Satisfaction resulting from intrinsic and extrinsic rewards affects the value (valence) of reward goals. Feedback from the actual relationship between performance and rewards influences the perceived effort-reward probability (expectancy). Together these elements determine whether a person will persist in exerting effort.

Feedback influences valences through needs, which in turn are determined by purposes. Purposes and goals are closely related. Both serve as standards for evaluating outcomes and making adjustments in behavior. Both are determined by a system's hierarchy of values. In the short run purposes may be served by internal or external acts, whereas goals call for acts directed toward the environment. In the long run purposes lead to goals, because maintenance of steady states in an open system requires inputs and outputs. For example, maintaining energy levels and avoiding hunger pangs requires that a person set goals for acquiring and ingesting food. A purpose of maintaining a secure relationship with a friend leads to goals such as paying back social debts and keeping contact.

Assuming that outcomes have positive value as expected, feedback to needs is negative. The better the outcome, the greater the reduction in stress and strain. Because other strains are usually present, a system may switch to other activities before a need is completely fulfilled.

Feedback to expectancies and instrumentalities comes from the perceived relationship of acts to task outcomes (expectancy) and task outcomes to reward outcomes (instrumentality), rather than from the outcomes themselves. As noted earlier, these relationships may be perceived on a conscious level or simply recorded as associations. In either case the effect of a successful outcome is to strengthen the association and increase the likelihood that the behavior will persist or recur. Positive reinforcement or operant conditioning may be explained by this feedback mechanism, operating noncognitively.

Environmental influence. In addition to the effects of internal feedback, persistence of behavior is also influenced by intrusion of environmental stimuli. Events may cause a sudden, urgent change in needs, forcing a disruption of behavior even though current goals or needs have not been met. A more subtle influence is represented by the presence of others who might evaluate a person's behavior and outcomes. This influence is modeled by several theories, including the social information processing approach (Salancik and Pfeffer 1978) and the social learning approach (Davis and Luthans 1980).

Ferris et al. (1978) offered a social facilitation model that combines approval from others with expectancy theory. Approval as an outcome of task performance influences the perceived instrumentality of task performance toward obtaining approval. Coupled with a need for social approval (which gives a positive valence to the goal of approval), this instrumentality contributes to motivation toward task performance.

Equity theory (Adams 1963; Carrell and Dittrich 1978) presents another model for evaluation of outcomes. According to this theory, people compare their own behavioral inputs and outcomes with the inputs and outcomes of others. If outcomes seem equitable according to this standard, task behavior persists. Otherwise, the person modifies inputs in order to try to rectify the perceived inequity.

Equity theory and the social-environmental approaches can be inserted into the living systems model as influences on the valences of acts and goals. That is, information concerning equity and the expectations or approval of others alters these valences. When a reward outcome seems inequitably low, it loses valence as a goal. Prior social approval of an act increases its valence; disapproval lowers its valence. As we saw earlier, approval or disapproval as an outcome may influence the instrumentality of the task goal.

Summary of the Single-System Model

The single-system model of motivation encompasses arousal, direction, and persistence of behavior. It is compatible with a wide variety of other theories, models, and approaches to motivation that can be inserted as interpretations or elaborations of its components. It can be interpreted as a cognitive model that is applicable to complex behavior of higher level systems, or as a noncognitive model applicable to all levels of living systems.

At the social-system levels the cognitive interpretation applies to the decision making of leaders. Thus Chapter 11 will draw upon this model of motivation in its discussion of the motivational role of leaders. The noncognitive interpretation would apply to emergent behavior of social systems. In a group, for instance, much behavior is governed by group norms rather than by the purposes and goals of any individual member. Like purposes and goals, norms serve as standards against which behavior and outcomes can be compared and controlled.

Given that the model applies to motivation of a group or organization as well as an individual, the remainder of this chapter will be devoted to exploring the interaction between individuals and higher level systems. How do the needs of an individual interact with the needs of a family group or a business firm? How do they influence each other's choice of goals? How are acts and outcomes shared? We will not be able to examine all of the interactions in detail, but we will explore them briefly in order to suggest the potential of the living systems model.

MOTIVATIONAL INTERACTION

As the single-system model indicates, the motivational process is open to influence at several points. Motivation may be affected through influence directed at perceptions of needs, valences, or associations, the choice of goals or

Figure 7–2
Resource Exchange in an Employer-Employee Dyad

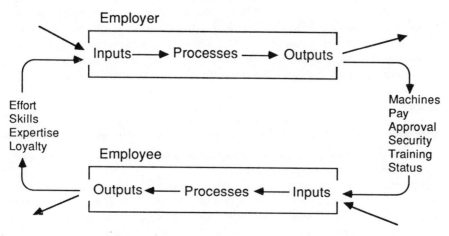

Source: From L. Tracy (1984: 201).

acts, and the evaluation of outcomes. Such influence typically comes from other living systems, as when a supervisor seeks to motivate the work performance of an employee or the government attempts to influence a business firm to control pollution.

Path-goal theory specifies several ways in which a supervisor can influence the motivation of subordinates (Georgopoulos, Mahoney, and Jones 1957; Evans 1970; House 1971; House and Mitchell 1974). The leader may try to (1) intensify needs for the available rewards, (2) convince subordinates of the attractiveness of the rewards (thereby increasing valences), (3) make the task easier or convince subordinates that they can do it (thereby increasing expectancies), and (4) provide assurance that performance will be rewarded and deliver rewards as promised (thereby increasing instrumentalities). As we noted earlier, various social-interaction approaches to motivation also model social influence on valences, expectancies, and instrumentalities.

A particularly prevalent form of motivational interaction is between a social system and its members, both of which have needs. The continuing relationship between social system and individual is based on mutual need fulfillment. In a business firm, for example, individual employees supply the organization with effort, skills, expertise, loyalty, obedience, regular attendance, perhaps even tools. In return employees may receive pay and benefits, recognition, security, supervision, training, tools, machinery and the energy to run it, safe and healthful working conditions, status, and loyalty.

This mutual exchange of needed resources between two living systems may be pictured in the form of a systems dyad (see Figure 7–2). Note that each system has alternative sources for need fulfillment (represented by unlabeled input arrows), such that their mutual dependency is not total.

An important aspect of the relationship between an organization and its members or employees is that, as part of the social contract, the latter cede some decision-making authority to the leaders of the organization. Individuals accept the legitimacy of orders (within limits) from the organization and agree to carry out the specified actions. For instance, an employee may willingly accept direction as to when to work, what to work on, how to perform the task, and how much to produce. Thus a leader can easily direct subordinate behavior.

⟵ Motivation of an individual's behavior still comes from the individual, but it is more or less strongly influenced by the organization. To the extent, for instance, that a person accepts the organization's goals as his or her own goals, their valences for the individual are enhanced.

Processes such as Management by Objectives (MBO) (Carroll and Tosi 1973; Raia 1974) or participative decision making (Marrow, Bowers, and Seashore 1967; Filley, House, and Kerr 1976) may be used to increase individual acceptance of organizational goals. It should not be overlooked, however, that these are two-way processes in which individuals may have some influence on organizational goals. Participative decision making is often used in conjunction with goal setting as a means of obtaining commitment to organizational goals. Some controversy exists, nevertheless, as to whether participation or goal setting alone, both additively or both interactively, leads to high task performance (Latham and Steele 1983).

Individual and social systems often merge at the stage of task performance. The amount of effort and skill that each individual puts into the task contributes to group or organizational performance and outcomes. Likewise, the quality of leadership and amount of capital investment that the social system puts into the task contributes to an individual's performance and outcomes. Just as a supervisor may attempt to influence an employee's motivation in order to increase his or her contribution to the task, so the employee has an interest in inducing the firm to increase its contribution.

Although the individual and social system receive different outcomes from their joint performance, these separate outcomes represent a division and sharing of the overall outcomes. Equity theory comes into play here. Collective bargaining or individual contract bargaining may be used to set the terms for this division. Each party to the dyadic relationship has an interest in influencing the division of the joint outcomes.

Figure 7-3 is a model of the motivational interaction between two living systems (Tracy in press). In this figure the motivation models for two single systems (Figure 7-1) have been broken out and placed in parallel, merging at the point of behavior because both systems must act in concert to accomplish the task. Mutual influence is shown as in the dyad (Figure 7-2), but with elaboration of the points of input. For simplicity, external inputs were not included in the model.

Figure 7–3
Model of Motivational Interaction between Systems

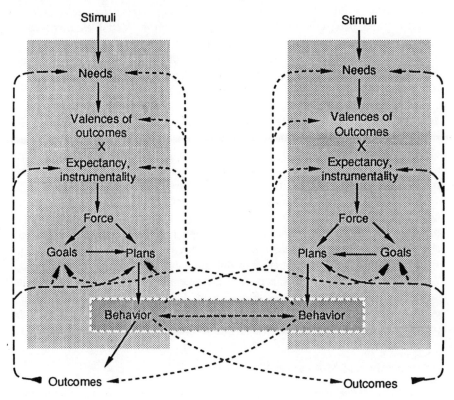

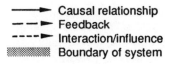

The model applies to any two systems that attempt to coordinate their behavior. The interaction of two individuals trying to plan an evening's entertainment or two governments negotiating a mutual arms reduction pact would be modeled in the same way. Of course, the interacting patterns of influence could exist even when behavior is not coordinated.

SUMMARY AND IMPLICATIONS

Motivation is defined as the processes of a living system that cause arousal, direction, and persistence of its purposeful behavior. Variables involved in these motivation processes include the presence of stimuli, the intensity of needs, alternative goals and acts that might fulfill those needs, valences and expectancies of anticipated outcomes, and feedback from actual outcomes.

Although no single current theory or model does justice to all aspects of motivation, a model was presented that integrates the living systems need concept with theories of expectancy, goal setting, reinforcement, social cognition, and social interaction. Many of the currently popular approaches to motivation are thus combined in one model. The model is dynamic, encompassing several mechanisms whereby motivation may change over time. It also indicates several points at which external stimuli may influence the motivational processes.

Using the systems dyad concept together with these points of influence, a model of motivational interaction was developed. Two major implications of this model for a pair of interacting systems are that motivation is a two-way street and that performance and outcomes are dependent on the contributions of both systems. Each system may attempt to influence the other's perception of needs, valences, expectancies, goals, acts, and outcomes. Research on motivation must take these interactive influences into account. People and organizations setting out to motivate others must consider the effects on their own motivation and be prepared to accept the mutual nature of the process.

Implications of Motivational Interaction

The previous discussion indicates that motivation involves extensive interaction between living systems. Motivation cannot be adequately modeled by looking at single-system processes alone. Individual work motivation, for example, occurs in the context of work groups and organizations. The motivation of employees interacts at many points with the motivation of the group and organization.

The discussion of interactive properties of living-systems motivation contains several practical implications for leaders and managers. First, unlike traditional models of motivation, it emphasizes that motivation is a two-way street. Members individually and collectively seek to motivate an organization to do certain things just as the organization seeks to motivate individual and group performance.

Furthermore, the model makes clear that performance is dependent on both individual and social system contributions. Managers, in seeking greater input of effort from employees, often overlook the possibility that poor supervision or poorly maintained machinery may be wasting much of the existing effort. Employees, on the other hand, may be well aware of that waste of effort but are discouraged from communicating to organizational decision makers about it. Recent innovations in management such as Quality Circles and Quality of Work

Life experiments are based on tapping the expertise of employees to reduce such waste. A motto of Quality Circles is "Work smarter, not harder!"

Motivation already exists for people to contribute ideas to improve the efficiency of their social systems. Most employees are able to see that improved performance, so long as it does not have a high cost (e.g. loss of job, increased effort), will enhance fulfillment of their own goals. Lowering the perceived cost by assuring job security or rewarding good ideas with recognition and bonuses can push employee motivation over the threshold into the realm of action. Participation and commitment to organizational goals may also become part of employees' self-concept.

The level of contribution to a social system by individual members is not based directly on their calculations of the valences of goals, likelihood of attaining them, and equity of the exchange. Rather, level of contribution is chosen as one element of the path that promises maximum fulfillment of needs. Individual inputs to the social system will increase if employees are convinced that the payoff gain is greater than the incremental cost.

Payoffs may be increased in various ways. For instance, through coaching or clarification of instructions a supervisor may increase an employee's expectancy of attaining a performance goal and thereby gaining additional rewards. Likewise, instrumentality of task performance for the employee may be strengthened by a firm promise of a reward for high performance and by consistent fulfillment of that promise. The living systems model emphasizes the influence of feedback from actual outcomes on future assessment of expectancies and instrumentalities, and thence on motivation.

Path-goal theory offers some of the same insights, but it fails to distinguish clearly between individual and organizational goals. Paths are seen as organizationally determined. The role of a supervisor is to smooth and clarify the organizationally defined path, provide organizationally determined rewards for good performance, and emphasize the value of those rewards. In contrast, the motivational interaction model suggests that defining and clarifying the path, smoothing it, and determining appropriate rewards is a mutual process between employees and organizational leaders. When supervisors attempt to make this a one-way process, they are likely to shut off valuable inputs and adversely affect employee motivation.

If employees are motivated to provide their best inputs of effort and skill to the joint enterprise, the outcome still depends on the organization doing the same. Employers should therefore expect employees to try to influence the organization in order to obtain better inputs of capital and direction, as well as to gain a larger share of the joint rewards.

The motivational interaction model may also be used to gain a better understanding of relationships between many other system dyads, such as husband/wife, parent/child, purchaser/supplier, and nation/nation. Not only does the model indicate the many sources and targets of motivational influence in such relationships, but also it emphasizes the interdependence of outcomes.

Research Implications

For research on motivation the import of the model is to focus attention on the need for recording interactions and measuring change in both systems during any attempt to influence motivation. In stimulus-response experiments, for instance, what is the effect on the experimenter of the subject's performance from trial to trial? In a goal-setting experiment how does the experimenter respond to various goal levels set by different individuals or to individual reactions to goals set by the experimenter? Such interactions may have a lot to do with the outcomes of research on motivation. Failure to consider the mutuality of motivational interaction may invalidate the research.

Overall, the single-system model and the model of motivational interaction suggest that future research on motivation must be much more complex and capable of handling multiple variables and relationships. It is all very well to begin by focusing on the effects of specific variables such as needs or goals, but it is time that we recognize these are only parts of a larger picture. Adoption of some common terms that do not obscure the relationships between variables is a start. A next step would be research on the interactions among these variables.

It is quite likely, for instance, that the difficulties in testing expectancy theory can be traced to a failure to recognize other variables affecting the experimental situation. Ignoring opportunity costs and the motivation toward ongoing acts, and treating effort as a dependent variable rather than a determinant of task valence, are examples of this short-sighted approach.

Similarly, goal-setting experiments have tended to overlook the question of whether the behavioral path to the goal is clear and easy or ambiguous and difficult. Furthermore, little interest has been shown in the mechanisms by which goal commitment might be linked to high performance. Social cognitive theory or cognitive dissonance theory may provide an answer.

Goal-setting research should be extended to groups and organizations. Living systems theory suggests that the setting of organizational goals, for instance, should have the same motivational effects on the organization that personal goals have on people. A particularly interesting question would be the effect of the organization's degree of commitment to its goals. When a firm decides to market a new product and sets a goal of 10 percent market share, for instance, how far is it willing to go to attain that goal?

Reinforcement studies have generally failed to consider the effects of rewards on instrumentality estimates as well as on need fulfillment, probably because most reinforcement theorists ignore cognitive variables such as instrumentality. But the complex and seemingly contradictory results with respect to variable reinforcement schedules strongly suggest that the relationship between reward and behavior is not a simple one, and that other variables are at work, such as the ones suggested by Bandura (1986).

Finally, research in all of these areas should recognize the two-way nature of motivation, since it virtually guarantees experimenter effects. Even if the researcher is totally isolated from the experimental situation and those who conduct the experiment are ignorant of what is being tested, they will be motivated to react to the subjects' behavior. If the assistants' behavior is programmed to avoid such influence, the subjects may detect a lack of normal interaction. A better procedure may be to permit normal reactions and to measure behavioral influence on both sides of the experiment.

8

Power and Influence

Power is a primitive concept, well known to writers in ancient China, Greece, and Rome. Certainly Machiavelli understood power as a political concept. Yet power is so elemental that it is also found as a concept in physical science (e.g., atomic and hydroelectric power), chemistry (the power of an explosive reaction or a chemical bond), military science (fire power), sociology (authority and the power of a work group), psychology (individual dominance and will power), and physiology (muscle power). There are obvious differences in the use of the term in these various fields, but such a broadly used concept must possess a common core of meaning.

The common core is often assumed to be capacity or ability to influence other systems. That is, physical power is seen as the capacity to do mechanical work, chemical power as the capacity to sustain a chemical reaction, military power as the ability to defeat an enemy, and so forth. Dahl (1957: 202–3), for instance, defined power thusly: "A has power over B to the extent that [A] can get B to do something that B would not otherwise do."

This seems like a reasonable definition until one realizes that it leaves no way to identify power other than by its effects. We aren't told what power is, but only what it can do. Dahl's definition of power tends to confuse the concept with influence, leadership, and motivation.

Bass (1981: 170-71) argued against such a definition, pointing out that it creates tautologies. A capacity or ability should not be identified with actual accomplishment. Bierstedt (1950) insisted that power is potential; it is a capacity to do something and should not be confused with the actual doing. Yet if power is a "capacity to influence," how could it be detected or measured other than through observation of actual influence? There must be some way to identify the capacity even when it isn't used.

Unlike such terms as "influence" and "control," power does not have a verb form. We can say "they influenced the president," but not "they powered the president." Wrong (1968) viewed the lack of a verb form as unfortunate because power is thus seen as a property rather than a relation. But power can refer as easily to a relation (e.g., A > B) as to a property (e.g., A possesses X); what it cannot express by itself is the act of assertion.

Power simply exists. In order to be influential it must be "exercised" on someone. Power also exists even when it does nothing; power can be stored. Thus a definition of power should focus on what it is, not on what it can do.

To get at the true common core of power, let us examine how the term is used. There are two different senses of the term. First is a general sense, as in the power of the atom or of the presidency. In this sense power represents a potential or potency based upon availability of resources. The atom possesses available nuclear energy and the presidency holds legal authority and charisma. Second is a relational sense of the term, the power of one system over another. In this second sense both systems have available resources; the key to power lies in the resource differential between the systems.

The common core of power in both senses seems to lie in possession or control of resources—that is, one system possessing or controlling something that other systems lack. This is true whether we are talking about living or nonliving systems. For instance, the power of a storage battery is in the electrical charge it holds. A battery has the power to supply electrons to a motor, light bulb, and so on. Yet it has no power when connected to another battery of the same charge; the other battery has no lack of electrons. The same is true of people. It is often said that "money is power." Yet the possessor of money may hold little or no power over a millionaire. The possession of money per se would also afford little power over an infant, because infants do not value money.

Power also inheres in possessing resources that threaten other systems. A nation's weapons confer power because other nations *don't* want them to be used. Weapons and other punishing resources provide power because they are capable of generating a strain in another system. In fact even the possibility of their use may create a strain.

When two nations possess equal weaponry, *ceteris paribus*, neither has military power with respect to the other. It would still be correct to say that each nation has power in the general sense, since their weapons tend to give them power over other nations, yet they possess no power in the relational sense (i.e., over each other) because there is no differential between them. They may still influence each other, but that is another matter to be discussed later.

Nations also lack power if they cannot afford to use their weapons or other resources. Power lies in *expendable* resources, that is, excesses. Pfeffer (1981: 103–6) uses the similar term *slack* resources in discussing organizational sources of power. In general a system must possess or control excess resources and must perceive them to be excess, otherwise they will not be regarded as expendable. To some extent, however, a system may redefine its purposes or lower its levels of acceptance in order to free resources for power applications. In wartime, for instance, nations tend to "tighten their belts" and transfer productive capacity from civilian goods to weapons and military manpower.

In the general sense, therefore, *power* may be defined as possession or control of excess resources. The distinction between possession and control, while not essential, is useful. Possession implies that the resource is part of, or within the boundary of, the living system holding power. Control means simply that the system is able to deliver the resource, as a manager is able to command organizational resources.

Relational power is defined as possession or control of excess resources that can relieve or create a strain in another system. That is, system A has relational power over B if A has excess resources that can (1) fulfill some of B's needs, (2) reduce some of B's excesses, or (3) create lacks or excesses for B. In the first two cases A's power is the power to reward; in the last case it is the power to punish.

Influence, on the other hand, is the effect of one system on another system's behavior. To paraphrase Dahl (1957), when A gets B to do something that B would not otherwise do, A has (or exerts) influence over B. Influence can only properly be defined in a relational sense. When we say that a person has influence or is influential, we must mean either that he or she has influence over several other systems or that he or she holds general power.

As we shall see, influence arises from effective exercise of power. On the other hand, influence may exist without apparent power. When A gives B a tip on the stock market and B thereupon purchases the recommended stock, it is clear that A influenced B. It is somewhat of a moot point, however, whether this is a demonstration of A's expertise power or B's motivation, particularly if A got nothing appreciable out of the transaction.

SOCIAL POWER

The field of organizational behavior is primarily concerned with a form of power called *social power*. As a basic concept of the social sciences, social power has received a multiplicity of definitions and treatments (Bass 1981: 169–71). Social power has been viewed as an *attribute* of a power holder who, depending on the level of analysis, might be an individual, group, organization, or nation. It has also been seen as a *relation* between two such systems.

Different ways of observing and measuring social power have also been described in the literature. Social power has been inferred from the holding of resources, from the use of resources in acts of attempted influence, and from the outcomes of such acts. Such a diversity of views makes it difficult to employ the concept in scientific discourse.

General and Relational Senses

Although social power is more often treated in the relational sense, the general sense is also encountered. Bierstedt (1950), for example, defined group power in the general sense as latent force stemming from three sources: (1) numbers of people in the group, (2) social organization of the group, and (3) control of resources such as money, property, prestige, and knowledge. Other authors, while clearly perceiving power as a relation between systems, have focused on characteristics of the power holder as sources or bases of social power. For instance, Burns (1978: 12) noted: "The two essentials of power are motive and resource." In Burns' view power lies in control over expendable resources and the will to use them in order to influence others toward one's own purposes.

This view applies to any human system in a power relationship. All such systems have resources. When A attempts to exert power over B, B may attempt to resist by exerting countervailing power (Galbraith 1952). Or each system may attempt to exert power over the other intercursively. As Wrong (1968: 674) described intercursive use of power, "the control of one person or group over the other with reference to a particular scope is balanced by the control of the other in a different scope." For example, elected officials have legitimate power over citizens, but citizens have the power to vote those officials out of office. When two nations hold equal military power, they may seek power over each other in other arenas, such as trade or world opinion.

It may turn out that A has more power and can exert more influence than B, but the issue is not determined until we know the reactions of both systems. Whereas the reaction to power in the physical world is predictable, living systems are unique in the unpredictability of their responses. Reactions to power depend not only upon the resources possessed by each system, but also upon the will to use them or to bluff. Even though resources may be objectively in excess, they are not effectively expendable unless the possessor is willing to spend them. Many a battle has been lost by superior forces because their commander lacked the will to commit resources to the fight or challenge a bluff.

Nor is it sufficient simply to consider the resources and will of power holders. Another key to power lies in the wants and perceptions of the respondent. In the first century A.D. Epictetus wrote that it is because we fear death, loss of property, prison, or disenfranchisement, and love wealth and public office, that those such as Caesar who control these things are masters over us.

In modern terms we might say that a system's social power depends on its ability to fulfill or generate needs or to relieve or create excesses in other social systems. A power holder must possess resources that have value (i.e., positive or negative valence) to other systems and can be shared at no expense or expended in exchange for something of greater worth to self or others. Implicit in the commentary of Epictetus is the notion that both parties often gain what they want from a power relationship. We do Caesar's bidding and Caesar gives us wealth (or refrains from punishing us). When resources can be exchanged to the benefit of both parties, it is not necessary for either party to hold a predominance of power in order to influence the other.

In accordance with the preceding discussion *general social power* is defined here as possession or control of resources that the holder regards as excess, where the holder is a person or social system. Likewise, *relational social power* is possession or control of resources that the holder regards as excess and that another living system values positively or negatively. Thus social power is properly defined for living systems in terms of the holding of excess resources, rather than the effects or outcomes of the use of those resources.

Other Views of Relational Social Power

Cartwright offered a different relational definition of social power, after explicitly rejecting the notion of general power. Drawing upon Lewin's (1951) field theory, Cartwright (1959: 193) defined the power of A over B as the maximum force that A can exert on B minus the maximum resisting force that B can exert on A. The term *force* is used in the sense of a psychological vector (Lewin 1951). French and Raven (1959) defined social power similarly.

We are now talking about application of power. Cartwright defined social power in terms of what it can do, rather than what it is. To distinguish this usage of the term from social power as I have defined it, I will henceforth call this *social force*.

Note that Cartwright's definition, while recognizing the importance of both parties, is asymmetrical; it rests on the intent of A and assumes only resistance on the part of B. If A and B are both purposeful systems, it would be more reasonable to accord intent to both of them. Furthermore, since social force is treated here as a resultant of two opposing forces, it might better be called *net social force*.

The *relational social force* of A with respect to B may be defined as the maximum force that A can exert on B. Similarly, the relational social force of B with respect to A is the maximum force that B can exert on A. Then A has positive net social force over B when A can exert more force on B than B can exert on A.

Translating this into the terms of social power as I have defined it, the *total relational social power* of system A over system B is the sum of B's values for all the excess resources possessed or controlled by A, and similarly for B's power over A. Whoever has the greater sum has net social power.

Both systems in a dyad tend to be motivated by relational power, because each can affect needs or excesses of the other. This is true regardless of the hierarchical levels of the two systems. In an employer-employee relationship, for example, each system has the ability to provide resources that the other system values as input, and to accept resources that the other regards as excess. Thus each has power with respect to the other.

Each system in a dyad is able to deny the power of the other to some extent by substituting other resources or alternative sources. A system's control over resources needed by another system is seldom absolute. Nevertheless, there is a power bond between the two systems to the extent that they are mutually able to fulfill each other's needs and relieve each other's excesses. To the degree that one system gains less than the other from the relationship, that system has less to lose and is in a position of positive net power.

Note that a lack can be a source of power. When system A's lack matches the excesses of system B, A is able to reduce a strain for B by absorbing B's excess. In the illustration above, the employer provides an outlet for the employee's excess energy and expertise while the employee puts the employer's excess machinery and ideas to good use. Each holds usable power with respect to the other, regardless of the total balance of power. This would be true even if the worker were a prisoner or a slave. Although the worker's power is diminished in such a situation, there are still subtle ways of withholding resources from the employer. Unfortunately, those who hold great resources often fail to perceive the power of others to withhold their few desired resources.

PERCEIVED SOCIAL POWER

For social power to be effective it must be perceived. In a relation between systems A and B, if B fails to perceive A's control over resources, then A cannot use those resources to influence B. Conversely, if B incorrectly perceives that A controls something of value, A can exert influence even though holding little general power.

When one person believes another's bluff, for instance, the bluffer has power over the believer without the assumed or promised resources to back it up. Power resides in the perceived credibility of the bluffer. Likewise, a threat is powerful if it is believed; no direct force need be applied. But the recipient of the threat must believe that the other has the will and the capacity to carry it out.

The respondent's perception is essential for effectiveness of all forms of social power except the direct application of coercive force. Even the power of authority lies in its acceptance by subordinates, according to Barnard (1938). Expectancy theory posits that the power of rewards to motivate performance lies in people's perceptions of the value (valence) of prospective outcomes and of the likelihood that those outcomes will occur (Vroom 1964).

Individual Sources of Power

According to French and Raven (1959: 155–66), person A's power over person B is based on B's perceptions of A. They defined five bases of A's social power as follows:

1. reward power, based on B's perception that A has the ability to mediate rewards for B;
2. coercive power, based on B's perception that A has the ability to mediate punishments for B;
3. legitimate power, based on B's perception that A has a right to prescribe behavior for B;
4. referent power, based on B's identification (i.e., perception of oneness) with A; and
5. expert power, based on B's perception that A has some special knowledge or expertise.

Note that social power is defined by French and Raven as *perception* of an ability to expend resources (i.e., to reward or punish) or share them (i.e., to confer legitimacy, status, or knowledge), not as actual expenditure or sharing. Power is not an act; it is a capacity to act, stemming from actual or perceived control of expendable resources.

Another source of social power that should be mentioned is obligation. Blau (1964) cited the development of obligations as a primary source of a leader's power. Like the sources cited by French and Raven, obligation must be perceived in order to be effective. The power of obligation stems from B perceiving that A has already expended or shared resources with B and that B therefore should return the favor.

A very different source of power is perceived excess capacity in the form of space or time. That is, B perceives that A has the capacity to absorb some of B's excesses. A customer can consume part of a retailer's excess inventory. A clinical psychologist is able to spend time to absorb a patient's anxiety. Any system having such excess capacity can perform a service for other systems, and thus holds power.

Organizational Sources of Power

Groups, organizations, and nations have sources of power beyond those possessed by individuals. Indeed, one of the reasons for forming these social systems is to gather power. The power of a social system may be greater than the sum of power held by the individual members, although that sum is a starting point.

Organizational power may be viewed in two ways: (1) power provided to members, especially leaders, and (2) the power of the social system itself. An organization legitimizes certain sources of individual power, thereby strengthening them. It also gives members access to the power of other members and to the resources of the organization.

Legitimacy stems first from the charter of a social system. If the purposes and goals of the system are regarded as appropriate and its structure and processes are effective, the system achieves a status of legitimacy in the eyes of other living systems. The United States of America was recognized as a legitimate nation and its representatives to other nations were accorded diplomatic status when the colonies were able to establish a federal government and defend themselves and their Constitution against the British forces. A new business firm is usually perceived as legitimate when it is able to establish a market for its goods and services, meet certain legal obligations, and pay its bills.

Legitimacy is enhanced by societal norms and laws. These norms and laws condition people and institutions to accord the power of legitimacy to others if certain rules are followed. An infant is "legitimate" if its parents were married when it was born. On the other hand, a profitable business firm dealing in illegal products or services would have difficulty getting a bank loan; it is not legitimate. The power of legitimacy lies in the conditioning of people and social systems to acknowledge the "rightness" of certain behavior. Galbraith (1983: 24–37) accordingly calls it conditioned power. Conditioning is backed up by a court system to which individuals and organizations may appeal if their rights are not respected.

Legitimacy is conferred upon individual members according to their roles in the social system. Leaders within the system are given authority, sometimes called legitimate power, over other members. Authority enhances the power of expertise and usually conveys ability to mediate organizational rewards and punishments. Other members accept the authority of leaders as a condition of membership in the system, relinquishing the right to direct some of their own behavior. In return they typically receive rights, rewards, and benefits of membership, including power to carry out certain specified duties. Acceptance of the leader's legitimate power also relieves strains caused by an excess of individual responsibility.

Members may also obtain power from their roles in the social system. A person's position in the structure of the organization often confers a degree of control over resources required by other members and groups. The person in this position may control the flow of materials, funds, or information. This source is often called position power.

The authority of members and the legitimate power of the system as a whole are limited by the system's charter. An organization founded as a business firm has no acknowledged right to meddle in the political affairs of a sovereign nation. If a supervisor tries to tell an employee how to dress and the employee does not accept that as a legitimate area of supervisory decision making, the supervisor effectively lacks authority in that area. Insistence on trying to apply authority where it is not perceived as legitimate may damage that source of power even where it is properly applied.

When legitimacy is not recognized or is insufficient, social systems call upon several other sources of power. Prominent among these is collective power, the resources of individual members applied in a coordinated fashion. A group thus may wield much more power than its members individually could apply. A labor union, frustrated in its attempts to obtain recognition from an employer, may require its members collectively to exercise their power to walk out. A lobbying organization may ask its members to exercise their individual right to petition their congressional representatives. Collective power uses the reward and punishment powers of individuals in a way that multiplies their effectiveness, particularly toward a higher level system. Part of the multiplier effect comes from restriction of respondent's alternative sources—that is, the power of monopoly.

Cohesiveness of a group or organization strengthens its power. Bierstedt (1950), Pfeffer (1981: 122–24) and Galbraith (1983: 54–64) all noted that commitment of members to group goals and the ability of leaders to command obedience to the will of the group contribute to organizational power. The power of a labor union is sapped, for instance, if members disobey a strike call and cross the picket lines. Japanese manufacturing firms, and some American firms as well, are reputed to beat their competitors because of the commitment of their employees to the goals of the firm.

The power of a cohesive organization may be explained partly in terms of its internal efficiency. Fewer resources are required to maintain channels of communication and coordinate the adaptive processes of a cohesive organization. Consequently, more resources are available as power sources to be applied externally.

In addition to the resources provided by members, social systems have their own excess resources that may be used for reward or punishment. A business firm may use some of its profits to entertain legislators, to woo a key employee away from a competitor, to buy advertising, to increase its market share by cutting prices, and so forth. A labor union may use its dues to hire more organizers or conduct political education campaigns. A nation's excess land and natural resources give it the power to attract immigrants and investment capital. Shopping centers use their space to offer plentiful free parking in order to attract customers.

Like individual power, organizational power must generally be perceived in order to be effective. Organizational rewards for superior performance often do not receive the expected response, either because employees are not sufficiently aware of the rewards or because they do not value them highly. Legitimate power, in particular, depends entirely on perception. The United Nations has on numerous occasions tried to assert its authority to mediate a dispute between nations, but has often been ineffective because the nations involved refused to acknowledge the right of the United Nations to intervene.

Power Holder Perceptions

The perceptions of the power holder are also important. Holders may fail to perceive certain sources of their own power. For example, a manager may not be aware that he or she has the positive regard of employees and may fail to employ referent power even though it exists in the general sense. Revolutionary governments often resort to excessive use of coercion because they fear that other sources of power, such as legitimacy and charisma, will not be acknowledged by the people.

An unperceived power source is an uncontrolled power source. A manager may misperceive the values of employees and may promise them rewards of little value or disregard rewards of considerable value to them. Power, though it may exist in the general sense, is often wasted by the misperceptions of the holder.

Power tends to dissipate through entropic processes. Thus it must be watched and cared for. Power-conscious systems often use power to gather more sources of power, not just to fulfill their own needs. In gathering or exchanging for resources to be used as power sources, the holder must correctly perceive the worth that other systems will ascribe to these resources. The stock market is a good example of this sort of exchange, and it amply illustrates the difficulties of correctly predicting the future perceived worth of resource holdings.

Communication of Power

If power must usually be perceived in order to be socially effective, communication obviously plays an important role in determining relational power. A power holder must advertise the resources that he or she is prepared to spend or share, as well as indicate the desired response. But as we noted in Chapter 6, the message received is the only one that counts. In other words the respondent is in ultimate control even of communications about power. If B is unable or unwilling to understand what A wants or to perceive A's power, A may have no recourse except to try to exercise direct physical control. Moreover, A may not have enough power or the right kind of power for that.

It cannot be assumed that the recipient of a power message, even if it is accurately perceived, will simply comply. The recipient has several options. Compliance is one of them, of course. Part I of Figure 8-1 displays this option.

Variants of this option are minimal or pretended compliance. Labor unions, for instance, sometimes use a tactic called "work to rule" whereby workers do exactly what the written contract requires. Since much of the true contract between employer and employee is unwritten, such compliance is far from optimal or desirable.

A second option for B is simply to ignore or pretend not to perceive the communication from A. This is a form of bluffing. It is likely to work if A is unsure of the net power situation or is unwilling to spend resources to challenge B's bluff.

A third option is to try to form a coalition with a third party in order to neutralize the power of the initial holder. The third party, C, may hold net power over A or may serve as an alternative source of resources to B.

Finally, B may try to exercise countervailing power, as shown in Part II of Figure 8-1. When A transmits a message about available resources and desired responses, B does likewise. This may result in a standoff or an exchange of resources and/or acts of compliance, perhaps after negotiation.

Countervailing power may come from the same sources as initial power. In the employer-employee relationship Mechanic (1964) noted that subordinates often possess information or expertise that is valuable to the organization. Much of their power comes from the threat of withholding their services from the organization. They hold many legal rights that permit them to call upon the power of regulatory bodies and law courts. Affluence also strengthens the hand of subordinates by providing an alternative source of resources.

Lee (1980: 247–48) has described several additional conditions that limit supervisory power or provide countervailing power to employees. Organizational policies and the design of jobs may limit the amount of control that employees or

Figure 8–1
Communication of Power and Response

I. Dominance and compliance

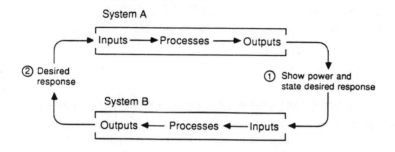

II. Reciprocation or resistance

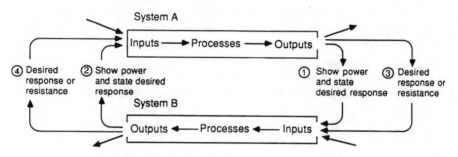

their supervisors have over task performance. In some organizations, employees have rights of appeal to higher levels of management. Finally, employees may be able to appeal to public sentiment. All of these sources must be perceived and communicated in order to be effective, although collective and legal powers may eventually result in direct application of force.

From the foregoing discussion we see that effective social power resides in some combination of the attributes of A and B, as well as the perceptions of each about the other. For A's power to be effective over B, the latter must (1) perceive that A possesses or controls excess resources, (2) value those resources positively or negatively, (3) believe that A will spend or share them, and (4) correctly perceive what response A wants. In most cases A must actually possess or control excess resources, perceive them as expendable, be willing to spend or share them, and accurately communicate to B an intention to do so, as well as indicating to B what response is desired. If A lacks sufficient excess resources, he may seek a coalition or contract with a third system to supply them.

Effective social power of system A over system B might be defined as the relational social power of A that is perceived by B and that B believes A is willing to use. It should also be recognized that the roles of A and B may easily be reversed. Both hold general power that may be the source of influence, if the power is appropriately perceived. *Net effective social power* is the difference in the power perceptions of each system vis-à-vis the other.

EXERCISING POWER

It may be of some interest to measure social power and note its sources, and power may sometimes be desired for its own sake, but the practical importance of power lies in its application. Power is exercised by the holder for the purpose of control or influence over other systems. Indeed, as we have noted, power is sometimes confused with influence.

If power is not influence, it nevertheless may be used for goals of influence. The exercise of power for influence may or may not require expenditure of resources. Under certain circumstances system A may simply communicate the desired behavior to system B, perhaps also citing a particular power base, and B will comply. Otherwise, A may expend resources through direct physical action on B (e.g., torture or imprisonment) or by means of rewards and punishments. Rewards may be given as reinforcement after B complies, or in advance as a means of creating an obligation. Punishments are used to discourage noncompliance when other applications of power have failed.

Methods of Application

Different resources require different methods of utilization. Power based on A's legitimacy, charisma, expertise, logic, or moral superiority, if perceived by B, generally leads to B's compliance without expenditure. A's authority is accepted if the order lies within B's zone of indifference. If A has referent power with respect to B, the latter will comply with A just to maintain the relationship. If B perceives that A has superior knowledge, skill, or moral authority, B may bow to A's judgment without question. If B sets a positive value on logic and perceives logic in A's arguments, they will be persuasive. If B feels an obligation to A based on past favors, B may do whatever A asks within the bounds of the obligation.

For application of power of this sort we often say that A is persuasive. Indeed, neither A nor B may be aware that power is involved in the exchange. Galbraith's (1983: 24-37) conditioned power is exercised in this fashion.

An interesting aspect of voluntary compliance is that it strengthens the power base. The power holder loses no resources, and acceptance tends to breed more acceptance. The only risk is that the respondent might reject an influence attempt, thereby reducing the value of the resource on which it was based. That is, authority or charisma or expertise, once denied, loses potency.

Coercive power used as a threat may also lead to compliance without expenditure. So long as B perceives the threat, is unable or unwilling to counter it, and believes that A will carry it out, B is likely to accept A's influence. The promise of a reward might also be influential without exchange initially, but the long-term effectiveness of promises is destroyed if they are not carried out. Threats, on the other hand, may be effective indefinitely if they are not challenged.

Respondent's perceptions are particularly important for the effectiveness of threats and promises. To respond as A desires, B must perceive not only that A possesses the necessary resources, but also that A has the will to carry out the threat or promise. Usually this requires that A at least occasionally follow through. For instance, a labor union that has not had a strike for many years may call one just to demonstrate the efficacy of the threat.

Costs of Power Exercise

Resources used as rewards must, in the long run, be expended through exchange. That is, system A pays for what it receives from B. Thus there is a cost associated with reward power, although it may be more than offset by what is received in exchange. The power of obligation, which is based upon prior exchange, also has a cost. Knowledge, once shared, likewise loses its relational power with respect to the receiver, although it may retain general power. In each of these cases, however, both systems may gain from the exchange because of differential values placed on the outputs and inputs.

Coercive power applied as punishment or physical force also has a cost, but there tends to be a net loss to the dyad. Typically, direct use of coercive power requires that A expend energy and/or consume material resources, but the expenditure has negative value for B, and A may gain only a cessation of noncompliance. Furthermore, coercive power operates by denying need fulfillment or creating an excess, thereby generating new sources of power for the respondent. For instance, a child whose energies have been bottled up by a threat of punishment may later erupt in destructive activity, to the detriment of everyone.

Direct physical force is the only application of power that does not depend on the perceptions of the respondent. Force may be used by A as a last resort precisely because B fails to perceive and acquiesce to other forms of power. But the lack of gain tends to encourage B to employ countervailing force. The net result may be a loss of relational power to both parties and a reduction of total power (bond) in the dyad.

According to Harsanyi, (1962: 68), "A's power over B is greater the smaller the costs of A's power and the greater the strength of A's power." It appears from the preceding discussion, however, that the stronger sources of power also tend to be more costly. There is little or no cost to A in using authority, logic, charisma, or expertise to influence B, because resources are shared rather than spent. But the strength of these power sources is very dependent on B's values.

Table 8–1
Cost and Effectiveness of Sources of Power

Source of power	Cost	Effectiveness
Legitimacy, Charisma, Expertise, Logic, Moral superiority	Low. Resources are shared rather than consumed.	High if resources are desired by recipient; low if they are not.
Threat of punishment	Low if recipient complies; high if user must consume resources to carry out threat.	High if recipient believes threat and decides not to employ countervailing power.
Obligation, Promise of reward	High. Resources must be transferred to recipient.	High if reward is desired by recipient; low if it is not.
Force	High. Resources are consumed.	High if user's power is dominant.

The values associated with threats of punishment and promises of reward tend to be greater; if credible, coercive and reward power are likely to be stronger than other forms. But threats and promises require at least occasional expenditure of resources in order to maintain credibility. Direct use of coercive and reward power is the most costly, but also the strongest because it is less dependent on respondent's perceptions. Table 8-1 summarizes the costs of exercising various forms of power.

Power and Motivation

At this point the link between power and motivation may be obvious, but it should nevertheless be delineated. Power can be exercised effectively only if the holder is motivated to use it and the respondent is motivated to act as the holder wishes. These linkages are seldom made explicit in the literature on power and influence.

The dynamic model of individual motivation presented in Chapter 7 indicated six points at which a system's motivation could be influenced by external forces. Each of these points offers an opening for the exercise of power. Different forms of power are appropriate at each point.

Stimulation of strains. The first point of influence is stimulation of strains within the system. External stimuli may arouse or create a need or excess or anticipation of one. For instance, B's perception that A is offering a particular resource as a reward may stimulate an existing need of that resource. Perception that A possesses charisma and expertise may arouse in B a need of leadership. Withholding the reward until a task is finished intensifies the need for that reward. If A threatens B with punishment, B may be motivated to avoid excess pain. The communication of power is usually aimed, first, at arousal of strains.

In cases where B is conditioned to respond in a certain way, A may only have to present the appropriate cue. When one of a group of boys decides he wants to race, he need only yell "Last one there is a rotten egg!" to elicit the desired response. The words create a competitive strain, or perhaps stimulate a need of conformity with the norms of the group. The only power the initiator must have is an understanding of the dynamics of the group; an uncompetitive group might not respond.

A subtler use of power is to relieve one strain so that another can become dominant. For instance, a manager might use control over budgets to authorize employment of additional people, so that a supervisor can concentrate on other productive matters. A peace negotiator might offer a pledge of nonaggression to relieve the strain of insecurity and allow the other party to concentrate on plans for laying down its arms.

Altering valences. A second aim of power communication is to change respondent's valences for resources that the power holder has. The holder may try to increase the valence of a resource by making it scarce, cutting off alternative sources. Other power tactics aimed at valences are persuasion and pointing out the valences that other systems ascribe to the resource. For instance, when Nestlé wanted to sell more infant formula in developing nations, the firm advertised the high valence given to the product in industrialized nations. Nestlé's power lay in perceived expertise, perhaps charisma (a respected, high-status brand name), and the money to conduct an intensive advertising campaign.

Influencing expectancies. Promises of reward and threats of punishment, if contingent on respondent's behavior, are aimed at expectancies. The power holder is attempting to strengthen the perceived link between respondent's behavior and outcomes. The perceived will of the holder to expend resources is the focus of this form of influence. Actual delivery of reward or punishment strengthens future expectancies, as well as influencing current perceived outcomes.

Changing goals and action plans. Commitment to organizational goals and acquiescence to prescribed ways of doing things are the primary foci of conditioned power in social systems. To the extent that members have already accepted these goals and acts as their own, other forms of power are unnecessary. Nevertheless, conditioned power is usually reinforced with a variety of other forms, including reward, coercive, legitimate, and referent power.

Controlling outcomes. Finally, power is used to define, control, and augment or reduce outcomes. The power of legitimacy, charisma, or expertise may be employed to convince the respondent that the outcome is fair and just. Authority to define tasks and dictate methods provides control over intrinsic rewards. Control over the division of resources resulting from joint performance is another source of power; it can be used to augment or diminish the respondent's outcomes. Ability to deliver or withhold extrinsic rewards and punishments may be used directly through reinforcement, or indirectly by creating expectancies. Thus power applied to outcomes influences the feedback to needs, goals, and expectancies. We have come full circle. Power may be used both to create strains and to relieve them.

To summarize, a system may use power in a variety of ways in order to influence or motivate (i.e., arouse, direct, and sustain) the behavior of another system. Most fundamentally, power can arouse, create, or fulfill needs and generate or relieve excesses. It can also alter valences and expectancies and influence goals and action plans. Through control of stimuli and outcomes a power holder can gain considerable influence over a responding system.

It must not be overlooked that the respondent also holds power and may attempt to exert it. The model of motivational interaction (Chapter 7) indicates that influence is a two-way street. The respondent may try either to block the initiator's use of power or to influence the initiator's behavior in return. The processes of conflict and cooperation (see Chapter 11) come into play here.

Influence without Power

Is power a necessary condition for influence? Some forms of influence seem to be based on the respondent's intrinsic motivation rather than on the power of the initiator. The example given earlier of boys responding to a dare is one instance. Another would be the response of a crowd to someone yelling "Fire!"

Should we regard these instances as examples of influence without power, or can they be explained in terms of referent or expert power? A boy shouting "Last one there is a rotten egg" may be seen as asserting referent power—if you respect me and want my respect, you'd better run—or even legitimate power—in this group anyone has the right to challenge other members. A person shouting "Fire!" may be assumed to hold important knowledge. The effect is enhanced by the referent power of the crowd as it starts to respond.

A subtler case is influence where none is intended. An employee may respond to the presence of the supervisor by working harder, even though the supervisor is not paying any attention to that employee. In this case power is not being "used," but it is nevertheless held by the supervisor and perceived by the employee, and it is that power to which the employee is responding. There is also no intent to communicate a power message. But communication is in the mind of the receiver, and a power message has been received.

Influence may occur through bluffing or threatening, even when objectively the initiator does not possess the power to back it up. Yet the respondent perceives the power to be there and responds to that perception. It appears that power is perceived whenever influence occurs, whether or not power is actually applied or available.

Powerlessness is, itself, a source of influence. In the game of "chicken" one strategy is to throw your steering wheel out the window in full view of the other competitor. The person who still has power—that is, the capability of steering— then has the choice of veering away and losing the game or staying on course and crashing.

Power is involved in all of these examples of apparent influence without power. Given that relational social power lies in perceived differences between systems with respect to resources held and the values put on those resources, and that such differences are ubiquitous, it seems likely that a power explanation can be found for any instance of influence. Nevertheless, power and influence are not the same thing. If influence cannot occur without perceived power, power can certainly exist without influencing anyone.

SUMMARY AND IMPLICATIONS

Social power is the possession or control of resources that the holder regards as excess. Net social power between two living systems is dependent on the expendable resources held by each system, the perception of own and other's resources and the value put on them by each system, each holder's willingness to expend or share resources, and the alternatives available to each system in terms of different sources or substitutable resources.

Exercising power involves all of these elements plus communication of a desired response. Power may be applied to arouse or fulfill needs, create or relieve excesses, influence valences and expectancies, alter goals and action plans, and control or define outcomes. Social power is often regarded negatively, because means such as unfulfilled promises, threats, and coercion are likely to lead to loss for one or both systems. But the exercise of social power often results in a net gain for both systems, particularly if resources such as rewards, legitimacy, expertise, and charisma are employed.

General power consists of possession or control of excess resources. This implies that power may be gained or maintained by (1) increasing inputs to the system, (2) decreasing consumption, (3) reducing outputs, and (4) increasing matter-energy storage and/or memory. These measures refer to possession of resources. Control of resources outside the system may be enhanced through the formation of alliances and contracts with other systems and through assumption of leadership in other systems. Power is often used in the acquisition of more power, either to obtain additional excess resources or to form alliances with other systems.

Relational power of A over B depends not only on A's excess resources but also on B's valences and perceptions. System A can increase relational power by such tactics as communicating effectively, demonstrating control over resources, bluffing, and restricting B's alternatives. When net power is considered, further tactics include inducing B to spend or waste resources, causing B to divert resources toward other systems, ignoring B's communications, and denying the value of B's resources. It should be noted that all of these tactics are familiar to students of the art of negotiation. That is not surprising, since bargaining theory focuses heavily on power as the determinant of negotiated settlements.

Application of power is often conceptualized in terms of using rewards and punishments to fulfill or create needs. The living systems analysis of power indicates, however, that a broader view should prevail. Power may be applied through withholding rewards and punishments in order to strengthen needs and relieve excesses; through creating obligations and developing exchanges of resources; and through altering valences, expectancies, goals, action plans, and perception of outcomes. Good communication and perception of power are often more important than the actual holding of resources.

A research implication of this chapter is that power research should focus on resources rather than outcomes. Questions that require more research include: How does a power holder determine what resources are expendable? How can a power holder assess the value of own resources from the point of view of a potential recipient? How can a power holder communicate a power message most effectively? How does a respondent decide whether to obey, resist, ignore, or counter a power message? What are the advantages and costs of using various sources of power? What are the most common modes of response to various sources of power? Are there particular combinations of resources that are more effective than other combinations?

9

Leadership Processes

Judging from the very large number of books and articles written about leadership, it is considered a very important topic in the study of organizational behavior. Living systems theory tells us why this is so. Leadership is the means of providing the top echelon of the decider subsystem for groups, organizations, societies, and supranational systems. Without leadership, human institutions are almost literally "headless."

Despite the great concern for leadership and the large volume of writings about it, there is relatively little agreement about what it is or how it functions. It has been written, not entirely in jest, that "there are almost as many different definitions of leadership as there are persons who have attempted to define the concept" (Bass 1981: 7). This chapter will add to that dismal record. None of the available definitions really fits living systems well, and most of them take too narrow a view of the concept. Fortunately, living systems theory provides a unique basis for a rigorous definition of leadership that reflects the common-sense notion of the term.

This chapter will first define leadership and then explore its properties and functions. Certain inherent problems will be identified. Links will be drawn to the topics of decision making, motivation, communication, power and influence.

DEFINITION OF LEADERSHIP

Miller (1978: 550) dismissed the concept of leadership in his presentation of living systems theory because he perceived a lack of clear definition or agreement on what leadership is. He suggested the use of his critical subsystem categories, instead. But leadership is a topic of interest to many people. It cannot be so easily dismissed or replaced.

Decider Processes

Despite the variety of definitions and uses of the term *leadership* and the multiplicity of functions ascribed to leaders, there is a core concept that is obviously related to the decider subsystems of groups, organizations, and societies. Under any definition, leadership involves making choices for a social system; it usually entails implementing them, as well. Where can this occur, other than in the decider?

As we noted in Chapter 6, the decider is defined as "the executive subsystem which receives information inputs from all other subsystems and transmits to them information outputs that control the entire system" (Miller 1978: 67). Some people would reject a definition of a leader as an "executive," but Miller includes much within that term. The decider processes include:

1. establishing purposes and goals for the system;
2. receiving and analyzing information from all subsystems and components (and thence from the environment);
3. synthesizing the data in order to narrow the range of alternatives to a choice of action; and
4. implementing the choice by transmitting commands or other forms of information that will cause other subsystems and components to carry out the chosen processes.

This description of decider processes, as it applies to groups and organizations, sounds very much like what we usually think of as leadership.

A problem with most definitions of leadership is that they proceed from an individual viewpoint. Their concern is with what the individual does to provide leadership for a group or organization. The approach taken in this chapter is to view leadership from the standpoint of higher level systems. What processes does the group or organization require of its decider subsystem, and how are those processes provided? It is in those processes that leadership is found.

The decider processes encompass virtually every aspect of leadership cited in other definitions. Some definitions may focus on the implementation stage and the role of the leader in inducing others to carry out the chosen action. Others emphasize the leader as generator of purposes and goals, for example, the "hero" as defined by Jennings (1960: 70–91). Many definitions treat leadership as the processing of information in order to make choices. Yet leaders, especially "great" leaders, are expected to do all of these things: establish values, set new goals, process information, choose a course of action, and mobilize followers to pursue that course.

There remains one other issue in establishing a living systems definition of leadership. Decider subsystems typically have several echelons. For instance, a government may have a president or prime minister, a congress or parliament, a bureaucracy, and a court system—all making decisions for the nation. Are they all part of the leadership of the nation? Such a view would not fit the common conception of leadership. To avoid such a diffuse concept of leadership, I will define it in terms of only the top echelon of the decider subsystem of a given system. As you will see, however, that may still allow multiple leaders and division of leadership responsibility.

Leadership may now be defined as purposeful assumption of some or all of the processes of the top echelon of the decider subsystem for a group, organization, society, or supranational system. All of the terms are as defined by Miller (1978).

Leadership usually is provided by individuals, or occasionally a group, although the definition does not rule out an organization or even a computer. Often a single leader cannot supply all of the necessary processes. Leadership may be shared by two or more component systems, which may be at the same or different levels. In the United States, for example, the structural relationship between the president and Congress allows each of them to assume some of the functions of leadership for the nation. The president serves primarily as the implementer and setter of goals, whereas Congress tends more to digest information and choose courses of action. The Supreme Court also performs processes of national leadership, but only with respect to a narrowly defined range of decisions. Within its defined sphere of responsibility each of these systems is supreme; each is in the top echelon of the nation's decider. Many other nations have a simpler, less-divided top echelon.

Levels of Leadership

The definition does not preclude the possibility of several levels of leadership within a large system such as a nation. By definition, each level of systems should have its own set of leaders. The board of directors of a company and/or its chief executive officer (CEO) may assume overall leadership of the firm, but each division, plant, department, and work group has its own top echelon. Lower level leaders are leaders of subsystems, being the top echelon of the deciders for those units. A leader of a work group, for instance, may receive orders from the head of the department, modify them to suit group goals, and then issue directions to individual group members.

Leadership is hierarchical. According to Simon (1962: 468), "in a hierarchical formal organization, each system consists of a 'boss' and a set of subordinate subsystems. Each of the subsystems has a boss, the immediate subordinate of the 'boss' in the system." These "bosses" generally fit the living systems definition of leadership.

Purpose

A key word in the definition of leadership is "purposeful." A person who randomly or playfully assumes some of the processes of the decider is not a leader. Likewise, a person who is thrust into the role against his or her will is not a leader, although he or she might become one. The U.S. Congress often fails to assert leadership for lack of any clear common purpose in its actions. A group or organization that is, itself, lacking in leadership cannot lead others. The definition asserts that the leader must have a purpose in assuming the reins.

Note that the definition says nothing about whether the purposes and goals of a leader's decisions are good or bad. Adolf Hitler was a leader, notwithstanding the poor quality of purposes and goals that he established for the Third Reich. A leader who formulates ineffective plans or fails to implement them properly may not retain leadership for long, but will remain the leader so long as no one else arises to assume the role. Neither Jimmy Carter nor Ronald Reagan may have been very effective as president of the United States, but no coup occurred to depose them. Each continued to perform many of the functions of national leadership until a new president was inaugurated. In other words, the quality of leadership may vary. We cannot limit the definition of leadership to good or effective decision making. Effectiveness is a matter of degree; we would not know where to put the cutting line.

What is required by the definition is that the leader must be trying to act in the interests of the system. A person who simply issues orders to others in pursuit of his or her own purposes and goals is not a leader. The leader has to be acting as part of the decider subsystem for the group or organization, not purely as his or her own decider. The ramifications of this point will now be explored.

Locus of Leadership

Much has been written about the problems caused by lack of leadership or weak leadership. Yet a key cause of weak leadership—sharing of the decider—remains almost unrecognized. Living systems theory makes it clear that every social system must share its decider with other systems, because its components are, themselves, living systems. This is true of all echelons of the decider but is especially critical at the top echelon. When a social system's leader is unavailable or is not acting on its behalf, the system is in jeopardy.

The cerebral cortex is the locus of the top echelon of a person's decider subsystem. A person may choose not to share that decider with any other system (although the brain may go astray by acting on its own desires rather than the good of the person as a whole). Furthermore, a person does not have to allow any other system to take over his or her decider processes.

In contrast, human social systems only borrow the components of their decider subsystems. Decider processes for an organization must be carried out by individuals or groups. Those individuals and groups have their own values, purposes, goals, and needs; yet they are expected to make decisions on the basis of the organization's values, purposes, goals, and needs. If any of the components of the organization's decider choose to act for their own benefit, to that degree the organization lacks a decider of its own and is less than a fully integrated living system. If *none* of the decider components act on behalf of the organization, the organization is dead.

The problem is especially critical with respect to the top echelon—namely, the leadership of the organization. The nature of leadership is such that all groups and organizations must from time to time be temporarily leaderless while their leaders sleep or attend to their own needs.

What are the effects of temporary loss of leadership? Miller (1978: 67) maintains that the decider is the one indispensable subsystem. Without a functioning decider of its own, a living system ceases to exist as an independent entity. Yet the decider seldom ceases to function entirely. When a person sleeps, lower echelons continue to monitor and control body processes. Likewise, many organizations have echelons that function around the clock, maintaining some minimal level of leadership.

Kerr and Jermier (1978) identified several "substitutes for leadership" that may serve to keep a leaderless organization functioning, at least in the short term. Pre-determined policies, procedures, rules, standards, and organizational structures serve as substitutes, so long as there are few exceptions and the environment remains stable. Tasks may be well-defined and routine, or they may be such that lower level members of the organization must make most of the choices anyway. Lower echelon deciders may be well-trained, committed to organizational goals, and capable of carrying on without a leader.

Multiple echelons also provide a group or organization with some continuity of decider processes when the top echelon chooses to act for itself or another system. For example, when the CEO of a firm acts solely in his or her own interests or those of the stockholders, ignoring the needs of the rest of the organization, lower level executives may fill the gap to some extent. But they must do so without the overall coordination that the top echelon is supposed to provide. The lower echelon executives are leaders of subsystems and are expected to make decisions on the basis of subsystem values. These decisions may be suboptimal for the system as a whole. The result for the organization may be a bit like the drunken person whose legs seem to have a mind of their own. Without top-level leadership a large organization or society soon dissolves into warring departments or tribes.

A group, organization, or society may not be able to recognize immediately whether its leaders are or are not acting in its interests. A Machiavellian leader is adept at disguising the fact that he or she is pursuing selfish interests. By playing off one group against another, a leader can often subvert any organized opposition and continue to rule for personal gain for many years.

Investment of authority in the leader's position increases the likelihood of blind acceptance of corrupt leadership. People tend to assume that anyone given the title of CEO or president will naturally try to act in the best interests of the firm or nation. It took more than two years of revelations and a final "smoking gun" to convince many Americans that President Nixon had anything to do with the Watergate incident.

The key question is: At any given moment, *where* is leadership located in the system and *for whose benefit* is it operating? I refer to this as the problem of the locus of leadership. The problem can be classified into five facets: shared leadership, conflict between leaders, divided loyalty, conflict of interest, and misperception of boundaries. Let us examine each facet separately.

Shared Leadership

Nothing in the definition of leadership requires that there be only one leader for a system. The processes of the top echelon of the decider can be shared by two or more people or groups. Indeed, leadership often is shared, but it is not an ideal arrangement. Studies of groups having two leaders have shown such groups to be less effective than similar groups with only one leader (Borg 1957; Osborn, Hunt, and Skaret 1977). In large, complex organizations, however, it may be difficult or impossible to avoid shared leadership. The decisions may be too numerous and too difficult for one person or group to handle, even with delegation of simpler decisions to the lower echelons.

Examples of shared leadership abound. In a business partnership, for example, two partners each typically assume some leadership duties. They are likely to divide responsibilities along functional lines, with one making financial decisions and the other making operational decisions. Certain types of decisions may require mutual agreement.

You could say that the partners form a group and it is the group that assumes leadership for the firm. Whether they actually form a group or not depends, however, on whether they are able to establish a decider subsystem for the two of them that is distinct from their own personal deciders and the firm's decider. In other words, do they develop a charter, values, purposes, and goals of the dyad that are separate from the charter, values, purposes, and goals of each individual or the business as a whole? In most cases that is unlikely. Leadership is simply divided between the partners, who act separately.

Leadership can be shared quite amicably and smoothly, provided that responsibility is clearly divided. Separate spheres of responsibility may be drawn and carefully adhered to, as in a family where one spouse makes the domestic decisions and the other deals with the family's "foreign relations." Or leadership may be divided temporally, as when day and night managers each make decisions for a store or restaurant.

A weakness of shared leadership is that decisions sometimes overlap or fall in the cracks. It is extremely difficult to define spheres of responsibility in such a way that everything is covered without overlap. When an event occurs that falls outside of the defined spheres, each leader may be reluctant to deal with it, perhaps for fear of stepping on another leader's toes. For example, when a night shift supervisor discovers a problem with the quality of parts produced on the day shift, it may simply be ignored as "not my problem." Yet it is a problem for the organization, of course. If the night supervisor does tackle it, he or she may be accused of meddling or exceeding authority.

Leadership Conflict

The opposite problem, leadership conflict, occurs when two or more leaders attempt to assume the same sphere of responsibility. When two partners issue conflicting orders about which job is to be completed first, that is leadership conflict. When President Reagan was wounded and Alexander Haig attempted to assume some of the duties of the presidency that had not been relinquished, that was leadership conflict.

Leadership conflict does not necessarily mean that conflicting orders have been issued. The leaders may happen to agree on some matters but still not be operating as a unit. If they both believe that they are providing leadership for the same activities, things will fall apart the moment they come to an area of disagreement. The conflict may also be over a less visible phase of leadership, such as establishing purposes and goals. Leadership conflict inheres in the fact that two or more systems are attempting to assume the same processes of the decider, not in the results of that fact.

Leadership conflict can be avoided or resolved in several ways. The conflicting parties can agree to elevate one of their number or an outside party to the top position. After a power struggle, ruling military juntas often resolve the problem in this manner. One of the junta members or an outsider may also oust the junta and take over. The conflicting parties may agree to form a unified group acting in concert, rather than acting as individuals. Finally, there can be a division of labor. One member of the junta may assume responsibility for foreign affairs, another for the military forces, a third for education, and so on. Another sort of division is to separate implementation from value setting, analysis, and synthesis. This sort of division will receive further discussion a bit later.

To the degree that leadership conflict exists in a living system, it is not a fully effective system. A living system must have clear, unitary direction from its decider subsystem. Resolving leadership conflict is a vital problem for any group, organization, or society.

Divided Loyalty

A key problem in leadership is the divided loyalty of the human components of a social system's decider. The problem is brought into sharp focus by living systems theory. Each living component must make decisions for itself as well as for the larger system of which it is a member. The question is this: At any given moment, for which system is the component working?

All leaders make decisions for themselves as well as for one or more other systems. A plant manager, in addition to being a company leader, may be a church deacon, head of the local Chamber of Commerce, and a family head. When the manager makes a decision about plant expansion, who is he or she representing? The company may or may not need a larger plant, but the community would benefit from new jobs and it may mean a promotion for the manager. How can the company be sure that the manager is acting in its best interests? In some cases even the manager may not know for sure.

It might seem that the problem would be resolved with an owner-manager. After all, the owner of a firm would be less likely to have divided loyalty between self and the firm. Yet such a division could still occur. Suppose that a physician tells the owner to cut back on hours spent at the office. Shall the owner protect the health of the body or the firm?

Even if we know in general where a leader's loyalties lie, the issue is not decided in any given instance. A leader ordinarily shifts focus many times every day. At breakfast the leader may make decisions for family and self. At the office the focus shifts to the company and self. At lunch or after work the leader may turn to working for one or more voluntary organizations (and self). At home again, the leader may engage in dyadic leadership with a son or daughter. The interests of these various systems are not necessarily opposed, but the chances are that there are some conflicts of interest. Self-interest is always present, but there may be several other conflicting loyalties in any given situation. Leaders, themselves, are often uncertain about whose interests they are serving.

It has been observed that situations seem to generate leaders. That is, a person of no great distinction suddenly arises to assume the role when leadership is needed. This observation can be explained from a living systems perspective. It is not that the situation suddenly causes leaders to "grow." The leadership ability may have been there all the time, but much of it was devoted to making decisions for self or for minor causes. What the situation does is to attract someone's commitment and focus their attention. Newly arisen leaders become loyal to a cause or a system that is bigger than themselves.

Winston Churchill hardly appeared to be a prime candidate for leadership before World War II. In his youth he seems to have had difficulty leading himself, let alone a nation. Yet the stress of war focused his talents and energies so that he emerged as a national leader. In other words, the emergence of leadership during times of stress can be understood as an effect of focusing the loyalty of the leader. In ordinary times a politician can play "politics as usual," figuring that the nation will muddle through somehow. In the face of a major threat to the nation, however, the politician may realize that the nation's fate is his or her own, and that the nation needs leadership more than the political party does.

Business firms are often able to survive a crisis, *if* the CEO is perceived as willing to make sacrifices for the firm. When other members see that the leader's loyalty is to the organization, they become more willing to commit their loyalty there also. Thus the situation can, for a while, solve the problem of divided loyalty. When the crisis is past, however, the problem tends to return.

Conflict of Interest

Conflict of interest is a legal concern. Laws are passed to prevent conflicts of interest among public officials between their governmental duties and their ties to business and other organizations. Similarly, some corporate mergers and interlocking directorates are forbidden in order to avoid conflicts of interest; but no amount of laws can eliminate such conflicts completely. A person cannot be divorced entirely from duties to self. The president of the United States may put stock holdings in a blind trust, but the president is still a family leader and a political party leader. If analysis shows that the nation needs a tax increase, but passing one would hurt the party's chances in the next election, whose interests will rule? Frequently the answer is that the leader tries to straddle the fence with a compromise decision that is not optimal for either system.

Social systems try various methods to assure that their leaders will act in the best interests of the system. Capitalist societies are based on the notion that leaders in a free-enterprise economy will naturally act in the best interests of society, because it is in their own best interest as well. With the same rationale, corporate boards of directors devise stock options for top company executives. Government employees are asked to sign loyalty oaths and no-strike pledges. Communist party leaders are pledged to party loyalty.

Your daily newspaper attests to the fact that these methods do not always work. The best interests of business leaders sometimes cause them to conspire to fix prices or to market goods that are known to be defective. Executive stock options often cause leaders to make decisions based on short-term profits or the price of the stock rather than the long-term viability of the company. Air traffic controllers violated their no-strike pledge when they believed their own interests were at stake. Communist party leaders have been accused of feathering their own nests with limousines and country estates.

Human institutions have no option but to accept the leadership of someone. The problem of loyalty will not go away; it cannot. Yet methods to assure loyalty of the leader do not always work. Sometimes more than one system is working simultaneously to assure the leader's loyalty to itself. A manager who feels pulled by company loyalty or public spirit to blow the whistle on the sale of defective goods may also be pressured by fellow managers to be loyal to the group and soft pedal the issue. When an executive is asked to relocate for the good of the firm, his or her family may counter with a plea for loyalty to them.

Sometimes the methods, themselves, are defective, as when stock options lead to short-term optimization, or reliance on free market forces is undercut by monopolies and oligopolies. But the answer does not lie in abandoning attempts to assure the loyalty of leaders. Probably the best answer is to devise institutions and choose leaders such that there is a natural congruence of interests between leader and institution. Short of that, one can only try to develop better reward systems that will motivate loyalty without distorting decision making. An executive compensation package that rewards both long- and short-term thinking, and concern for employees as well as stockholders, is better than one with a single focus.

Another common method of dealing with the problem of divided loyalty of the decider is to use a system of checks and balances. The assumption is that if several leaders approach a system decision with a mixture of system loyalty and hidden agendas, the hidden agendas will tend to cancel each other out. The division of powers in the United States between the president, Congress, and the Supreme Court is an example of this approach. Communist countries sometimes divide power between the premier and the head of the party, with military leaders as another force. Advocates of corporate takeovers say that the power of stockholders should be used as a check on the decisions of the board of directors (Pickens 1988). The board can in turn check the decisions of the CEO. Some decision makers appoint a devil's advocate to try to assure that they will not unknowingly fall into the trap of pursuing their own interests.

Again these methods are not perfect. The devil's advocate may have personal reasons for not raising certain issues. Stockholders and boards often lack the time, expertise, and cohesion to do an effective job of checking the CEO. The chairperson of the board may choke off debate from stockholders. The president, Congress, and Supreme Court may get into conflict about the limits of each other's powers. The military may stage a coup. However, checks and balances often do help to assure that leaders will act in the best interests of the system.

Misperception of Boundaries

One method mentioned earlier for reducing problems of divided loyalty and conflicts of interest is to gain congruence between the values of the social system and its leader. To the degree that the leader identifies with the organization, there can be no conflict or division. The ultimate example of this solution might be a hereditary ruler who is raised and educated to assume the role of leader for a nation. To a king, L'état c'est moi. The purposes and goals of the king are the purposes and goals of the nation. The problem with this solution is that it is very easy to slip from "I am the state" to "the state is mine." This is an example of misperception of the boundaries of the system. Instead of perceiving himself as the leader of a system that includes all citizens, the king may see himself as the system and the citizens as mere possessions or, in Miller's (1978: 33) term, *inclusions*.

A common example of this problem is the perception of a firm's CEO that he or she represents the owners or stockholders. If so, then the CEO acts as leader of the owners rather than the firm. The CEO acts to protect the capital investment of the firm, but neglects what Likert (1967) called the "human capital." It is certainly legitimate to perceive the owners and capital as *part* of the system to be led, but so are the employees. Who, then, is leader of the organization as a whole?

Perhaps a more frequent misperception is that the organization consists of stockholders and salaried employees, with hourly paid employees treated as inclusions. This misperception often leads employees to form a labor union, because they perceive that the firm's leadership is not acting on their behalf. The organization is thereby divided into two distinct parts, management and labor, with two sets of leaders attempting to direct the activities of the labor half.

In order to assume properly the leadership role in any social system, the would-be leader must correctly perceive the extent and boundaries of the system. Any part of the system that is excluded from consideration is likely to secede and seek its own leadership, as did the states of the Confederacy when they perceived that the U.S. federal government was not heeding their economic interests. On the other hand, it is possible for the leader to take too broad a view. Woodrow Wilson's leadership was rejected when he was perceived as pushing the objective of establishing the League of Nations ahead of U.S. national objectives. Nevertheless, probably the most common misperception by leaders is to equate the boundary of the system with their own boundary. Entrepreneurs who regard themselves as the firm are all too common. Perhaps the firm could not exist without them, just as a person could not exist without a head, but the system won't last long if the head or leader ignores its needs.

Misperception of the boundary, conflict of interest, divided loyalty, leadership conflict, and shared leadership are problems that cannot be solved totally, because more than one system is relying on the same decider for leadership. Nevertheless, these problems must be recognized and addressed in order to obtain effective leadership of any social system.

FOCI OF DECISION

Many studies and theories of leadership indicate that there are two distinct foci of leader decision making. One focus is on the environment and the goal-oriented tasks that must be carried out in order for the system to survive. The other focus is on relationships among the subsystems and components of the social system. In the long run both task accomplishment and internal cohesion and efficiency of the system are important for survival.

These two foci have manifested themselves empirically in many different ways. A series of studies at the University of Michigan found that supervisors of highly productive work groups were more likely to be employee-centered than production-centered (Katz, Maccoby, and Morse 1950; Katz et al. 1951). At Ohio State University factorial studies revealed two factors, labeled consideration and initiating structure, that accounted for most of the variance in descriptions of leader behavior (Stogdill and Coons 1957). Observing interactions in small groups, Bales and Slater (1955) found that leaders performed separate functions associated with productivity and with socioemotional support of group members. Based on their Least-Preferred Coworker (LPC) score, leaders were characterized by Fiedler (1967) as being task-oriented (low-LPC) or relations-oriented (high-LPC). Several popular leadership models and training tools are based on dimensions such as concern for production and concern for people (Blake and Mouton 1964; Hersey and Blanchard 1969; Reddin 1970). Despite criticism of some of the studies in which this dichotomy of leadership focus has been found, there seems little doubt that leader behavior can be divided into separate facets of external goal orientation and internal process orientation.

That these two foci of leadership are ubiquitous is not surprising. From a living systems viewpoint decisions must be made about internal purposes as well as external goals. Efficiency of internal processes and effectiveness in coping with the environment are both essential to success of the system. Leaders must be concerned about the subsystems and components (i.e., individuals, groups, and organizations) that carry out system processes as well as about the processes themselves and the goals they are intended to achieve.

Leaders must also be concerned about the three imperatives of living systems: maintenance of steady states, actualization of system potential, and propagation of the system and its products. With respect to members, therefore, leaders offer support to maintain existing relationships within the group or organization, strive to improve relationships and morale, and attempt to recruit and socialize new members. For task performance, leaders establish and maintain standards, push for improvement and innovation, and represent the system to potential customers and investors. Although some of these areas of decision making may be delegated to lower echelons, the leader must see that all are covered.

LEADERSHIP ROLES

The definition of leadership in terms of decider processes and the description of those processes suggest four basic roles for the leader: (1) value setter, (2) analyzer, (3) planner, and (4) implementer. Each of these roles has been the focus of research on leadership. They are also contained within the traditional list of primary functions of management: planning, organizing, controlling, and coordinating. Value setting is an intrinsic part of organizing, while controlling involves collection and analysis of data.

Studies of the behavior of business executives and military leaders have shown that they devote time to each of these roles, although in varying proportions. A study of navy officers found eight factors for use of time, including (1) high-level policy making, (2) administrative coordination, and (3) methods planning, which correspond to the value setter, implementer, and planner roles respectively (Stogdill, Wherry, and Jaynes 1953). In a longitudinal study of five chief executives Mintzberg (1973) identified ten roles, among which were an entrepreneurial (value setter) role, liaison and monitor (analyzer) roles, a resource allocator (planner) role, and a "leader" (implementer) role involving motivation of subordinates to achieve organizational goals.

A study of 348 business executives found that they spent 39 percent of their time in supervision, 18 percent in planning, 14 percent in generalist activities, 8 percent in investigation, 6 percent in coordination, 5 percent in negotiation, 4 percent in evaluation, and 7 percent in miscellaneous activities (Mahoney 1961). Since supervision, coordination, and negotiation would fall mostly within the implementer role, this role apparently consumed at least half their time. The planner role consumed more identifiable time than the analyzer role (i.e. investigation and evaluation). The time categories in this study did not identify a use corresponding to the value setter role.

Other roles identified in studies of executive behavior often focus on maintenance of interpersonal relationships, information flow, and power. Although not directly associated with the four decision-making roles that I have defined as leadership, these additional roles are necessary adjuncts of leadership. Good interpersonal relationships and information flow are important to the health of the system. They determine the readiness of the system to accomplish other tasks. The central decider for the system must monitor and maintain the system's health. Power must be maintained in order for the leader to carry out the implementer role effectively. Thus each of these additional roles supports the four decision-making roles of leadership. Let us now examine those four roles.

Value Setter

Social systems may have certain values built into their templates, but these values are subject to change and additional purposes and goals must be set as circumstances dictate. It is a primary role of leadership, first, to maintain the values of the system whenever possible and, second, to augment and adjust those values as the system grows or the environment changes. This role has been recognized by many writers. Barnard (1946) called it "determination of objectives"; Krech and Crutchfield (1948) referred to the policy-maker and ideologist roles; Selznick (1957), to definition of institutional mission and goals; Cattell (1957), to selecting and clarifying goals; Katz and Kahn (1978), to policy formation; and Hollander (1978), to goal setting and reality definition.

One of the benefits expected, if not demanded, of leadership is innovation. Leaders must, at times, act as change agents for the group or organization, evolving new purposes, setting new goals, and introducing new ideas. This role emphasizes the value setter phase of the decider processes, although effective innovation requires the other phases as well. Among those who have emphasized this aspect of leadership is Burns (1978), who stressed the importance of transformational, as opposed to transactional, leaders. In the political arena transformational leaders are the intellectual innovators, the reformers and revolutionaries.

Creativity is required as the first step toward innovation. Oddly, although trait theorists have found originality to be strongly correlated with leadership, the topic of creativity is rarely mentioned in the leadership literature (Bass 1981: 54). Yet the new ideas must spring from somewhere. Sometimes they may come full-blown to the mind of the innovator, through a process such as intuition. At other times creativity involves a logical process of gathering information and putting it together in novel ways. In other words, it makes use of the processes of analysis and synthesis.

Creativity may occur without any apparent stimulus, but more often it is a response to a perceived problem. Creativity involves finding new solutions to old problems. A leader who, consciously or intuitively, considers a broader range of data and analyzes more alternatives is likely to discover better solutions. Perhaps that is why trait researchers have generally found moderate positive correlations of leadership to knowledge, scholarship and intelligence (Bass 1981: 50–52).

A creative leader often sees problems that would otherwise be ignored, or defines problems differently from other members of the group. This may result from a more central viewpoint, a larger stock of information, or a different set of needs. The world perceived by the leader may be more complex than that perceived by others.

Groups and organizations are generally less effective than individuals in this phase of leadership. Although great strides have been made in developing methods such as brainstorming (Osborn 1957) and nominal group technique (Delbecq, Van de Ven, and Gustafson 1975) to tap the creativity of groups, they lack the data processing speed and integration of the individual mind. They do have the advantage of a greater store of information, however. Individual leaders may gain much of the value of that store of knowledge through participative leadership techniques. More will be said about that in the next chapter.

It should not be expected that leaders will always be creative or innovative. Often the situation does not call for innovation. When the environment is stable and the system is coping well, the best leader may be one who maintains current values and steers a steady course.

Analyzer

Analysis of data is the first step in directing events toward a chosen purpose or goal. It is also an essential step in the process of monitoring and controlling events once they are under way.

The analyzer role is the least recognized phase of leadership. Perhaps this is because it is the phase most likely to be delegated to lower echelons of the decider subsystem. Many managers and other leaders rely on their staff to gather and analyze data. The leader receives only filtered and predigested information, often in a form that severely limits the range of options. Wise leaders maintain secondary channels of information, so that they are not totally dependent on their staff for this critical step of the decision-making process.

Little research has been done on leaders as analyzers of information. Good analysis requires intelligence, a broad base of knowledge, and insight or good judgment in putting the pieces together. Most trait studies that have included such variables as intelligence, scholarship, knowledge, insight, and judgment have confirmed that these traits are moderately or strongly correlated with leadership (Bass 1981: 50–54). Yet the research that has been done on leadership of creative groups has focused on the role of the leader as process manager. Rather than contributing his or her own ideas, the leader is expected to monitor and direct group processes so as to optimize the inputs of other members. The information base required of such a leader is knowledge of group processes and methods of influence and control.

Because the leadership literature has paid so little attention to the process of data gathering and analysis, we must look to the research and writings on decision making. Here we find discussion of such topics as bounded rationality, cost of information, logical versus intuitive analysis, and biases in information processing. These topics were covered in Chapter 6 and will not be repeated here. Suffice it to say that, when we are talking about decision making for a social system, such topics speak to the question of quality of leadership.

Planner

The planner or synthesizer role is much better represented in writings about leadership. In the management literature, for instance, the CEO's role and performance in strategic planning for the firm receives a great deal of attention. How the planning role is carried out by the leader is also the focus of attention in research on participative management. Beginning with the pioneering work of Lewin and Lippitt (1938), researchers have thoroughly investigated the relative effects of leaders doing the planning themselves or involving other group members in the process (Bass 1981: 296–308). Overall, results appear to indicate that the effects of autocratic or democratic leadership on performance depend on the nature of the task and, perhaps, the followers. Democratic leadership, however, generally has the better effects on satisfaction and morale of the group.

Tannenbaum and Schmidt (1958) expanded the scope of research on sharing of the planning role by noting that there are several intermediate stages between fully autocratic and democratic leader behavior. Bass and Valenzi (1974) and Vroom and Yetton (1974) developed categories of leader behavior, depending on the extent to which leaders explain, consult, and share final decision-making power with the group. These categories of leader decision-making style, ranging from directive through consultative and participative to delegative, have been found to affect group acceptance of the decision, follower satisfaction, group commitment and loyalty, and task performance (Bass 1981: 319–330). The Vroom-Yetton model will be presented in more detail in Chapter 10.

As to *what* is planned by the leader or under the leader's direction, it should be remembered that action is necessary with respect to internal processes as well as external goals. Plans must be formulated to maintain morale, train members, obtain commitment to group or organizational goals, resolve conflicts, reorganize, and so forth. Plans are also needed to obtain resources, market products and services, recruit new members, acquire new customers, react to new competitive forces, enhance the reputation of the organization, and cope with decline. Note that the imperatives of maintenance, actualization, and propagation are reflected in these plans.

Implementer

The most visible role of leadership is implementation of plans. Many definitions of leadership focus solely on this role. Much research has been done on the leader's style of implementation, and there are several models purporting to link style to effectiveness.

It is possible, and often effective, to lead by example. Military leaders, at least at the lower echelons, may personally lead the charge. Team leaders are expected to display the skill and aggressiveness that they ask of other team members. Heads of states and corporations must display honesty and integrity if they expect it of their subordinates. Curiously, leadership by example has received almost no serious study in the United States.

Nevertheless, leaders usually implement plans by issuing orders or suggestions. It is in the implementer role that power and effective communication become especially important to the leader. Followers must have reason to follow, and that is supplied by the various forms of power. They must also know *how* to follow; goals and means must be communicated clearly and actions must be coordinated.

Leadership effectiveness has been linked with style of implementation by trait theories, the Ohio State leader behavior studies (Stogdill and Coons 1957) and their offshoots, Likert's (1967) four systems, Fiedler's (1967) contingency theory, and path-goal theory (Georgopoulos, Mahoney, and Jones 1957). Of these models, the one that relates best to living systems is path-goal theory. Models of effective leadership will be reviewed in the next chapter.

SUMMARY AND IMPLICATIONS

From a living systems viewpoint leadership may be defined as the purposeful assumption of some or all of the processes of the top echelon of a social system's decider subsystem. These processes are value setting, data analysis, synthesis and choice of action plans, and implementation. Among the implications of this definition are the facts that social systems must share their leaders with other living systems and that leadership may be divided among two or more entities. The sharing of leaders' attention creates problems of divided loyalty, conflict of interests, misperception of boundaries, and periodic loss of leadership. Division of leadership causes internal conflict as well as gaps and overlaps in decision making.

Social systems have evolved various methods to counter these problems, including systems of checks and balances, bureaucratic division of duties, loyalty oaths, and executive compensation systems. None of these methods is perfect, and there is a need for more creative thought about these problems.

Among the research questions raised by this chapter are the following: How often and to what degree do organizations lack leadership? That is, how often is the attention of the organization's leader(s) turned elsewhere, and what processes or functional areas are left uncovered? How do the four leadership processes tend to be dispersed within organizations, and how is this dispersion affected by the size and nature of the organization? To what extent can substitutes for leadership and aids such as decision support systems ameliorate the problems of lack of leadership? If, as I suspect, value setting is the phase of leadership that is most often lacking, how can organizations encourage more attention to this process? How is the organizational loyalty of a leader affected by external forces such as a family crisis or concurrent leadership of another social system? How can organizations obtain more loyalty from their leaders?

10

Models of Leader Effectiveness

Effectiveness, for a living system, means survival. Beyond that it means health; that is, the ability to fulfill the system's imperatives of maintenance, actualization, and propagation. An effective living system must be able to acquire and/or produce the resources it needs, cope with changes in its environment, and attain its purposes and goals.

Effective groups and organizations require effective leadership. A social system may remain healthy for short periods without leadership, simply by luck or by being in a benevolent environment. In the long run, however, critical choices must be made as the system and/or its environment change. Effective leadership means making and implementing choices for the system that permit it to prosper.

There are many models of leader effectiveness, and they measure effectiveness in a variety of ways. The simplest criterion of effectiveness is that the leader succeeds in inducing followers to do what he or she wants done. While that criterion might serve for the implementer role of leadership, it ignores the quality of the value setting, analysis, and synthesis that precede implementation. It also misses the basic purpose of leadership, which is to maintain the effectiveness of a social system. Given our inclusive definition of leadership, a true criterion of leader effectiveness must be some measure of the health of the system.

CRITERIA OF EFFECTIVENESS

How do we know when a living system is healthy? For an organism we might monitor certain steady states, such as temperature, blood pressure, heartbeat, and respiration. If these signs are within normal limits, the organism is presumed to be at least minimally healthy. But it might have a disease that can be detected only by a blood test or X ray, or by a psychiatric examination.

Obviously, determination of the health of an organism is not easy. To be reasonably certain, a large number of steady states must be measured. The same is true for groups, organizations, and societies. These are complex systems striving to maintain many different sorts of steady states. Most attempts to measure the health or effectiveness of organizations do not come close to a full examination of these states.

A group is generally regarded as healthy if it maintains morale, keeps internal conflict to a minimum, and fulfills certain needs of its members so that they maintain their membership. If the group has a specific task or goal, task performance or goal attainment would be added as a criterion. Models that have focused on group leadership, such as Fiedler's (1967) contingency model, have generally measured task performance or goal attainment as *the* indicator of effectiveness. Note that such a measurement ignores the second focus of leadership, internal process, that was discussed in Chapter 9. It also ignores growth and the ability of the group to propagate its values.

Measurement of organizational effectiveness is much more complex and sophisticated. A number of models of organizational effectiveness have been proposed and many varieties of techniques have been developed for measuring an organization's state of health. These models and techniques focus on both external goal attainment and internal processes, although not necessarily together. Certain elements of growth and dissemination may also be measured. Variables such as market share, customer loyalty, stock price, and credit rating serve as external indicators of the effectiveness of a business firm. The health of internal processes is measured by indexes such as return on equity or investment, value added, budget variance, cash flow, inventory of raw materials and finished products, accident rate, and grievance rate.

At this point I will define effectiveness and examine several models of organizational effectiveness. Then I will evaluate some of the many models of leader effectiveness that have been proposed. Finally, the implications for research and practice will be discussed.

ORGANIZATIONAL EFFECTIVENESS

Living systems are purposive, and their specific purposes are guided by the general imperatives of maintenance, actualization, and propagation. A healthy living system is one that is able to attain its purposes and goals. Equivalently, a healthy system is able to fulfill its needs and eliminate its excesses.

Defining Effectiveness

Organizational effectiveness has been defined as "the ability of the organization to achieve all of its purposes" (Hodge and Anthony 1979: 219) or "the degree to which an organization realizes its goals" (Daft 1986: 102). Goals, according to Daft, define and operationalize an organization's primary purpose. These definitions are roughly equivalent to the definition of health given earlier. They differ, however, as to whether effectiveness is an absolute (i.e., achieving all purposes) or a matter of degree. Must an organization fulfill *all* of its needs in order to be healthy?

From the previous discussion of needs we know that they are seldom, if ever, completely fulfilled. Need fulfillment is a dynamic, continuing process. As the system acts to fulfill one set of needs, others are being generated by consumption, loss, and extrusion. Indeed, as we noted in Chapter 5, a certain amount of strain is probably healthy, provided that the system is able to do something about it. It seems sensible, therefore, to treat effectiveness as a matter of degree. There may be a minimum level of effectiveness below which the system is in decline, but absolute effectiveness is an ideal never to be realized.

Organizational effectiveness may now be defined as the degree of attainment of an organization's avowed purposes and goals. Group effectiveness would be defined similarly. The term *avowed* means that the purposes and goals must be known and understood. An organization cannot be held accountable, except by death, for purposes of which it is not even aware, nor could we measure attainment of such purposes.

Measuring Effectiveness

Organizations have purposes with respect to survival, growth, development, dissemination, and (sometimes) replication. These purposes are expressed as preferred values for various internal and external states. Internal preferred values are needs; preferences for external states become goals. To measure organizational effectiveness directly, therefore, one must measure need fulfillment and goal attainment.

Some business organizations seem to focus primarily on goals such as high profit, increasing market share, or capital acquisition. Others are more concerned with purposes such as maintaining equilibrium or improving efficiency. These avowed purposes and goals indicate what the primary measures of organizational effectiveness should be.

Quinn and Rohrbaugh (1983) developed this notion into the competing values approach to measuring effectiveness. They defined four distinct value models, each leading to different criteria of effectiveness. The Open Systems and Rational Goal models both focus on external measures but the Open System model emphasizes flexibility (growth, resource acquisition), whereas the Rational Goal model emphasizes control (productivity, profit). The flexibility versus control dimension is also reflected in two models that focus on internal values, the Human Relations and Internal Process models. Criteria for these models, respectively, might be employee development and stability.

Various other approaches to measuring organizational effectiveness have been proposed and applied. One approach is to focus on internal processes as the best indicators of organizational health (Likert 1967; Beckhard 1969; Cunningham 1977). Other approaches concentrate on the organization's ability to acquire needed resources (Yuchtman and Seashore 1967; Cunningham 1978) or attain its output goals (Price 1972). A wide variety of measurements is employed, depending on the discipline of the researcher. For business firms these include measures of performance in business strategy (Venkatraman and Ramanujam 1986), finance (Myers 1984), and marketing (Walker and Ruekert 1987).

Any single focus—whether it be on internal processes, inputs or outputs, or on strategy, finances, or markets—presents a limited picture of organizational effectiveness. Even if an organization emphasizes a single goal, it must recognize other aspects of its relationship to the environment. One attempt to broaden the measurement of effectiveness is the multiple-constituency approach (Keely 1978; Connolly, Conlon, and Deutsch 1980). Some constituencies (e.g., owners and employees) are internal; others provide inputs to the organization (e.g., suppliers, labor unions, creditors, government) or receive outputs from it (e.g., customers and the community). Each constituency has its own criteria of effectiveness of the organization. A balanced assessment of organizational effectiveness may be obtained by sampling the evaluations of a variety of these constituencies.

The multiple constituency approach is consonant with the stakeholder concept. Mitroff (1983: 4) defines *stakeholders* as "all those parties who either affect or who are affected by a corporation's actions, behavior, and policies." Included among these parties would be suppliers and customers, as well as competitors and government regulatory bodies.

LEADER EFFECTIVENESS

Having defined organizational effectiveness and indicated how it may be measured in terms of attainment of purposes and goals, we may now consider the effectiveness of leaders in directing organizational effort toward those ends. Ultimately, the effectiveness of the leader is measured by the effectiveness of the group or organization. We should not overlook the fact, however, that leaders may avow purposes and goals that are different from those of the organization. It seems reasonable to reflect these personal ends in the criteria by which leader effectiveness is judged, although this is seldom done.

Most models of leader effectiveness focus on the implementation phase of leadership. They do not raise questions about the quality of a leader's values, goals, analysis, or plans, but are concerned with how well the leader is able to effectuate a plan through collective action. For a model of effective leadership in value setting we will look to the literature on corporate culture. Locke's (1968) goal-setting theory of motivation, which was reviewed in Chapter 7, will provide a model of effective goal setting. The Vroom-Yetton (1974) normative model of leadership will serve for effective analysis and synthesis of plans. Fiedler's (1967) contingency theory and path-goal theory provide models of effective implementation. Each of these models will now be reviewed.

Value Leadership

We know little about how leaders decide what values, purposes, and goals a social system should have. In many cases it appears that leaders begin by assimilating and representing the values of the majority of members. Hollander (1964) found that leaders must first conform and earn "idiosyncracy credits" before they can deviate from group norms or attempt to change them. Leaders tend to rank high in conformity to group norms, although this may be because they were influential in setting those norms (Jones, Gergen, and Jones 1963; Tannenbaum and Bachman 1966).

Group norms codify the shared values and beliefs of group members. At the organization level shared values and beliefs are termed *organizational culture* (Smircich 1983). Cultural values may have much to do with an organization's success. Peters and Waterman (1982: 285), studying 62 successful companies, found them to be guided by a few basic values implicit in the following dominant beliefs:

1. A belief in being the "best,"
2. A belief in the importance of the details of execution . . . ,
3. A belief in the importance of people as individuals,
4. A belief in superior quality and service,
5. A belief that most members of the organization should be innovators . . . ,
6. A belief in the importance of informality to enhance communication,
7. Explicit belief in . . . the importance of economic growth and profits.

Authors such as Ouchi (1981) and Pascale and Athos (1981) noted how the values of large Japanese firms differ in general from those of their U.S. counterparts. Many Japanese firms exhibit shared beliefs in collective responsibility for corporate action, consensus in decision making, and corporate responsibility for employee welfare, for instance. Ouchi advocated adaptation of some of these values into a new American organizational value system, which he called Theory Z.

Recognition of the importance of organizational values is a recent phenomenon. Thus lack of research on the value setting and value maintenance role of leadership is not surprising. So far, research has concentrated on the ways in which organizational values are communicated, emphasized, and reinforced.

Transmitting values. Leaders employ ceremonies, rites, myths, slogans and symbols to inculcate and reinforce organizational values (Deal and Kennedy 1982). These methods of communicating culture are used not only to indoctrinate new members but also to assure that every member perceives the organization's commitment to the values they represent. In order to be effective, culture must be pervasive and members must believe that the values are shared.

Ceremonies and rites are special, planned events that dramatically underline organizational values. Ceremonies may focus on members who particularly represent certain values or beliefs. Peters and Waterman (1982: 123–24) cited the example of the weekly Tupperware Rally and annual Jubilee in which employees receive public recognition for their sales volume. The value being emphasized is the importance of sales goals. An example from another sort of organization would be the school graduation ceremony, in which the values of scholarship are annually extolled and awards are presented.

Legends and myths are stories, based on real events or not, that illustrate the success of those who embody the "right" values, or perhaps the failure of those who do not. According to L. W. Lehr (1980), former CEO of Minnesota Mining and Manufacturing (3M), company executives liked to repeat stories about employees who defied top management and continued working on an idea, sometimes in secret, even after they were ordered not to, until they finally succeeded. Such stories emphasize the value of hard work and persistence, as well as the importance that 3M places on innovation.

Stories provide a less formal, and perhaps less obvious, means than ceremonies for communicating shared values. Stories can be told by anyone at any time; they don't require a special occasion. Of course, there is a danger that they may become distorted as they circulate. Consequently, leaders periodically need to retell the official version.

Symbols and slogans are used to emphasize specific, usually simple, values. Symbols vary widely in form. They may be pictorial, as in a company logo (e.g., Prudential Life's Rock of Gibraltar, a symbol of stability) or in advertising copy (e.g., Ford's shining light bulb symbolizing a "better idea"). They may be architectural, as exemplified by the White House, which symbolizes the constancy of the presidency even as individual presidents come and go. They may consist of a private code or vocabulary, such as football teams and the Central Intelligence Agency use to emphasize the importance of secrecy and to enhance the team concept.

Slogans are brief verbal messages, often aimed at customers or clients as well as organization members. The slogan "Quality is job 1" was used in advertising to sell automobiles, but it was also intended to sell the value of quality to those who build the product.

Symbols and slogans have the advantages that they are brief, simple, perhaps dramatic, and possibly omnipresent. Usually they cannot carry a complicated message but may be ideal for emphasizing a single primary value. Many large business firms devote huge sums of money and elaborate care to devising logos and slogans.

A leader who makes appropriate and consistent use of ceremonies, rites, myths, slogans, and symbols tends to be more effective than one who ignores these means of transmitting values. Peters and Waterman (1982) stress that lesson with multiple examples. Research linking value transmission to effectiveness is generally lacking, however.

Setting goals. Goal setting is another important area of leader effectiveness. Pascale and Athos (1981) enshrined the establishment of superordinate goals as the central element of their Seven S's—the others are strategy, structure, systems, staff, skills, and style—for successful corporate leadership. Superordinate goals unify and sustain the other elements. A full set of superordinate goals includes goals for the organization as an entity, its markets and internal operations, its employees, and its relationship to the society, state, and culture.

Research on the setting of effective organizational goals has been largely anecdotal. Based on a study of thirty-four firms in Japan and the United States, Pascale and Athos (1981: 289) concluded: "Effective superordinate goals should be (1) significant, (2) durable, and (3) achievable." They cited Matsushita Electric Company as an outstanding example of a firm guided by such goals even after the retirement of its founder, Konosuke Matsushita, who promulgated them. Although American cultural values make it more difficult for employees to accept the significance of corporate goals as a central part of their lives, companies like IBM, Procter & Gamble, Delta Airlines, and 3M appear to have succeeded in establishing effective superordinate goals.

At individual and group levels the focus of research has been on effectiveness of goals as motivators of performance, not on the quality of the goals themselves. Locke (1968) found in a series of studies that the key variables determining the effectiveness of goal setting were (1) difficulty, (2) specificity, and (3) acceptance of the goal. A leader, he noted, may influence individual or group performance most directly by issuing specific, challenging goal instructions (provided that they are accepted and are within the person's or group's capabilities) and setting time limits. Feedback of results and encouragement of competition may be used somewhat more indirectly to suggest goals.

Participation in the goal-setting process, as well as rewards such as money and praise, may be used to reinforce commitment to goals. People tend to become more committed to a goal when they have had a role in setting it. Management by objectives is based on that premise. But participation may also lead to the setting of a lower goal. Subsequent research has tended to confirm the primary roles of goal difficulty, specificity, and acceptance or commitment, but with mixed results as to such variables as participation, monetary reward, and task difficulty. These issues were discussed more fully in Chapter 7.

Decision Leadership

We know little about how leaders collect and analyze data or synthesize and choose action plans, other than what is known about the decision-making process in general. If leaders are better decision makers than the general population, it appears that their superiority stems from traits such as greater intelligence and knowledge, rather than from a different way of thinking. Perhaps leaders incorporate a broader range of data or a longer time frame in their processing of data, but there is no evidence that they are inherently more rational or logical. Thus the basic processes of decision making discussed in Chapter 6 serve for leaders as well as followers.

There is a distinct role for effective leadership, however, in the choice of *how* and *by whom* decisions are made for a social system. Should the decision be made by the leader alone or in consultation, by a subgroup of members, or by all members? If the members are involved, should the decision be by majority or consensus? Who should perform the initial collection and analysis of data? How can the expertise and problem-solving talents of the members best be utilized? These are questions that must often be answered by a leader.

Beginning in the early 1950s many researchers attempted to establish a relationship between group performance and the directive or participative decision-making style of the leader (Bass 1981: 319–24). Measures of effectiveness included group acceptance of decisions and commitment to them, follower satisfaction, task performance, and productivity. Regardless of the criterion, results were mixed.

Attention therefore shifted to characteristics of the situation that might moderate the relationship, such as information distribution, personality, and the nature of the task. Fairly consistent findings were that a directive style is more effective with passive or authoritarian followers and with structured tasks in a stable environment; whereas participative leadership is more effective with egalitarian subordinates and in situations involving complex, unstructured tasks or a turbulent environment (Bass 1981: 325–26).

There are many shades and mixtures of directiveness and participation. Tannenbaum and Schmidt (1958) developed a model depicting a continuum of seven decision-making styles varying by degree of participation. Vroom and Yetton (1974), in their normative model of leadership, offered logical advice about what styles should prove effective under various circumstances. The model assumes that a group leader chooses one of the following five ways to make a decision:

AI: Leader alone analyzes data and synthesizes plan.

AII: Subordinates provide information, leader synthesizes plan.

CI: Leader consults subordinates individually for information and synthesis, then makes own synthesis.

CII: Leader consults subordinates as a group for information and synthesis, then makes own synthesis.

GII: Leader and subordinates together analyze data and synthesize plan.

These five categories do not exhaust the possibilities. In style AII, for instance, subordinates might provide raw data or fully analyzed information; their degree of influence on the decision will vary accordingly. A leader might consult subordinates individually for information and as a group for synthesis, or vice versa. Going beyond GII, a leader might decide to delegate the decision to an individual or group of subordinates. Nevertheless, the five categories cover a useful range of possibilities.

The heart of the model is a set of seven situational characteristics that limit the number of feasible or effective ways of making a decision. These seven limiting characteristics are:

Table 10–1
Elimination Rules and Feasible Sets of Decision Methods

Elimination rule	Feasible set
If (1) solution quality is important and (2) leader lacks information, eliminate AI.	AII, CI, CII, GII
If (1) quality is important and (6) subordinates do not share organizational goals, eliminate GII.	AI, AII, CI, CII
If (1) quality is important, (2) leader lacks information, and (3) problem is unstructured, eliminate AI, AII and CI.	CII, GII
If (4) subordinate acceptance is important and (5) subordinates probably won't accept leader's unilateral decision, eliminate AI and AII.	CI, CII, GII
If (4) acceptance is important and (7) conflict over solution is likely, eliminate AI, AII, and CI.	CII, GII
If (4) acceptance is important but (1A) quality is not, eliminate AI, AII, CI and CII.	GII
If (4) acceptance is important and (6) subordinates don't share organizational goals, eliminate AI, AII, CI and CII.	GII

Source: Vroom (1964).

1. A high-quality plan is required.
2. The leader lacks sufficient information.
3. The problem is unstructured.
4. Acceptance of the plan by subordinates is important for effective implementation.
5. The plan would probably not be accepted and implemented properly if leader makes decision alone.
6. Subordinates do not share the organizational goals to be obtained by solving the problem.
7. Subordinates are likely to disagree about the preferred solution.

There are seven rules, based on logic and research results, for eliminating decision methods from the feasible set of decision methods, according to the situation. The rules and resulting feasible sets are shown in Table 10-1.

Elimination of decision methods is cumulative over the seven rules. When the situation matches the second and third rules, for instance, only CII remains feasible. The model is often displayed as a decision tree showing the remaining feasible set for each possible combination of rules.

Some combinations are regarded as impossible or irrelevant; for example, if solution quality is not important, it doesn't matter whether the problem is unstructured or the leader lacks information. Nevertheless, there are twelve possible combinations of rules, making the model cumbersome and difficult to use. In practice it may be easier and more sensible to apply the seven rules, which are relatively logical and straightforward. Field (1979) suggested that a much simpler model, involving only procedures CII and GII, would suffice since one of these two options is always in the feasible set.

Evidence relating the model to leader effectiveness is slim. A self-report study of 96 managers found that they were significantly more likely to have been effective in situations when their reported decision procedure fit the model than when it didn't (Vroom and Jago 1978). Jago and Vroom (1980) showed that two simpler models proposed by Field (1979) were less effective.

A weakness of the Vroom-Yetton model is that it assumes the seven limiting characteristics are static. If the leader lacks sufficient information or subordinates do not share organizational goals, for example, these are deficiencies that might be corrected, rather than designing the decision-making system around them. In the short run, however, the seven characteristics probably do limit leaders' options.

Implementation Leadership

As noted earlier, most models of leader effectiveness focus on the role of the leader as implementer. A leader is regarded as effective to the extent that he or she is able to get the group or organization to carry out a plan or task. This in turn depends on the willingness and ability of the followers or subordinates to accept and implement instructions.

Leader behavior and effectiveness. Early research focused on the autocratic-democratic dimension of leader behavior and its relationship to group performance. This dimension mixes style of implementation with decision-making style. As with research on the directive-participative dimension, results were mixed. When researchers at the University of Michigan (Katz et al. 1950, 1951) and Ohio State University (Stogdill and Coons 1957) divided leader behavior into two or more dimensions, however, some fairly consistent relationships of leadership style to effectiveness were found (Bass 1981: chs. 20, 21).

The two most prominent dimensions or factors of leader behavior were labeled production (or task) orientation and relations orientation by the Michigan researchers, and initiation of structure and consideration by the Ohio State group. These dimensions correspond respectively to the external and internal foci of leader decisions discussed in Chapter 9. That is, production orientation/initiation of structure focuses on the external goals of the group, whereas relations orientation/consideration is concerned with internal processes.

In most studies measuring production and relations orientation it was found that both variables related positively to subordinate satisfaction and performance.

There were many exceptions, however, and the relationships were found to be moderated by variables such as the ambiguity and difficulty of the task, and followers' need for achievement (Bass 1981: 335–41).

Studies measuring initiation of structure and consideration produced less consistent results. These studies were conducted in a wide variety of contexts, including industrial, military, educational, medical, and nonprofit organizations. They also employed four different instruments: the original Leader Behavior Description Questionnaire or LBDQ (Hemphill and Coons 1957; Halpin and Winer 1957); the Supervisory Behavior Description Questionnaire or SBDQ (Fleishman 1953); the Leadership Opinion Questionnaire (Fleishman 1957); and the revised and expanded Form XII of the LBDQ (Stogdill 1963). These instruments differ considerably in item content, factor structure, and reliability of the scales (Schriesheim and Stogdill 1975), probably thereby causing differences in research results.

The most consistent finding was that consideration is related to subordinate satisfaction. In many cases productivity or task performance was found to be related to a combination of consideration and initiation of structure. But the nature of the task, as well as characteristics of the organization and the followers, proved to be significant modifiers.

The validity of these results may be questioned on the grounds that consideration and initiation of structure are not "pure" factors of leader behavior, but also reflect loadings of evaluation and dynamism of the leader, respectively (Tracy 1987). Consequently, a strong relationship between the "leader behavior" dimensions and evaluative criteria such as satisfaction and performance ratings is built into the instruments themselves. The idea that leader behavior is divided into concern for tasks and concern for relationships fits well with living systems theory. Unfortunately, it is difficult to separate measurement of behavior from implicit criterion measurement in attempting to demonstrate relationships of leader behavior to system effectiveness.

Subordinate ability and maturity. In leadership research the ability of followers to accomplish the task is often assumed. It is up to the leader to select and train competent subordinates, or to choose plans that match their capacity. If their performance is inadequate, it is assumed that the leader has failed to motivate them properly. The focus of research is on the factors affecting the willingness of subordinates to follow orders.

One model that attempts to incorporate the factor of subordinate ability into determination of effective leader behavior is the Life Cycle theory of Hersey and Blanchard (1969). The model recommends that leaders vary their emphasis on task and relationships according to the willingness and ability of their subordinates. Unfortunately, the theory suffers from inadequate conceptualization and lack of validation (Graeff 1983). It also contradicts logic and experience in at least one respect. Hersey and Blanchard argued that immature workers (i.e., those who lack both willingness and ability) require high task-low relationships supervisory behavior. But the literature on supervision of workers recruited from the ranks of the hard-core unemployed, who initially lack both willingness and ability to perform well, indicates that they need high relationships (considerate) leadership even more than most workers (Friedlander and Greenberg 1971). They require training and lots of structure but, if it is given without flexibility and consideration, they quickly quit and drop back into unemployment.

A more logical theory of effective leader behavior might relate the amount of task-oriented behavior to subordinate ability and the amount of relations-oriented behavior to willingness to work. The assumption underlying the latter relationship is that, if subordinates are not intrinsically motivated toward the task, consideration may generate motivation through greater identification with the group and its goals. With respect to ability, the more able subordinates become, the less direction they require, and the more it becomes annoying if given in excess by the leader.

Leader's style and contingency theory. Fiedler (1967) proposed and tested a theory of contingent relationships between situational variables and two styles of leadership. The two styles were supposedly personality-based and were measured by instruments called the Assumed Similarity of opposites (ASo) and Least-Preferred Coworker scales. The situational variables were, in supposedly descending order of importance, the quality of leader-follower relationships, degree of task structure, and leader's position power. These elements were combined into a complex model showing that leaders with high LPC (or ASo) scores tend to be more effective in situations of moderate difficulty, whereas low-LPC leaders are more effective in easy or very difficult situations.

The exact nature of the two styles supposedly indicated by high and low LPC scores is unclear. High scores have often been equated with consideration and concern for relationships, and low scores with initiation of structure and task orientation, but the scores have been subjected to a wide and changing variety of interpretations. Fiedler (1978) concluded that the leader's style interacts with the situation, and that LPC scores reflect different patterns of interaction.

The model was originally constructed with data from studies of a wide variety of task groups, including basketball teams, military task groups, industrial work groups, consumer sales cooperatives, and ad hoc study groups. It then received further testing with groups in military and industrial settings. Leadership effectiveness was measured in term of the task performance of the group. Task performance was measured either by objective criteria or by multiple expert ratings. Internal process criteria were generally ignored.

Although a great many studies have tested the theory, results were equivocal. Even though the preponderance of correlations reported by Fiedler (1967) between ASo or LPC scores and group performance were in the predicted direction, there were many exceptions and *none* of the correlations was statistically significant (Lee 1980: 224–25). Situational variables were measured, and situations classified, in a variety of ways (Graen et al. 1970). The ASo and LPC scales likewise were not standardized. LPC scores were usually trichotomized, but no standard cutoff points were established for classification of a leader as high or low. Although the LPC scale was presumed to measure a relatively stable response pattern of the leader, LPC scores exhibited low test-retest reliability over a period of a few weeks, as well as differences in the way people responded to the instrument (Stinson and Tracy 1974). A review of evidence for the theory led Schriesheim and Kerr (1977) to conclude that it has little empirical support.

Path-goal theory. The path-goal theory of leadership (Georgopoulos, Mahoney, and Jones 1957; Evans 1970; House 1971) views leader effectiveness as a function of the leader's behavior in clarifying subordinates' goals and smoothing the paths to goal attainment. The theory indicates that a leader motivates subordinates by influencing their perceptions of work goals and the means of attaining them. Path-goal theory is closely related to the dynamic model of motivation presented in Chapter 7.

According to House and Mitchell (1974: 84), a leader may affect the subordinate's choice of behavior in several ways:

1. recognizing and/or arousing the subordinate's needs for outcomes over which the leader has some control;
2. increasing the personal payoffs to subordinates for work-goal attainment;
3. making the path to those payoffs easier to travel through coaching and direction;
4. helping subordinates to clarify expectancies;
5. reducing frustrating barriers; and
6. increasing the opportunities for personal satisfaction contingent on effective performance.

It is obvious from this list that path-goal theory forms an intimate link between leader behavior and subordinate needs. The leader recognizes or arouses these needs (item 1), applies need-fulfilling rewards (item 2), and helps subordinates in various ways to perceive and attain rewarding outcomes (items 3-6). Note that items 3 and 5 involve reducing the costs to the subordinate, items 2 and 6 increase the subordinate's payoffs, and items 1 and 4 increase awareness of the expected link between performance and need fulfillment.

The effectiveness of all these forms of leader behavior would be predicted by expectancy theory. The dynamic model of motivation, as well as Porter and Lawler's (1968) theoretical model, would suggest the addition of feedback concerning outcomes and their link to performance.

House and others tested path-goal propositions relating subordinate attitudes and performance to leadership style (House and Dessler 1974; House and Mitchell 1974; Szilagyi and Sims 1974; Stinson and Johnson 1975; Downey, Sheridan, and Slocum 1975). In particular, the predicted effects of initiation of structure and consideration under various contingencies of subordinate characteristics and work environment were investigated. As with the earlier studies of leader behavior, results were often mixed, and for much the same reasons (Mitchell 1979). The concepts of initiation of structure and consideration were too broad and the instruments for measuring them were too contaminated with other factors such as coercion (Schriesheim and Von Glinow 1977). Thus, the measured leadership styles did not relate closely enough to the leader behaviors specified by path-goal theory. A better strategy for testing the theory might be to relate effectiveness to specific leader behavior that clarifies the goal or smooths the path, rather than trying to relate it to a "style."

SUMMARY AND IMPLICATIONS

Effective leadership means making and implementing decisions for a social system that permit it to prosper. The effectiveness of a group or organization in attaining its purposes and goals is, in part, a measure of the effectiveness of its leader. But leader effectiveness may also involve attainment of the leader's own purposes and goals, and group or organizational effectiveness depends partly on the ability and maturity of subordinates.

Group effectiveness is often measured in terms of task performance or goal attainment. Other indicators such as morale, consensus, and growth are typically ignored. Measurement of organizational effectiveness tends to be broader and more sophisticated. For a business firm external indicators such as market share, customer loyalty, stock price and credit rating might be used. The health of internal processes might be measured by indexes such as return on equity or investment, value added, budget variance, cash flow, inventory of raw materials and finished products, accident rate, and grievance rate. Some indexes such as the price/earnings ratio may combine external and internal measures.

Effective leadership requires setting and inculcating appropriate purposes and goals for the system, making good decisions aimed at those purposes and goals, and seeing that the decisions are implemented. No single model encompasses all of these aspects of effective leadership, but models dealing with each phase were reviewed.

One conclusion that may be drawn from this review is that measurement problems pervade our attempts to assess leader effectiveness and test theories about it. Not only are the criteria of effectiveness typically too narrow, but even those simple criteria are often measured through instruments that lack validation, are unstandardized from study to study, and are biased or contaminated with other variables. We theorize much about what makes leaders effective, but we have proven virtually nothing about it.

If leader effectiveness is ever to be studied in a thorough, systematic manner, the first step would be agreement on a definition of leadership. By the very nature of the phenomenon I would argue that the definition must be broad and based on systems theory. Without purposeful social systems, leadership has no meaning.

Second, the study of leader effectiveness must recognize that overall success of a leader depends on performance or direction of several different phases of decision making for the system. These phases include the setting and transmission of values, purposes, and goals; analysis of data; synthesis and choice of plans for coping with or initiating change; and implementation and monitoring of the chosen plans. Effectiveness depends on proper performance of *all* of these phases. Not only the methods used, but also the quality of choices affect the health of the system. To date, very little attention has been paid to academic research on the quality of leaders' choices.

Third, we must do a much more careful job of developing instruments for measurement of leader behavior and outcomes. Currently available instruments suffer from serious problems of subjectivity, bias, contamination of variables, lack of standardization, uncertainty as to meaning, poor reliability, and lack of validation. Furthermore, many studies using these instruments have employed samples of convenience, often lacking a full range on the relevant variables.

From a practical standpoint the most basic implication of this chapter is that effectiveness should be measured over a broad set of criteria. Both external and internal indicators should be employed. Reliance on a single criterion of effectiveness (e.g., the "bottom line") risks missing important indicators of illness in the system. A lack of profits may indicate problems in the firm, but a healthy surplus does not mean that all is well. Morale may be deteriorating, the research that leads to future growth may be suffocating, or creative tension may be dissipating in favor of groupthink. On the other hand a firm with high morale and good internal communications may decline because it fails to keep in touch with the needs of its customers. Only through a broad assessment of internal and external indicators—a thorough physical and fiscal examination, so to speak—can the effectiveness of the system or its leadership be measured.

11

Exchange and Conflict between Systems

At several points in this book we have dealt with exchange between systems, depicted by the systems dyad. All living systems above the cellular level rely upon constant exchange between living components. Motivation, communication, roles, influence, and leadership all involve exchange of matter-energy and/or information between systems.

We have also frequently encountered the concept of conflict. Conflict is found both within and between living systems. Within a living system there are many conflicting values that must be arranged in a hierarchy in order to sort them out. Purposes and goals derived from one imperative often conflict with those required for another. Multiple needs compete for attention. Messages compete for channels to carry them. Conflicting action plans vie for implementation. Groups and organizations suffer from divided loyalties and conflict over whose purposes their leaders are serving.

Between systems there are even greater sources of conflict. Each system seeks to propagate its values to other systems. Fulfillment of needs involves living systems in competition for resources. One system chooses an action plan that involves others, who have plans of their own. Conflicting role demands are sent to a group member. Two systems each try to exert power to influence the other. Two or more people or groups vie for leadership of the same system.

Like many English words, conflict has multiple meanings. Conflict may refer to (1) opposition (of values, goals, power), (2) overt action (war, interference, dominance), or (3) a feeling of emotional disturbance caused by opposition. The last meaning will not concern us here, because it does not apply generally to living systems. Conflict within and between living systems will be defined both as a condition of opposition and as behavior caused by opposition.

A condition of opposition may or may not result in overt conflict behavior. Relationships with other systems or the energy required for an overt clash may tip the balance in favor of doing nothing. Another alternative is simply to withdraw from the relationship and seek cooperative interaction with another system.

Despite the prevalence of conflict, the essence of living systems is cooperation. A large accumulation of cells must work together in order to form a living organ. Many organs must cooperate to keep an organism going. Groups and organizations require the cooperation of members in order to function. Individual members must cooperate not only with the suprasystem but also with each other. The subsystems and components of any living system must accept the coordination provided by the decider, or else the system ceases to exist.

Cooperation is defined as behavior that results in a sharing of benefits. Cooperation results from a condition in which two or more systems can help each other to achieve their purposes and goals. In biology this condition is called symbiosis.

Cooperation is based upon the need for exchange between systems. Exchange is a vital part of the input and output processes of living systems. If inputs obtainable from the nonliving environment were sufficient for all purposes, there would be no reason to cooperate with other living systems. But life forms long ago found many advantages in intersystem exchange. Often the continuing nature of these advantages caused systems to form higher level systems capable of maintaining and coordinating the exchange relationship.

Are there specific characteristics of an exchange relationship that induce conflict or cooperation? Is conflict a tear in the fabric of the system, or does it have positive value? How do living systems attempt to manage conflict? How can systems promote increased cooperation? These are some of the questions that this chapter will seek to answer.

EXCHANGE

Exchange between systems takes many forms. First, there is the question of what is exchanged. It may be matter, energy, information, or any combination of these. The exchange does not have to be symmetrical. Matter may be exchanged for information, as when goods are purchased with money. Or information may be traded for energy, as in a group member's energetic response to a suggestion from the leader.

Second, the resources that one system offers to another may be of positive or negative worth, both to self and other. The most stable, cooperative exchange relationships stem from a situation in which each system is able to trade its excesses (i.e., resources of negative worth to itself) to a system that places a positive value on them. When a system must offer resources of positive worth to itself, cooperation is still possible provided that it receives resources of greater worth in exchange. But cooperation requires that the long-term net value of the exchange be perceived as positive for both systems.

A condition of conflict exists when the net worth of the exchange is negative for one or both systems. If the resources available for exchange are negatively valued by the holder, it costs nothing to inflict punishment on the other system, although retaliation can be expected. Conflict can be quite stable, so long as each system gets rid of more negative worth than it absorbs from its opponent. When a system must use resources of positive worth to itself in order to oppose another system, the net worth of conflict and the likelihood of conflict behavior are reduced. Yet conflict may be profitable because it enables a system to obtain resources from the environment or a favorable exchange with a third system.

Some exchanges become positive in value only when additional systems are involved. An exchange involving money or credit, for instance, would not be worthwhile to the recipient of the money if there were not another system willing to accept cash or credit in exchange for goods and services. In periods of very rapid inflation, in fact, this becomes a problem for exchange relationships based on money. "Full faith and credit" of the government are needed to make the monetary exchange system work.

Conflict behavior, in particular, is likely to assume positive net worth only when other relationships are taken into account. Two nations may find it useful to engage in armed conflict, even though each suffers damage at the hands of the other, because it solidifies their bonds with other nations and with their own citizens. Another example of positive net worth from conflict when other systems are considered is the benefit that an organization derives from competition between work groups, who may gain also through earning bonuses.

When one system stands to gain while the other loses, domination and exploitation are likely to occur. This exchange relationship is inherently unstable, however, because the losing system will seek to escape from it. Living systems must actively seek positive exchange, or else face extinction because of inability to replace consumed resources.

Bonding

Very long-lasting relationships may be built upon mutually net positive exchanges between systems. If the exchanges meet constantly recurring needs, a permanent bond may be formed. The strongest bonds are found between components and subsystems of higher level systems. The bonds between organs of an organism, members of a family, employer and employee, citizen and nation are based upon mutually beneficial exchange. Over time a template develops that codifies the terms of the exchange and enables the bond to replicate itself.

Other, less permanent relationships, such as between buyer and seller or audience and performer, are also built on mutually beneficial exchange. The relationship may lack permanency because the needs that are met are evanescent or because there are many other systems offering similarly beneficial exchanges. The degree of interdependency, as discussed in Chapter 8, is an important factor in establishment of a bond. The greater the interdependency, the stronger the bond.

Some bonds appear to be "odd couples" from the point of view of an observer. Although the mutual benefits of marriage as an institution are recognizable, it is often difficult to understand what two particular people see in each other. Indeed, they may come to the same conclusion after having a go at marriage for a while. Perception is an important factor in social bonds. The exchange creates a bond so long as both parties *perceive* it to be mutually beneficial. But bonding may occur without perception, so long as it is mutually fulfilling, and may persist without perceived benefit if the partners see no better options.

Theories of Exchange

There have been attempts to develop theories of exchange in such fields as physiology, sociology, economics, and ecology. Exchange between human individuals as the basis for formation of groups was modeled by Homans (1958) and Thibaut and Kelley (1959). According to Homans the likelihood of bonding into a group increases as the amount of shared sentiments, activities, and interactions increases. Thibaut and Kelley proposed that affiliation with a group is based on a positive level (i.e., rewards greater than costs) of outcomes from the interaction. This is similar to the positive net-worth-of-exchange criterion discussed earlier.

Adams' (1965) equity theory, as noted in Chapter 7, posits that an individual's motivation to work is based upon the perceived ratio of exchange between the person and the employer, as compared with the perceived ratio for other employees. In other words, it is not simply a question of whether organizational rewards exceed personal costs. That may only determine willingness to associate with the organization (i.e., take the job). How hard the employee is willing to work depends on how well his or her personal ratio of exchange compares with that of other employees. To put the idea more broadly, conflict between components develops if the system does not distribute rewards equitably, or at least in a manner that is perceived to be equitable.

Sources of power are based upon the anticipated worth of various sorts of exchange. Reward power stems from being able to offer resources that are worth more than the cost of compliance. Coercive power is based on the recipient's perception that compliance offers a better exchange (even if negatively valued) than does risking punishment through noncompliance. Authority is accepted only when subordinates believe they are receiving a reasonable exchange for their obedience.

Hollander and Julian (1969) based their theory of leadership on social exchange theory. In their view followers accord status, esteem, and influence to the leader in exchange for the leader's aid in achieving group goals and fulfilling expectations of rewarding outcomes. Influence between leaders and followers is a two-way process.

Thus we see exchange theory employed to model a variety of interpersonal and intersystem processes. It may not be going too far to assert that positive exchange is the basis of *all* linkages between living systems. Because living systems seek to fulfill needs and to maintain a positive balance of inputs over outputs, it follows that they will be attracted to any relationship with another system that offers a favorable exchange, and opposed to any relationship offering a negative balance. This principle serves to explain bonding between living systems just as positive and negative charges explain chemical bonding between elements and compounds.

CONFLICT AND COOPERATION

Opposition involves values. Conflict occurs when two systems set the same value on a resource that is insufficient to satisfy both of them. The systems oppose each other over possession of the resource. Conflict also occurs when different sets of values (ideologies) attempt to propagate themselves among the same carriers.

Difference in values sets up an opportunity for cooperation. When systems value resources differently, a mutually satisfactory exchange is possible. For example, a person can exchange excess time, energy, and skills for an organization's excess money or goods. Each system's excess resources have low or negative worth to itself, but high worth to another system. Similarly, two people may help each other to cut down some trees because one wants the timber and the other wants to farm the land. Each acquires something different from the interaction that is worth more than he or she put into it. Cooperation and exchange between systems is based on such differences in values.

As noted, values themselves may be a source of conflict. When one system decides to propagate its values to another system, the other system will oppose the exchange unless its own value system sets a positive worth on accepting the new values. The positive worth may come from the new values themselves or from some other aspect of the exchange, such as a bribe or the charisma of the value giver.

Conflict between Systems

Conflict may or may not be inherent in the relationship between two systems. If the systems occupy the same niche, need the same resources, and available resources are insufficient to fulfill both sets of needs, then the two systems are inherently in opposition. In such a situation conflict behavior is probable because it is the only way, other than finding a new niche, that either system can fulfill its needs.

Such a condition of absolute opposition is unlikely. Typically, there is inherent conflict over some resources and a potential for sharing or exchanging others. It then becomes a matter of the perceptions of both systems as to whether the potential for cooperation or withdrawal outweighs the advantages of conflict. Since a system never fulfills all of its needs, it may choose to act on those that can be fulfilled cooperatively. When alternative sources or substitutes are available, it may also choose to withdraw from the relationship and seek fulfillment elsewhere.

A situation in which both systems may benefit from interaction does not guarantee cooperation. For cooperation to occur, the systems must perceive the opportunity and must agree on terms of the interaction, or else must fall into a mutually beneficial exchange through a process of trial and error. Agreement is commonly achieved through a process of negotiation or mutual decision making. Part of the process may involve making each other aware of the potential benefits of cooperation.

Conflict within a System

The foregoing discussion of conflict *between* systems does not seem to account for conflict *within* a system. Yet a shift in the frame of reference allows us to see internal conflict as a special case of intersystem conflict. Internal conflict occurs between subsystems or components. The conflict stems from the values of these units, rather than (or in opposition to) the values of the system itself.

When the desires of the head oppose those of the heart, or the needs of management conflict with those of labor, the conflict is between systems that are components of a larger system. In such cases the benefits of cooperation are already known, as they are the basis for the suprasystem, but there is a downward shift in the level of decision making. Instead of acting as part of the decider for the suprasystem, each component is making decisions for itself.

Internal value conflict may also be interpreted as intersystem conflict. There is conflict between innate values and those learned from other systems, for instance. But what about the innately conflicting values of maintenance, actualization, and propagation? Are there any specific subsystems or components associated with these values? I would argue that there are.

A certain degree of maintenance is required by all critical subsystems, but the boundary, distributor, supporter, channel and net, decoder, and internal transducer subsystems seem to be most concerned with maintenance of steady states. The basic function of the boundary is to maintain the integrity of the system and protect it from the environment. The supporter maintains the physical relationship of the components. The internal transducer provides feedback for control of system processes. The roles of the distributor, decoder, and channel and net are more passive, but involve maintaining stable conditions for the flow of matter-energy and information.

The functions of other subsystems can be seen to contribute more directly to growth and elaboration of the system. The ingestor and input transducer subsystems act in opposition to the boundary in order to bring in new resources that may help to actualize the system. The matter-energy storage and memory subsystems contribute to the growth of the system by storing resources. The converter and associator combine resources into new and more elaborate forms.

The motor subsystem opposes the supporter to enable the system to act upon its environment. Each of these subsystems also contributes to maintenance, of course, but there is a subtle shift of emphasis toward growth and elaboration.

Propagation involves output of some or all aspects of the system. The reproducer subsystem is obviously devoted to propagation, but the producer, extruder, encoder, and output transducer subsystems also enable dissemination of aspects of the system. The producer generates artifacts bearing the stamp of the system (e.g., products carrying the designs and brand name of the company). The extruder opposes the boundary in order to remove these products from the system and disseminate them to other systems. The encoder and output transducer propagate information, some of it proprietary, in a form designed to influence and educate other systems. Some output is necessary simply to maintain the system, but these subsystems are enablers of propagation.

The decider subsystem serves all three imperatives, balancing the needs of each. The decider controls system processes in order to meet established purposes and goals, but it also generates many of those purposes and goals, synthesizes new action plans, and disseminates the orders to implement them. To sort out the conflicting demands of the subsystems for maintenance, actualization, and propagation, the decider employs the system's hierarchy of values.

This picture implies that conflict among subsystems is inherent in the template of the system. The three imperatives inevitably pull the system and its critical subsystems in different directions. All living systems above the cell level contain components that are themselves living systems with their own values, purposes, and goals. The critical subsystems lack deciders of their own, but their varying interests are known to the system's decider, which must balance them. Fortunately, the template also carries the seed of a mechanism to resolve these innate conflicts, namely the hierarchy of values.

FORMS OF CONFLICT AND THEIR MANAGEMENT

There are three distinct types of conflict behavior. Type 1 consists of pursuit of the same goal (or resource) as another system; type 2 involves interference with another system's pursuit of that goal; and type 3 is direct attack on another system. Type 1 behavior is commonly called competition, and is characteristic of sports such as track and golf. Ideally, it is also characteristic of business behavior in a free-market economy. Interference with another system's pursuit of the goal (type 2) is found in many sports, such as football and basketball. It is also found in business in such forms as industrial espionage, deceptive advertising, and erection of trade barriers. Type 3, direct attack on another system, is characteristic of war. It may also be found in sports such as boxing, and in business in the form of corporate raids and hiring executives away from a competitor.

In type 1 behavior the exchange between the systems may be valued positively or neutrally. The chief source of negative value is loss of some or all of a desired resource to the other system. Behavior of types 2 and 3, on the other hand, involves direct exchanges of negative value. Consequently, the behavior is less likely to result in net benefit to either system. Systems would not choose to engage in conflict behavior if they expected a net loss in the long run or there appeared to be a better alternative, but they may misjudge the strength or tenacity of the other system. There are also intrinsic rewards from conflict, such as the joy of winning and the thrill of competition.

Type 1 conflict is managed by means of rules. These rules may be agreed upon by the parties or imposed by a suprasystem. Although both systems may try to abide by the rules, there is often disagreement about interpretation, or motivation to cheat. The employment of a third party as referee to interpret and enforce the rules is a typical solution.

Conflict of type 2 is sometimes managed by rules and referees, but more often through negotiation and compromise. The best interests of the opposing systems usually lie in minimizing the costs of interference with each other and dividing available resources equitably. Third-party mediation or arbitration may aid them in seeing the wisdom of managing their conflict in this manner.

Systems engaged in type 3 conflict are unlikely to be able to manage their conflict on their own. Rules, if any exist, are often thrown out the window in such conflict, although the systems may be able to abide by some minimal conventions (e.g., conventional weapons but no chemical or biological warfare). Type 3 conflict is often resolved by surrender of one of the combatants. A strong suprasystem or coalition of peer systems may be able to impose peace or act as a mediator to bring the opposing systems to the bargaining table.

Conflict may also be categorized by the forms of behavior in which it occurs. In our traversal of OB topics we have seen many different kinds of conflict. Chapter 2 mentioned role conflict and the opposition of differentiation and integration in organizational structure. Both internal and external conflicts of values, purposes, and goals were discussed in Chapter 3. Competition among needs and desires for attention and fulfillment was noted in Chapters 5 and 7. In Chapter 6 we found competition among messages for attention, and conflict in the rejection of messages. Chapter 8 discussed competition for sources of power, and conflict in the use of power. Conflicting loyalties and conflicts of interest were discussed in Chapter 9. Let us reexamine a few of these forms of conflict.

Role Conflict

A person's role in a group or organization consists of the set of system processes to which the person is assigned. Role performance represents an exchange of specified behavior for organizational rewards. Conflict may occur because there are inconsistencies within the role definition or because it clashes with the role holder's values.

The concept of role conflict could be put on a firmer basis by recognizing its sources in the values of interacting systems. The primary source of role conflict lies in the different purposes and goals of a social system and its individual members. Secondarily, there is conflict engendered by differences between individuals. Disagreement between superior and subordinate about the role of the subordinate is likely to stem from both sources, as the superior's decider subsystem represents both the organization and the self.

A subordinate's discomfort with the sent role may also come from both individual and organizational values. For instance, a subordinate may believe that certain role demands are not only unethical but also harmful to the company. Management of the conflict must recognize the integrity of the values of both systems.

In managing role conflict, it should be kept in mind that a role would not be given or accepted if the parties did not see some mutual advantage in the exchange. There is usually a vested interest for both systems in maintaining the long-term viability of the relationship, which often translates into loyalty toward the suprasystem. Given that people on both sides of a role dispute may be motivated by what they believe is good for the organization, conflict should not be resolved simply by an assertion of power. The best resolution probably involves appeal to a higher echelon of the organization's decider subsystem.

Differentiation and Integration

Roles represent differentiation within a group, organization, or society. Such differentiation, as we noted in Chapter 2, is necessary in any complex system in order to obtain the benefits of efficiency through specialization of function. But differentiation engenders parochial attitudes within the system. People and groups become identified with their roles, often forming new living systems around those roles. This leads to conflicts of values, purposes, and goals.

In order to counter the conflict-generating side effects of differentiation, organizations must provide various means of integrating the components of the system into a well-coordinated unit. These means of integration include (1) assigning linking-pin roles that bridge two or more subunits, (2) incorporating both functional and product responsibilities in roles, (3) employing joint committees in planning and problem solving, (4) assigning people to serve as troubleshooters and boundary spanners, and (5) emphasizing superordinate goals of the organization and designing reward systems accordingly. As a general principle, these means of integration involve setting up auxiliary channels of two-way communication, as well as providing the mutually beneficial conditions required for cooperation.

Differentiation is required for growth and elaboration of the system. It is driven by the actualization imperative, whereas integration is required for maintenance. Maintaining a proper balance of differentiation and integration does not just happen. To some extent the template can build such balance into the structure of the system, but it also requires active intervention from the decider subsystem to monitor and control the competing forces.

Values, Purposes, and Goals

Conflicts between and among values, purposes, and goals may exist at three distinct levels. First, there are conflicts within a given system engendered by differing demands of the three imperatives, by collision of innate and learned values, and by incompatibility of certain purposes and goals. Second, there are value conflicts between systems that are components of a suprasystem, such as between employees of a firm. Third, there are conflicts between systems that have no suprasystem.

Conflicts of the first kind are generally resolved by the system's hierarchy of values. Pathology occurs when the hierarchy is unable to resolve the conflict in any stable way. Neurosis and apathy may be symptoms of such unresolved conflict.

The second kind of conflict can be resolved or managed by the suprasystem. A basic strategy is to inculcate the suprasystem's own set of values and superordinate goals within all component systems, so that a common set of values may govern all behavior within the suprasystem. Successful business organizations try to teach their employees a set of corporate cultural values and to reinforce these values through example, repetition, and reward (Pascale and Athos 1981; Peters and Waterman 1982). The role assignments of group leaders, supervisors, and managers include serving as exemplars and senders of the suprasystem's values and norms. These people may also seek to resolve specific conflicts through instruction, influence, and negotiation.

It is not good for the suprasystem to try to eliminate all value differences between component systems. Some conflicts in values, purposes, and goals are required for differentiation within the suprasystem. Value differences contribute to creativity and innovation, whereas too much conformity can lead to pathologies such as groupthink (Janis 1982) and totalitarianism. As with differentiation and integration, the decider of the suprasystem must try to maintain a balance between value conflict and conformity, preserving the virtues of diversity while minimizing the loss of efficiency from overt conflict. According to Pascale and Athos (1981: 270), Ed Carlson accomplished this as CEO of United Air Lines by encouraging substantive conflict while keeping personal conflict to a minimum. His rule was: "Disagree without being disagreeable."

In the third type of value conflict there is no suprasystem to resolve the issue. The two systems may find in their differences an opportunity for exchange, in which case negotiation is the usual method of resolution. Other methods of resolving the conflict include domination through power, withdrawal, and appeal to a third party.

Negotiation. Negotiation is a joint decision-making process whereby two systems come to an agreement about their behavior toward each other. The mutually agreeable terms of their interaction form a contract, which is a template for the dyadic behavior of the systems. The negotiation process can be modeled by linking together two decision models (see Chapter 6). Each system in turn decides on an offer of terms, which motivates the other system to search for a better alternative. When one of the systems can find no better alternative, it decides to agree to the terms that the other system has already decided upon (Tracy 1985). The model of motivational interaction presented in Chapter 7 also represents the negotiation process.

Negotiation may be directed at compromise, an equitable sharing of available resources. In this case both systems decide that it is better to accept half a loaf rather than fight and perhaps lose it all. Power may be relatively equal, such that neither system can be confident of winning a battle. Overt conflict would involve resource consumption that might not be justified by the result. Negotiation toward compromise is largely devoted to exploring the values of the two systems to discover the differences that would permit a mutually beneficial exchange, as well as to determine what each system regards as an equitable division of resources.

Negotiation may also be employed to find ways in which the two systems can cooperate to increase the available resources. Used in this way, negotiation becomes a joint problem-solving process. Walton and McKersie (1965) called this process *integrative bargaining*, whereas the more traditional process of compromise was named *distributive bargaining*. The techniques involved in these two types of negotiation are different, though not necessarily at odds (Tracy and Peterson 1986). When two systems succeed in integrative bargaining, they strengthen the bonds between them because they increase the worth of their interaction.

Part of the negotiation process may also be directed at changing attitudes so that the differences are reduced. Walton and McKersie (1965) called this process *attitudinal structuring*. Besides enabling a better result from distributive or integrative bargaining, attitudinal structuring is aimed at improving the ongoing relationship between the systems. This, in itself, can be mutually satisfying, and it also increases the likelihood of cooperative implementation of the contract.

Domination. Instead of negotiating, one or both systems may seek to dominate the other through exercise of power. If one system perceives that the other has sufficient net power to make resistance too costly, the weaker system will usually submit to control of some of its behavior by the other system. Domination may not eliminate the underlying value conflicts, however, but may simply submerge them to erupt again at a later date. Furthermore, if neither system perceives itself as weak, a battle may result in which both systems lose. The costs of exercise of power were discussed in Chapter 8.

Power may also be used indirectly to support influence attempts aimed at changing the other system's attitudes and goals. This may be a one-way process, in which case it is a subtle form of domination. But influence is often a two-way process. As noted earlier, it may be an integral part of negotiation.

Figure 11–1
Dimensions of Conflict and Cooperation

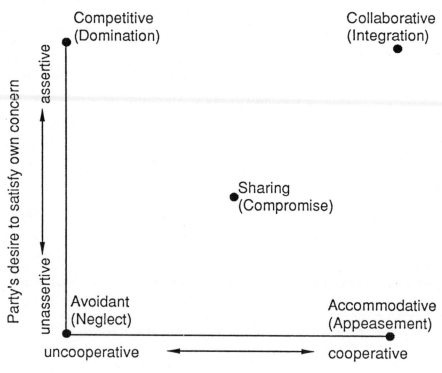

Source: From Thomas (1983: 900).

When neither system thinks it can dominate the other or sees any benefit from negotiation, the final option is for one or both to withdraw and not engage in interaction with the other. Thus the four basic options for two systems that must resolve their differences without the aid of a third party are (1) dominance and accommodation, (2) compromise, (3) cooperation, or (4) withdrawal. Thomas (1983) showed that these options result from two dimensions: concern for own benefits and for opponent's benefits from the exchange. The model representing these dimensions is shown in Figure 11-1.

Third party. A third party or system may be called upon to resolve a conflict of goals between two other systems. There are several ways in which a third party may be used. Appeal may be made to a neutral system to serve as mediator or arbitrator of the dispute, or one system may form a coalition with a third party in order to change the power balance.   Use of a third party is particularly likely when the two systems hold relatively equal power and are unable to resolve their conflict through negotiation.

Acting as a mediator, a third party simply tries to help the two systems to negotiate an agreement. A mediator may facilitate bargaining by acting as a process consultant, a go-between in communications, or a fact finder. As a consultant the mediator tries to structure or focus the negotiation process into channels that emphasize mutual benefits. When direct negotiation degenerates into distrust and recriminations, a mediator may act as a trusted messenger to restore communication between the systems. In the fact-finding role a neutral system may seek to improve the quality of information on which the disputing systems are making their decisions.

Although arbitration also involves a neutral third party, it differs from mediation in one fundamental respect. Whereas a mediator only aids the disputing systems to decide on an agreement, an arbitrator has the power to make, and sometimes to enforce, a decision for the two systems. The systems decide, in effect, to abide by the decision of the neutral party.

One might ask, "What's in it for the third party?" Mediators and arbitrators are usually paid for their services by the conflicting systems, or else are employed by a higher level system such as government, whose interest is to avoid conflict and improve cooperation among its components. When employed by the conflicting systems, neutrals are usually paid equally by both of them in order to preserve neutrality.

When a third party enters a coalition with one of two conflicting systems, on the other hand, its motive is likely to be a share of the resources acquired by its partner, or else a gain in power that may be exercised at a later date. Coalitions are usually formed to settle a dispute through domination, although they can serve simply to provide greater influence in negotiation. A coalition is, itself, a dyadic interaction in which the partners anticipate mutual satisfaction.

SUMMARY AND IMPLICATIONS

Exchange and bonding between systems are essential to all forms of life above the level of the cell. Exchange forms the basis for both cooperation and conflict. Two systems are likely to cooperate when they hold different values for resources and the net benefits of exchange are positive for both systems. If the exchange fulfills mutual needs on a continuing basis, the dyad may bond into a new living system.

Conflict occurs when two systems hold similar values for a scarce resource, such that it cannot be obtained or exchanged without net loss to one or both systems. Techniques of conflict management depend on the nature of the conflict and the power of the manager. Conflict within a system may often be managed by the system's decider, by application of its hierarchy of values, or through such techniques as emphasizing superordinate goals, designing reward systems to encourage behavior directed at organizational goals, developing integrative links within the structure of the organization, devising rules to regulate behavior, and imposing order from above when necessary. When the conflict is between the system and its components, negotiation is a useful tool, perhaps aided by intervention of a third party.

Conflict between systems of relatively equal power may consist of competitive pursuit of a goal, interference with another system's goal pursuit, or direct attack on another system. Methods of conflict management include negotiation, dominance, and appeal to a third party. Even though conflict exists with respect to some resources, it is often possible to find other exchanges between the two systems or with a third system that generate a net positive value for the dyadic relationship.

One implication of this chapter is that exchange between living systems is a very central topic for organizational behavior. It is the basis for formation of all social systems. It is linked to issues of motivation, communication, influence, cohesiveness, and cooperation; and to conflicts in roles, values, purposes, goals, perceptions, motives, power, and leadership. To understand, predict, and control organizational behavior, we need to know more about the processes of exchange between systems.

One point that should be emphasized is the fact that the potential for cooperative exchange stems from *differences* in values. That fact is codified in such conventional wisdom as "opposites attract," but we often forget it when we talk about the value of homogeneity and a common corporate culture. Some similarities, some common values and sentiments are useful, but so are the differences. Perhaps it is no coincidence that the institution of marriage is falling apart in the United States as we move toward greater equality and similarity of functions between the sexes. When each marriage partner can do everything the other can, the benefits of partnership decline and the bonds loosen.

The basis of international trade and cooperation is in the differences in natural resources, products, wage rates, infrastructures, skills, tastes, and so forth between nations. The United States and the Soviet Union want some of the same things, but the very considerable differences between the two nations offer many opportunities for mutually beneficial exchange. Such differences cause conflict only when the nations attempt to impose their values on each other. The recent thaw in relations and ratification of an arms reduction treaty may signal a recognition of that fact.

Excellent business firms find a way to differentiate themselves from their competitors. They build a better mousetrap, offer better service, establish a reputation for quality and service, generate a positive public image, attract superior employees by offering higher wages or better working conditions. They constantly search for new products and services, knowing that other firms will enter the established markets and homogenize them. By differentiating themselves from other firms, they increase the chances that their products and services will offer a mutually beneficial exchange with their customers.

Conflict is not inherently bad and cooperation is not inherently good. Opposition of values represents a potentially useful energy differential between systems. Conflict may lead to mutual destruction or to new ways of resolution that are good for both systems. Cooperation is usually beneficial to the systems involved in the exchange, but it may lead to exploitation of other systems.

Cooperation and conflict are dynamic processes stemming from tension between systems. Two systems may cooperate in some matters and compete in others at the same time. Conflict and cooperation require active *management* by the respective decider subsystems or by a suprasystem in order to extract the most beneficial consequences from the exchange.

12

New Perspectives on People and Organizations

If you have read this far without skipping anything, you must have noticed that certain themes and concepts kept repeating themselves. The imperatives of maintenance, actualization, and propagation; dynamic homeostasis and the importance of values, needs, excesses, purposes, and goals as control standards; the systems dyad and exchange between systems; conflict and cooperation; and the decider subsystem as the central coordinator are themes that pervade this book. Indeed, certain themes have been repeated so often that you may have thought I was running out of material. Actually, the repetition of themes and concepts was entirely intentional. It was meant to highlight the fact that organizational behavior is a much more closely knit field of knowledge than is commonly realized. There is also, in some cases, less to it than meets the eye.

The usual presentation of OB is a bit like viewing a partially completed picture puzzle. Several clumps of pieces have been assembled, but there are many gaps in the border and you cannot be certain that the clumps are all part of the same puzzle. In contrast I have tried to present a view of OB that is more like a completed transparent plastic scale model of the human body or of a factory and its people. Each separate topic is a different perspective on the model with a different section in the foreground, but with the other parts still visible in the background. Even this simile is not accurate, because organizational behavior is dynamic, not static. The emphasis is on process rather than structure. Thus the models should be animated.

It turns out that much of conventional OB may be represented by a relatively small number of concepts and models. The apparent proliferation of concepts is caused by specialization of knowledge and the failure to see parallels between the behavior of individuals, groups, organizations, and societies, or to perceive connections between such topics as values, motivation, learning, and leadership.

At this point I will review those concepts and models that seem to be most central to our understanding of OB. I hope you will pardon me if this seems like déjà vu, but I want to be sure that the overall picture has not been obscured by the level of detail in the preceding chapters. I will then offer a prescription for the further study of organizational behavior.

GENERAL CONCEPTS AND MODELS

The book began with a recitation of the characteristics of life. The characteristics of a living system that most clearly differentiate it from nonliving systems are:

1. the possession of a template and ability to replicate itself;
2. the ability to grow and develop its capabilities;
3. the ability to maintain a variety of steady states in the face of change both within itself and in the environment;
4. the possession of a decider subsystem able, in conjunction with other critical subsystems such as the memory and associator, to coordinate the activities of the system;
5. the holding of values that govern the choices made by the decider subsystem; and
6. the ability to act upon and influence the environment, including other living systems.

This short list is not intended to slight other important characteristics of living systems, such as their organic composition, the narrow range of environments in which they can exist, or the other critical subsystems.

From the first three numbered characteristics come the imperatives of propagation, actualization, and maintenance, respectively. It is the existence of *three* imperatives, rather than just one, that generates much of the dynamism and conflict in organizational behavior. Life would be relatively simple if organisms and organizations were born full grown, fully developed, and immortal. Then they would only have to cope with change in the environment in order to maintain themselves. But that is not the case. Change must often be generated from inside the system and steady states must be disturbed, in response to values supplied by the template or through learning. Living systems must grow and develop, reproduce and disseminate. It is part of their nature.

Characteristics 4 and 5, possession of a decider and of values, define the homcostatic nature of living systems. But the three imperatives make this a very dynamic homeostasis. Many values are subject to long-term change in accordance with the metavalues of actualization and propagation. Maintenance often requires short-term change in values in response to change in the environment. Also, of course, there is the fluctuation of values caused by the processes of consumption, extrusion, and replenishment of resources. As values change, so do the preferred target states toward which behavior is directed.

Homeostasis implies passivity, yet living systems are anything but passive in their interaction with their environments. In order to maintain conditions that are favorable for their health, living systems actively intervene in natural processes and attempt to influence other living systems. Nor are these simply reactions. Upper-level living systems, at least, try to understand and predict change in the environment in order to control or avoid it. Furthermore, they deliberately introduce change in order to "improve" the conditions under which they must live.

The existence of three different imperatives, a multiplicity of shifting values, and attempts to influence the environment, including other living systems, guarantee that living systems will encounter much conflict. I did not include conflict in the basic list of characteristics of living systems, because it is a resultant of the other characteristics. But conflict and the processes of conflict management are pervasive in organizational behavior. Any search for lasting peace and stability in relationships within or between living systems is futile. The very essence of management is dealing with conflict.

Pictures of a "best" organization structure or leadership style are dreams. Reality is that, even though organizational behavior involves homeostatic processes, it is extremely dynamic. We have begun to recognize this fact with various contingency theories, but we have difficulty in handling a sufficient number of variables at one time. Simple models are "user friendly" but, as economists discovered long ago, they run the risk of being very wrong.

Dyadic Exchange

A recurring theme of this book has been dyadic exchange between living systems. The learning of new values, communication and influence processes, performance motivation, the gathering and use of power, and leadership all involve exchange of resources between systems. Exchange is the basis of formation of bonds between systems that may culminate in the development of higher level systems. Living systems are built on mutually beneficial exchange between component systems. The exchange may be multiway, but it can be modeled by a set of dyadic relationships, keeping in mind that relations between levels are also part of the set.

A subtheme has been the idea that exchange between living systems is almost always two-way. Living systems tend to avoid interaction that holds no benefit for them. In any observed instance of behavioral interaction between living systems, investigation should first center on what is being exchanged and the worth that each system places on the traded resources. Conflict or a brief relationship can be predicted from any exchange in which one or more parties perceive an imbalance or a lack of net benefit. On the other hand a close bond may develop if the trade is fair, the resources have continuing high worth, and alternative sources are not readily available.

Another subtheme is that exchange often occurs between systems at different levels. Corporation and employee, or corporation and nation, may form a dyad just as two individuals do. The difference in level of the systems may pose problems of communication, interdependence, and power, but the exchange is still between two living systems. If the exchange is not satisfactory to both parties, the weaker system may seek to withdraw or to equalize power through formation of a coalition or a higher level system. If a stable relationship is desired between systems at different levels, it behooves the higher level system to take special consideration of the needs of the lower level system.

Those who design incentive systems might take these precepts as a starting point, keeping in mind that employees are also trying to motivate the employer. Communicators should think in terms of what their messages hold of worth to the recipients and how that worth will be perceived. If it is not worth what the communicator is asking in return, the message is likely to be ignored or rejected. (That goes for teachers and authors, as well.) Leaders must consider what benefit their leadership holds for members of the group or organization. Wise leaders often expend considerable effort on developing obligations among their followers, thereby strengthening bonds with them and storing a ready source of power. The realization that you are involved in an exchange, not a one-way process, and that all parties must benefit for the exchange to work well, will go far toward avoiding problems in communication, teaching, motivation, and leadership.

One other activity in which dyadic exchange should be emphasized is research on organizational behavior. Interaction between subjects and the researcher or observer is all too often ignored. There is some awareness of the so-called Hawthorne effect for observers, of course, and some experimenters use blind and double-blind techniques, but far too much research in OB is conducted on student groups and by means of questionnaires. The motivation of student groups to participate in a study is always suspect. They may do it for fun, in which case they may respond in unpredictable fashion; or they may participate to please the teacher, motivated to give the "right" responses. Even a double-blind experimental setup does not eliminate this sort of tacit exchange, although the subjects may incorrectly perceive "rightness."

Questionnaires provide all sorts of hidden cues as to what the researcher is looking for, cues that are both correctly and incorrectly perceived. Respondents react to these cues in various ways, depending on what they think they are getting out of the exchange. Often they perceive that they are getting nothing out of it, which may account for the usually low rate of response to questionnaire surveys. Worse yet, the responses that are received are likely to be from people who have an axe to grind or a message to send. It is little wonder that such research generally leads to results that, even if statistically significant, contradict other findings or account for less than 10 percent of the variance in outcomes. In order to make progress in testing our understanding of organizational behavior, we *must* develop better instruments and research techniques.

The Decider Problem

This book has emphasized the importance of the decider subsystem and its deficiencies. The problems of bias, distorted perceptions, and inadequate search that plague individual decision making are magnified when individuals must serve as deciders for groups, organizations, and societies. The fact that living systems must share the components of their decider subsystem with other systems creates all sorts of difficulties. Chief among them is the fact that neither the system nor its components may know from moment to moment precisely which system the components are serving. For a group or organization, obtaining the commitment of its deciders, and particularly its leader(s), may be more crucial than we have heretofore realized.

The problem of whom we serve as deciders is highlighted by research on the Prisoners' Dilemma game. In this game each player has a choice of cooperating (C) and sharing a joint payoff, or defecting (D) and possibly receiving a much larger personal payoff. The D choice results in a large payoff for the defector if the other player chooses C, but they both lose if both choose D. The payoff matrix is usually set up so that, assuming a 50/50 chance that the other will choose C, the expected payoff for D is higher than for C. Thus each player's choice centers on what he or she thinks the other will do. Will the other act for the good of the dyad (i.e., choose C) or for personal gain (D)?

Variations of the game involve iterated play versus a one-shot game, and expansion to many players. When the same dyad is involved in several rounds of the game, the parties often learn to cooperate (Axelrod 1984). The expectation that they will have to continue to interact in the future seems to lead to making choices for the good of the group, if only from fear that failure to do so will result in loss of benefits. But trust is involved. Each player must trust that the other player is committed to cooperation. A single act of defection may quickly lead to retaliation and a continuing cycle of mutual defection and loss.

Multiple players make the choice more difficult, in one sense, because more people must be trusted. A multiplayer game is usually set up so that, if one or a few players defect, they fare better than the cooperators. If all cooperate, they each receive a payoff larger than if they all defect, but a single defector would receive a much larger payoff and lower the payoff for everyone else. Many real situations in groups and organizations have these characteristics.

Hofstadter (1985: 740–51) conducted an ad hoc game of this sort with twenty players. If they all cooperated they would each receive $57; if they all defected each would be paid $19. But if one person defected, the defector would receive $95 and the others only $54 each, and so on. In his letter to the players Hofstadter emphasized that they were all rational people and that they should make a rational choice. He reasoned that, if they all assumed the others were rational, they would further assume that all would make the same play. In that case, all choosing C and receiving $57 each is clearly better than all choosing D and receiving $19 each. In fact, however, fourteen presumably rational people chose D and six chose C. Their stated reasons boiled down to the facts that either they did not trust others to be rational or they did not accept their role as part of a group and therefore made an individual choice.

What does this story tell us about the ability of individuals to act as part of the decider subsystem for a group? It tells us that people, or Americans at least, are too prone to think only of their own good. (Hofstadter speculated that his results might have been different with a Japanese sample.) They do not trust the commitment of their fellow players to the common good, perhaps because they do not trust their own commitment. Consequently, they contribute to fouling the nest that they all must live in. The majority choose to litter, pollute, exceed the speed limit, waste energy, ignore recycling, loaf on the job, not vote in elections, and so forth because they do not perceive their own decisions as being part of the decision-making process of the groups, organizations, and society to which they belong. As a society—and worse, as a democracy—we have failed to teach good citizenship.

Our people do not realize that the social systems on which they depend require their commitment. Consequently, those social systems are ill and dying at a phenomenal rate. Indicators include the high rate of failure of small businesses; loss of markets by large firms, particularly in areas of heavy international competition; failure of military operations such as the attempted rescue of hostages in Iran; the difficulty experienced by NASA in launching a rocket without mishap; billion- and trillion-dollar cost overruns on defense contracts; the inability of our government to stop drug trafficking and the failure of individual addicts or their friends to stop them from killing themselves with drugs; suffocating litigation caused both by failure to perform and by greedy litigants and attorneys; repeated failure to pass school levies and the consequent inadequate preparation of our youth; refusal of sports stars to play because a few million dollars isn't enough; and the high rate of divorce, depriving many children of a proper upbringing because their parents can't curb their own appetites for other sex partners or a completely compliant and compatible spouse. These societal ills are not going to get better unless and until we begin to realize that we each have a responsibility to the social systems of which we are members and decider-subsystem components.

Axelrod (1984) has shown that cooperation is possible, even on decisions of the form of the Prisoner's Dilemma, if we can develop mutual trust and a sense of commitment to the common good. But how do we learn this sense of citizenship, of being part of the decider to the group or society, when our families, schools, newspapers, religious and other institutions are a shambles? What can the study of organizational behavior contribute to solving the problem?

PRESCRIPTIONS

The admonition, "physician, heal thyself!" applies not only to individuals but also to all higher levels of living systems. If the ills of society are to be cured, we must look to those who purport to study or "fix" social systems. Social psychologists, sociologists, anthropologists, organizational behaviorists, and political scientists are the "medical research team" for groups, organizations, and societies. They study the parameters of healthy systems and classify the pathologies of sick ones. Teachers, managers, consultants, and politicians are the physicians. They use the knowledge supplied by research and experience to diagnose illness and to prescribe for or operate upon the patient.

Medical knowledge has advanced rapidly in the last few decades. Thanks in part to the development of new instruments such as the electron microscope, fiber optics, and computer-processed X-ray and ultrasound scanners, we know much more about the functioning of both healthy and sick bodies. A great amount of money has been poured into the development of these instruments and their use in finding cures for illnesses such as cancer and heart disease.

Meanwhile, research on instruments to measure the health of social systems and on study of the pathologies of those systems has been starved for funds. The same societal mechanisms that favor individual decision making over commitment to social systems has governed the allocation of time, energy, and money to medical research rather than social research. Social researchers have fallen back on convenience samples and questionnaires for lack of time and money to develop or employ more elaborate techniques. It is as if we were still in the dark ages of medicine, when the only data a doctor had to go on were a pulse rate, the feeling of the forehead, and the complaints of the patient. Lack of good, objective data on social behavior has left a clear field for academic charlatans, quack consultants, and political hacks, who trumpet faulty research findings and sell phony nostrums and panaceas to unsuspecting corporations and governments.

If people realize that most of their social institutions are sick, and *if* they accept that the health of these institutions is as important as their own health (indeed, that their own health is partly dependent on the health of their social systems), and *if* they understand that something can be done about it, then a cure is possible. But it will not come quickly or cheaply, any more than the search for a cancer cure has been quick and cheap.

Millions of dollars will have to be spent, first, on developing better instruments and training better researchers and, second, on employing them to learn more about the healthy functioning and pathologies of groups, organizations, and societies. Throwing money at the problems will not cure them, but failure to throw money will guarantee that nobody looks for a cure. Research funds not only buy groceries for researchers and their families, but also signal that, as a society, we have finally realized the importance of the health of our social systems.

Judging from our experience with medical research, cures for our social ills will require decades even if the commitment is there. For the most part we do not have the necessary instruments on hand and will have to develop them from scratch. The kinds of research tools we need are those that obtain objective data without interfering with the processes they are measuring, or else record both sides of the interaction. I suspect that audio and video recorders and computers will figure prominently in these instruments. Techniques are already available for processing a video image in such a way as to elicit objective data about interactions, but they are time consuming and have not been employed in social research, as far as I am aware. Much more difficult will be the development of instruments to measure people's thoughts and attitudes. It will be somewhat easier to measure organizational attributes such as communication flow and culture.

We have a substantial body of theory on which to develop testable hypotheses, once the instruments are available, but a lot of research will be needed just to sort the wheat from the chaff among these theories. It is my hope that this book may aid the process of sifting, even though I have not followed Miller (1978) in stating a large number of cross-level hypotheses. Miller's work will probably be more useful in generating ideas for ethological inquiry.

Finally, even after better knowledge about social system processes becomes available, it will require many years to disseminate this knowledge to the practitioners of the social healing arts. Just as physicians become obsolescent if they don't keep up with the medical journals, so managers and politicians will fall behind if they don't follow the latest research findings (assuming that the research is of good quality). Most such practitioners do not currently keep up with the literature, but they can be excused on the grounds that so much of it is irrelevant or contrary to experience. If we ever do develop a science of social systems, managers and politicians will have to become more professional about their craft. For now I can only prescribe that they understand the importance of their role as deciders for other living systems, that they take the role seriously, and that they try to maintain commitment to those systems.

References

Acar, W. 1984. What's a problem?—A summary. *Proceedings of the 1984 annual conference*. Atlanta: American Institute for Decision Sciences.

Ackoff, R. L. 1962. *Scientific method*. New York: Wiley.

———. 1978. *The art of problem solving*. New York: Wiley.

Ackoff, R. L., and F. E. Emery. 1972. *On purposeful systems*. Chicago: Aldine-Atherton.

Adams, J. S. 1963. Toward an understanding of inequity. *Journal of Abnormal and Social Psychology* 67:422-36.

———. 1965. Inequity in social exchange. In L. Berkowitz (Ed.), *Advances in experimental social psychology*, Vol. 2, 267-99. New York: Academic Press.

Alderfer, C. P. 1969. An empirical test of a new theory of human needs. *Organizational Behavior and Human Performance* 4:142-75.

———. 1972. *Existence, relatedness, and growth: human needs in organizational settings*. New York: Free Press.

Arkes, H. R., and K. R. Hammond (Eds.). 1985. *Judgment and decision making: an interdisciplinary reader*. Cambridge: Cambridge University Press.

Ashmos, D. P., and G. P. Huber. 1987. The systems paradigm: correcting the record and suggesting the future. *Academy of Management Review* 12:607-21.

Atkinson, J. W. (Ed.) 1958. *Motives in fantasy, action, and society*. Princeton, NJ: Van Nostrand.

Atkinson, J. W. 1964. *An introduction to motivation*. Princeton, NJ: Van Nostrand.

Axelrod, R. 1984. *The evolution of cooperation*. New York: Basic Books.

Bales, R. F., and P. E. Slater. 1955. Role differentiation in small decision-making groups. In T. Parsons et al. (Eds.), *Family, socialization, and interaction processes*, 259-306. New York: Free Press.

Bandura, A. 1986. *Social foundations of thought and action: a social cognitive theory*. Englewood Cliffs, NJ: Prentice-Hall.

Barash, D. 1979. *The whisperings within*. New York: Harper & Row.

Barnard, C. I. 1938. *The functions of the executive*. Cambridge, MA: Harvard University Press.

———. 1946. The nature of leadership. In S. D. Hoslett (Ed.), *Human factors in management*. New York: McGraw-Hill.

Bass, B. M. 1960. *Leadership, psychology, and organizational behavior*. New York: Harper.

————. 1981. *Stogdill's handbook of leadership*. New York: Free Press.

Bass, B. M., and E. R. Valenzi. 1974. Contingent aspects of effective management styles. In J. G. Hunt and L. L. Larson (Eds.), *Contingency approaches to leadership*, 130-52. Carbondale, IL: Southern Illinois University Press.

Beach, L. R., and T. R. Mitchell. 1978. A contingency model for the selection of decision strategies. *Academy of Management Review* 3: 439-49.

Beckhard, R. 1969. *Organization development: strategies and models*. Reading, MA: Addison-Wesley.

Berelson, B., and G. A. Steiner. 1964. *Human behavior: an inventory of scientific findings*. New York: Harcourt Brace and World.

Berne, E. 1964. *Games people play*. New York: Grove Press.

Bierstedt, R. 1950. An analysis of social power. *American Sociological Review* 15:730-38.

Blake, R., and J. S. Mouton. 1964. *The managerial grid*. Houston: Gulf.

Blau, P. M. 1964. *Exchange and power in social life*. New York: Wiley.

Borg, W. R. 1957. The behavior of emergent and designated leaders in situational tests. *Sociometry* 20:95-104.

Brayfield, A. H., and W. H. Crockett. 1955. Employee attitudes and employee performance. *Psychological Bulletin* 52:396-424.

Brehmer, B. 1969. Cognitive dependence on additive and configural cue-criterion relations. *The American Journal of Psychology* 32:490-503.

Burns, J. M. 1978. *Leadership*. New York: Harper & Row.

Campbell, J. P., M. D. Dunnette, E. E. Lawler, III, and K. E. Weick, Jr. 1970. *Managerial behavior, performance, and effectiveness*. New York: McGraw-Hill.

Campbell, J. P., and R. D. Pritchard. 1983. Motivation theory in industrial and organizational psychology. In M. D. Dunnette (Ed.), *Handbook of industrial and organizational psychology*, 63-130. New York: Wiley.

Carrell, M. R., and J. E. Dittrich. 1978. Equity theory: the recent literature, methodological considerations, and new directions. *Academy of Management Review* 3:202-10.

Carroll, S. J., and H. L. Tosi. 1973. *Management by objectives: applications and research*. New York: Macmillan.

Cartwright, D. (Ed.). 1959. *Studies in social power*. Ann Arbor: University of Michigan, Institute for Social Research.

Cattell, R. B. 1957. A mathematical model for the leadership role and other personality-role relations. In M. Sherif and M. Wilson (Eds.), *Emerging problems in social psychology*. Norman: University of Oklahoma.

Checkland, P. B. 1981. *Systems thinking, systems practice*. New York: Wiley.

Christensen-Szalanski, J. J. 1980. A further examination of the selection of problem-solving strategies: the effects of deadlines and analytical aptitudes. *Organizational Behavior and Human Performance* 25:107-22.

Connolly, T. 1976. Some conceptual and methodological issues in expectancy models of work performance motivation. *Academy of Management Review* 1:37-47.

Connolly, T., E. J. Conlon, and S. J. Deutsch. 1980. Organizational effectiveness: a multiple-constituency approach. *Academy of Management Review* 5:211-17.

Cunningham, J. B. 1977. Approaches to the evaluation of organizational effectiveness. *Academy of Management Review* 2:463-74.

————. 1978. A systems-resource approach for evaluating organizational effectiveness. *Human Relations* 31:631-56.

Cyert, R. M., and J. G. March. 1963. *A behavioral theory of the firm.* Englewood Cliffs, NJ: Prentice-Hall.

Dachler, H. P., and W. H. Mobley. 1973. Construct validation of an instrumentality-expectancy-task-goal model of mork motivation. *Journal of Applied Psychology Monograph* 58:397-418.

Daft, R. L. 1986. *Organization theory and design,* 2nd ed. St. Paul: West.

Dahl, R. A. 1957. The concept of power. *Behavioral Science* 2:201-15.

Davis, T.R.V., and F. Luthans. 1980. A social learning approach to organizational behavior. *Academy of Management Review* 5:281-90.

Dawkins, R. L. 1976. *The selfish gene.* New York: Oxford.

Deal, T. E., and A. A. Kennedy. 1982. *Corporate cultures.* Reading, MA: Addison-Wesley.

Delbecq, A. L., A. H. Van de Ven, and D. H Gustafson. 1975. *Group techniques for program planning: a guide to nominal group and Delphi processes.* Glenview, IL: Scott, Foresman.

Downey, H. K., J. E. Sheridan, and J. W. Slocum, Jr. 1975. Analysis of relationships among leader behavior, subordinate job performance and satisfaction: a path goal approach. *Academy of Management Journal* 18:253-62.

Drexler, K. E. 1986. *Engines of creation.* Garden City, NY: Anchor Press.

Driver, M. J., and S. Streufert. 1969. Integrative complexity: an approach to individuals and groups as information-processing systems. *Administrative Science Quarterly* 14:272-85.

Dudycha, L., and J. C. Naylor. 1966a. Characteristics of human inference process in complex choice behavior situations. *Organizational Behavior and Human Performance* 1:110-28.

————. 1966b. The effect of variations in the cue R matrix upon the obtained policy equation of judges. *Educational and Psychological Measurement* 26:583-603.

Ebert, R. J., and T. R. Mitchell. 1975. *Organizational decision processes.* New York: Crane, Russak and Co.

Ekeh, P. P. 1974. *Social exchange theory.* Cambridge, MA: Harvard University Press.

Emory, C. W., and P. Niland. 1968. *Making management decisions.* Boston: Houghton-Mifflin.

Evans, M. G. 1970. The effects of supervisory behavior on the path-goal relationship. *Organizational Behavior and Human Performance* 5:277-98.

Ferris, G. R., T. A. Beehr, and D. C. Gilmore. 1978. Social facilitation: a review and alternative conceptual model. *Academy of Management Review* 3:338-47.

Fiedler, F. E. 1967. *A theory of leadership effectiveness.* New York: McGraw-Hill.

————. 1978. The contingency model and the dynamics of the leadership process. In L. Berkowitz (Ed.), *Advances in experimental social psychology,* Vol. 11. New York: Academic Press.

Field, R. H. G. 1979. A critique of the Vroom-Yetton contingency model of leadership behavior. *Academy of Management Review* 4:249-57.

Filley, A. C., R. J. House, and S. Kerr. 1976. *Managerial process and organizational behavior,* 2nd ed. Glenview, IL: Scott, Foresman.

Fleishman, E. A. 1953. The description of supervisory behavior. *Journal of Applied Psychology* 37:1-6.

—————. 1957. The leadership opinion questionnaire. In R. M. Stogdill and A. E. Coons (Eds.), *Leader behavior: its description and measurement*, 120-33. Columbus: Ohio State University.

Foster, D. 1975. *The intelligent universe*. New York: Putnam's Sons.

French, J. R. P., and B. Raven. 1959. The bases of social power. In D. Cartwright (Ed.), *Studies in social power*, 150-67. Ann Arbor: University of Michigan.

Friedlander, F., and S. Greenberg. 1971. Effect of job attitudes, training, and organizational climate on performance of the hard-core unemployed. *Journal of Applied Psychology* 55:287-95.

Galbraith, J. K. 1952. *American capitalism: the concept of countervailing power*. Boston: Houghton Mifflin.

—————. 1983. *The anatomy of power*. Boston: Houghton Mifflin.

Galbraith, J., and L. L. Cummings. 1967. An empirical investigation of the motivational determinants of task performance: interactive effects between instrumentality-valence and motivation-ability. *Organizational Behavior and Human Performance* 2:237-57.

Georgopoulos, B. S., G. M. Mahoney, and N. W. Jones. 1957. A path-goal approach to productivity. *Journal of Applied Psychology* 41:345-53.

Graeff, C. L. 1983. The situational leadership theory: a critical review. *Academy of Management Review* 8:285-91.

Graen, G. 1969. Instrumentality theory of work motivation. *Journal of Applied Psychology Monograph* 53:1-25.

Graen, G., D. Alvares, J. B. Orris, and J. Martella. 1970. The contingency model of leadership effectiveness: antecedent and evidential results. *Psychological Bulletin* 74:285-95.

Hackman, J. R., and G. R. Oldham. 1980. *Work redesign*. Reading, MA: Addison-Wesley.

Hall, D. T., and K. E. Nougaim. 1968. An examination of Maslow's need hierarchy in an organizational setting. *Organizational Behavior and Human Performance* 3:12-35.

Halpin, A. W., and B. J. Winer. 1957. A factorial study of the leader behavior descriptions. In R. M. Stogdill and A. E. Coons (Eds.), *Leader behavior: its description and measurement*, 39-51. Columbus: Ohio State University.

Hammond, K. R., C. J. Hursch, and F. J. Todd. 1964. Analyzing the components of clinical inference. *Psychological Review* 71:438-56.

Hammond, K. R., T. R. Stewart, B. Brehmer, and D. O. Steinmann. 1975. Social judgment theory. In M. F. Kaplan and S. Schwartz (Eds.), *Human judgment and decision processes*, 271-312. New York: Academic Press.

Hammond, K. R., and D. A. Summers. 1965. Cognitive dependence on linear and nonlinear cues. *Psychological Review* 72:215-24.

Hamner, W. C., and D. W. Organ. 1978. *Organizational behavior: an applied psychological approach*. Dallas: Business Publications.

Harsanyi, J. C. 1962. Measurement of social power, opportunity costs, and the theory of two-person bargaining games. *Behavioral Science* 7:67-80.

Hayek, F. A. 1978. *The three sources of human values*. London: London School of Economics and Political Science.

Hemphill, J. K., and A. E. Coons. 1957. Development of the Leader Behavior Description Questionnaire. In R. M. Stogdill and A. E. Coons (Eds.), *Leader behavior: its description and measurement*, 6-38. Columbus: Ohio State University.

Heneman, H. G., III, and D. P. Schwab. 1972. Evaluation of research on expectancy theory predictions of employee performance. *Psychological Bulletin* 78:1-9

Hersey, P., and K. H. Blanchard. 1969. Life cycle theory of leadership. *Training and Development Journal* 23:26-34.

Herzberg, F. 1966. *Work and the nature of man*. Cleveland: World.

Herzberg, F., B. Mausner, R. O. Peterson, and D. F. Capwell. 1957. *Job attitudes: review of research and opinion*. Pittsburg: Psychological Services of Pittsburg.

Herzberg, F., B. Mausner, and B. B. Snyderman. 1959. *The motivation to work*. New York: Wiley.

Hodge, B. J., and W. P. Anthony. 1979. *Organization theory: an environmental approach*. Boston: Allyn and Bacon.

Hofstadter, D. R. 1985. *Metamagical themas*. New York: Basic Books.

Hollander, E. P. 1964. *Leaders, groups, and influence*. New York: Oxford.

————. 1978. *Leadership dynamics*. New York: Free Press.

Hollander, E. P., and J. W. Julian. 1969. Contemporary trends in the analysis of leadership processes. *Psychological Bulletin* 71:387-97.

Homans, G. C. 1958. Social behavior as exchange. *American Journal of Sociology* 63:597-606.

House, R. J. 1971. A path goal theory of leader effectiveness. *Administrative Science Quarterly* 16:321-38.

House, R. J., and G. Dessler. 1974. The path goal theory of leadership: some post hoc and a priori tests. In J. G. Hunt and L. L. Larson (Eds.), *Contingency approaches to leadership*, 29-59. Carbondale: Southern Illinois University Press.

House, R. J., and T. R. Mitchell. 1974. Path goal theory of leadership. *Journal of Contemporary Business* 3(4):81-97.

House, R. J., R. S. Schuler, and E. Levanoni. 1983. Role conflict and ambiguity scales: reality or artifacts? *Journal of Applied Psychology* 68:334-37.

House, R. J., and L. A. Wigdor. 1967. Herzberg's dual-factor theory of job satisfaction and motivation: a review of the evidence and a criticism. *Personnel Psychology* 20:369-89.

Hulin, C. L., and M. R. Blood. 1968. Job enlargement, individual differences, and worker responses. *Psychological Bulletin* 69:41-55.

Hull, C. L. 1943. *Principles of behavior*. New York: Appleton-Century-Crofts.

Ivancevich, J. M., and M. T. Matteson. 1980. *Stress at work: a managerial perspective*. Glenview, IL: Scott, Foresman.

Jago, A. G., and V. H. Vroom. 1980. An evaluation of two alternatives to the Vroom/Yetton normative model. *Academy of Management Journal* 23:347-55.

James, L. R., W. F. Joyce, and J. W. Slocum, Jr. 1988. Comment: organizations do not cognize. *Academy of Management Review* 13:129-32.

Janis, I. L. 1982. *Groupthink*, 2nd ed. Boston: Houghton Mifflin.

Jennings, E. E. 1960. *An anatomy of leadership*. New York: McGraw-Hill.

Johnson, T. W., and J. Stinson. 1975. Role ambiguity, role conflict, and satisfaction: moderating effects of individual differences. *Journal of Applied Psychology* 60:329-33.

Jones, E. E., K. J. Gergen, and R. E. Jones. 1963. Tactics of ingratiation among leaders and subordinates in a status hierarchy. *Psychological Monographs* 77(3):No. 566.

Kahn, R. L., D. M. Wolfe, R. P. Quinn, J. D. Snoek, and R. A. Rosenthal. 1964. *Organizational stress: studies in role conflict and ambiguity.* New York: Wiley.

Kaplan, M. F., and S. Schwartz. 1975. *Human judgment and decision processes.* New York: Academic Press.

Katz, D., N. Maccoby, and N. C. Morse. 1950. *Productivity, supervision, and morale in an office situation.* Ann Arbor: University of Michigan.

Katz, D., N. Maccoby, G. Gurin, and L. Floor. 1951. *Productivity, supervision, and morale among railroad workers.* Ann Arbor: University of Michigan.

Katz, D., and R. L. Kahn. 1966. *The social psychology of organizations.* New York: Wiley.

———. 1978. *The social psychology of organizations*, 2nd ed. New York: Wiley.

Kaufman, H. 1985. *Time, chance, and organizations.* Chatham, NJ: Chatham House.

Keely, M. 1978. A social-justice approach to organizational evaluation. *Administrative Science Quarterly* 23:272-92.

Kepner, C. H., and B. B. Tregoe. 1965. *The rational manager.* New York: McGraw-Hill.

Kerr, S., and J. M. Jermier. 1978. Substitutes for leadership. *Organizational Behavior and Human Performance* 22:375-403.

Kleinmuntz, B. 1968. The processing of clinical information by man and machine. In B. Kleinmuntz (Ed.), *Formal representation of human judgment*, ch. 6. New York: Wiley.

Krech, D., and R. S. Crutchfield. 1948. *Theory and problems of social psychology.* New York: McGraw-Hill.

Latham, G. P., and T. P. Steele. 1983. The motivational effects of participation versus goal setting on performance. *Academy of Management Journal* 26:406-17.

Latham, G. P., and G. A. Yukl. 1975. A review of research on the application of goal setting in organizations. *Academy of Management Journal* 18:824-45.

Lawler, E. E., III. 1973. *Motivation in work organizations.* Monterey, CA: Brooks/Cole.

Lawrence, P. R., and J. W. Lorsch. 1969. *Organization and environment.* Homewood, IL: Irwin.

Lederer, K. 1980. Introduction. In K. Lederer (Ed.), *Human needs*, 1-14. Cambridge, MA: Oelgeschlager, Gunn & Hain.

Lee, J. A. 1980. *The gold and the garbage in management theories and prescriptions.* Athens: Ohio University Press.

Lehr, L. W. 1980. How 3M develops entrepreneurial spirit throughout the organization. *Management Review* 69(10):31.

Lewin, K. 1951. *Field theory in social science.* New York: Harper.

Lewin, K., and R. Lippitt. 1938. An experimental approach to the study of autocracy and democracy: a preliminary note. *Sociometry* 1:292-300.

Likert, R. 1961. *New patterns of management.* New York: McGraw-Hill.

———. 1967. *The human organization.* New York: McGraw-Hill.

Locke, E. A. 1968. Toward a theory of task motivation and incentives. *Organizational Behavior and Human Performance* 3:157-89.

———. 1978. The ubiquity of the technique of goal setting in theories of and approaches to employee motivation. *Academy of Management Review* 3:594-601.

Locke, E. A., G. P. Latham, and M. Erez. 1988. The determinants of goal commitment. *Academy of Management Review* 13:23-39.

MacKinnon, N. J. 1978. Role strain: an assessment of a measure and its invariance of factor structure across studies. *Journal of Applied Psychology* 63:321-28.

Mahoney, T. A. 1961. *Building the executive team*. Englewood Cliffs, NJ: Prentice-Hall.

March, J. G., and H. A. Simon. 1958. *Organizations*. New York: Wiley.

Marrow, A. J., D. G. Bowers, and S. E. Seashore. 1967. *Management by participation*. New York: Harper & Row.

Maslow, A. H. 1943. A theory of human motivation. *Psychological Review* 50:370-96.

———. 1970. *Motivation and personality*, 2nd ed. New York: Harper & Row.

McAllister, D. W., T. R. Mitchell, and L. R. Beach. 1979. The contingency model for the selection of decision strategies: an empirical test of the effects of significance, accountability, reversibility. *Organizational Behavior and Human Performance* 24:228-44.

McClelland, D. C. 1961. *The achieving society*. Princeton: Van Nostrand.

Mechanic, D. 1964. Sources of power of lower participants in complex organizations. In W. Cooper, R. Leavitt, and M. Shelly, II (Eds.), *New perspectives in organization research*, Chap. 4. New York: Wiley.

Mento, A. J., R. P. Steele, and R. J. Karren. 1987. A meta-analytic study of the effects of goal setting on task performance: 1966-1984. *Organizational Behavior and Human Decision Processes* 39:52-83.

Merker, S. L. 1983. Living systems processes: nineteen more or less. In G. E. Lasker (Ed.), *The relation between major world problems and systems learning*, 233-36. Seaside, CA: Intersystems Publications.

Miller, J. G. 1978. *Living systems*. New York: McGraw-Hill.

Mintzberg, H. 1973. *The nature of managerial work*. New York: Harper & Row.

Mitchell, T. R. 1974. Expectancy models of job satisfaction, occupational preference and effort: a theoretical, methodological and empirical appraisal. *Psychological Bulletin* 81:1053-77.

———. 1979. Organizational behavior. *Annual Review of Psychology* 30:243-81.

———. 1982. Expectancy-value models in organizational psychology. In N. Feather (Ed.), *Expectations and actions: expectancy-value models in psychology*, 293-312. Hillsdale, NJ: Lawrence Erlbaum Associates.

Mitroff, I. I. 1983. *Stakeholders of the organizational mind*. San Francisco: Jossey-Bass.

Murray, H. A. 1938. *Explorations in personality*. New York: Oxford.

Myers, S. C. 1984. Financial theory and financial strategy. *Interfaces* 14(1):126-37.

Oparin, A. I. 1957. *The origin of life on the earth*, 3rd ed. New York: Academic Press.

Osborn, A. F. 1957. *Applied imagination*. New York: Scribner.

Osborn, R. N., J. G. Hunt, and D. J. Skaret. 1977. Managerial influence in a complex configuration with two unit heads. *Human Relations* 30:1025-38.

Ouchi, W. G. 1981. *Theory Z: how American business can meet the Japanese challenge*. Reading, MA: Addison-Wesley.

Parnes, S. J. 1964. Research on developing creative behavior. In C. W. Taylor (Ed.), *Widening horizons in creativity*, 145-69. New York: Wiley.

Pascale, R., and A. Athos. 1981. *The art of Japanese management*. New York: Warner Books.

Peters, T. J., and R. H. Waterman, Jr. 1982. *In search of excellence*. New York: Harper & Row.

Peterson, C. R., K. R. Hammond, and D. A. Summers. 1965a. Multiple probability learning with shifting weights and cues. *American Journal of Psychology* 78:660-63.

————. 1965b. Optimal responding in multiple-cue probability learning. *Journal of Experimental Psychology* 70:270-76.

Pfeffer, J. 1981. *Power in organizations*. Cambridge, MA: Ballinger.

Pfeffer, J., and G. R. Salancik. 1978. *The external control of organizations: a resource dependence perspective*. New York: Harper & Row.

Pickens, T. B., Jr. 1988. The restructuring of corporate America. *Mid-American Journal of Business*, 3(1):3-5.

Porter, L. W. 1962. Job attitudes in management: I. perceived deficiencies in need fulfillment as a function of job level. *Journal of Applied Psychology* 46:375-84.

Porter, L. W., and E. E. Lawler, III. 1968. *Managerial attitudes and performance*. Homewood, IL: Irwin.

Porter, L. W., E. E. Lawler, III, and J. R. Hackman. 1975. *Behavior in organizations*. New York: McGraw-Hill.

Price, J. L. 1972. The study of organizational effectiveness. *The Sociological Quarterly* 13:3-15.

Quinn, R. E., and J. Rohrbaugh. 1983. A spatial model of effectiveness criteria. *Management Science* 29:363-77.

Raia, A. P. 1974. *Managing by objectives*. Glenview, IL: Scott, Foresman.

Reddin, W. J. 1970. *Managerial effectiveness*. New York: McGraw-Hill.

Redding, W. C. 1972. *Communication within the organization*. New York: Industrial Communication Council.

Rist, G. 1980. Basic questions about basic human needs. In K. Lederer (Ed.), *Human needs*, pp. 223-53. Cambridge, MA: Oelgeschlager, Gunn & Hain.

Rizzo, J. R., R. J. House, and S. I. Lirtzman. 1970. Role conflict and ambiguity in complex organizations. *Administrative Science Quarterly* 15:150-63.

Rush, J. H. 1957. *The dawn of life*. Garden City, NY: Hanover House.

Salancik, G. R., and J. Pfeffer. 1977. An examination of need satisfaction models of job attitudes. *Administrative Science Quarterly* 22:427-56.

————. 1978. A social information processing approach to job attitudes and task design. *Administrative Science Quarterly* 23:224-53.

Schriesheim, C. A., and S. Kerr. 1977. Theories and measures of leadership: a critical appraisal of present and future directions. In J. G. Hunt and L. L. Larson (Eds.), *Leadership: the cutting edge*. Carbondale: Southern Illinois University Press.

Schriesheim, C. A., and R. M. Stogdill. 1975. Differences in factor structure across three versions of the Ohio State leadership scales. *Personnel Psychology* 28:189-206.

Schriesheim, C. A., and M. A. Von Glinow. 1977. The path-goal theory of leadership: a theoretical and empirical analysis. *Academy of Management Journal* 20:398-405.

Scott, W. R. 1981. *Organizations: rational, natural and open systems*. Englewood Cliffs, NJ: Prentice-Hall.

Selye, H. 1956. *The stress of life*. New York: McGraw-Hill.

Selznick, P. 1957. *Leadership in administration: a sociological interpretation*. Evanston, IL: Row, Peterson.

Shaw, M. E. 1971. *Group dynamics: the psychology of small group behavior*. New York: McGraw-Hill.

Siciński, A. 1978. The concepts of "need" and "value" in the light of the systems approach. *Social Science Information* 17:71-91.

Simon, H. A. 1957. *Models of man*. New York: Wiley.

———. 1962. The architecture of complexity. *Proceedings of the American Philosophical Society* 106:467-82.

Skinner, B. F. 1938. *The behavior of organisms*. New York: Appleton-Century-Crofts.

———. 1953. *Science and human behavior*. New York: Macmillan.

Slovic, P., D. Fleissner, and W. S. Bauman. 1972. Analyzing the use of information in investment decision making. *Journal of Business* 45: 283-301.

Smircich, L. 1983. Concepts of culture and organizational analysis. *Administrative Science Quarterly*, 28:339-358.

Spitz, R. A. 1945. Hospitalism: an inquiry into the genesis of psychiatric conditions in early childhood. *Psychoanalytic Study of the Child* 1:53-74.

Steers, R. M., and L. W. Porter. 1974. The role of task-goal attributes in employee performance. *Psychological Bulletin* 81:434-52.

Stinson, J. E., and T. W. Johnson. 1975. The path-goal theory of leadership: a partial test and suggested refinement. *Academy of Management Journal* 18:242-52.

Stinson, J. E., and L. Tracy. 1974. Some disturbing characteristics of the LPC score. *Personnel Psychology* 24:477-85.

Stogdill, R. M. 1963. *Manual for the Leader Behavior Description Questionnaire-Form XII*. Columbus: Ohio State University.

Stogdill, R. M., and A. E. Coons (Eds.). 1957. *Leader behavior: its description and measurement*. Columbus: Ohio State University.

Stogdill, R. M., R. J. Wherry, and W. E. Jaynes. 1953. *Patterns of leader behavior: a factorial study of navy officer performance*. Columbus: Ohio State University.

Stoner, J.A.F. 1961. A comparison of individual and group decisions involving risk. Masters thesis, Massachusetts Institute of Technology.

Summers, D. A. 1969. Adaptation to change in multiple probability tasks. *American Journal of Psychology* 82:235-40.

Szilagyi, A. D., and H. P. Sims. 1974. An exploration of the path-goal theory of leadership in a health care environment. *Academy of Management Journal* 17:622-34.

Tannenbaum, A. S., and J. G. Bachman. 1966. Attitude uniformity and role in a voluntary organization. *Human Relations* 19:309-23.

Tannenbaum, R., and W. H. Schmidt. 1958. How to choose a leadership pattern. *Harvard Business Review* 36(2):95-101.

Thibaut, J. W., and H. H. Kelley. 1959. *The social psychology of groups*. New York: Wiley.

Thomas, K. W. 1983. Conflict and conflict management. In M. D. Dunnette (Ed.), *Handbook of industrial and organizational psychology*, 889-935. New York: Wiley.

Thorndike, E. L. 1911. *Animal intelligence*. New York: Macmillan.

Tolman, E. C. 1932. *Purposive behavior in animals and men*. New York: Century.

Tracy, L. 1984. A dynamic living-systems model of work motivation. *Systems Research* 1:191-203.

———. 1985. Cross-fertilization of decision theory and bargaining theory. In T. Martin (Ed.), *Proceedings, 28th annual conference, Midwest Academy of Management*, 44-48. Carbondale: Southern Illinois University.

———. 1986. Toward an improved need theory. *Behavioral Science* 31:205-18.

———. 1987. Consideration and initiating structure: basic dimensions of leader behavior? *Social Behavior and Personality* 15:21-33.

———. In press. Motivational interaction between living systems. *Systems Practice*.

Tracy, L., and T. W. Johnson. 1981. What do the role conflict and role ambiguity scales measure? *Journal of Applied Psychology* 66:464-69.

———. 1983. Measurement of role stress. *Social Behavior and Personality* 11:1-7.

Tracy, L., and R. B. Peterson. 1986. A behavioral theory of labor negotiations—how well has it aged? *Negotiation Journal* 2:93-108.

Tubbs, M. E. 1986. Goal Setting: a meta-analytic examination of the empirical evidence. *Journal of Applied Psychology* 71:474-83.

Turner, A. N., and P. R. Lawrence. 1965. *Industrial jobs and the worker*. Boston: Harvard Graduate School of Business Administration.

Venkatraman, N., and V. Ramanujam. 1986. Measurement of business performance in strategy research: a comparison of approaches. *Academy of Management Review* 11:801-14.

Vinokur, A. 1971. Review and theoretical analysis of the effects of group processes upon individual and group decisions involving risk. *Psychological Bulletin* 76:231-50.

Vroom, V. H. 1964. *Work and motivation*. New York: McGraw-Hill.

Vroom, V. H., and A. G. Jago. 1978. On the validity of the Vroom-Yetton model. *Journal of Applied Psychology* 63:151-62.

Vroom, V. H., and P. W. Yetton. 1974. *Leadership and decision making*. New York: Wiley.

Wahba, M. A., and L. G. Bridwell. 1976. Maslow reconsidered: a review of research on the need hierarchy theory. *Organizational Behavior and Human Performance* 15:212-40.

Wahba, M. A., and R. J. House. 1974. Expectancy theory in work and motivation: some logical and methodological issues. *Human Relations* 27:121-47.

Walker, O. C., Jr., and R. W. Ruekert. 1987. Marketing's role in the implementation of business strategies: a critical review and conceptual framework. *Journal of Marketing* 51(3):15-33.

Walton, R. E., and R. B. McKersie. 1965. *A behavioral theory of labor negotiations*. New York: McGraw-Hill.

Wanous, J. P., and A. Zwany. 1977. A cross-sectional test of need hierarchy theory. *Organizational Behavior and Human Performance* 18:78-97.

Wiggins, N., and P. J. Hoffman. 1968. The three models of clinical judgment. *Journal of Abnormal Psychology* 73:70-77.

Wilson, E. O. 1975. *Sociobiology: the new synthesis*. Cambridge, MA: Harvard University Press.

Winterfeldt, D. von, and W. Edwards. 1986. *Decision analysis and behavioral research*. Cambridge: Cambridge University Press.

Wright, W. F. 1979. Properties of judgment models in a financial setting. *Organizational Behavior and Human Performance* 23:73-85.

Wrong, D. H. 1968. Some problems in defining social power. *American Journal of Sociology* 73:673-81.

Yuchtman, E., and S. E. Seashore. 1967. A system resource approach to organizational effectiveness. *Administrative Science Quarterly* 12:377-95.

Index

ABOUT THE AUTHOR

LANE TRACY is a professor of management at the College of Business Administration, Ohio University, where he has taught for seventeen years. He has also taught in Malaysia and Ethiopia. He received a Ph.D. in business administration in 1971 from the University of Washington. He worked for Cooper Industries in 1981–82 under an AACSB Corporate Faculty Fellowship and has served as a consultant for several business firms and government agencies. He was the first editor-in-chief of the *Mid-American Journal of Business*, serving from 1985 to 1988.

Professor Tracy is the author or coauthor of many works on industrial relations, human resource management, research methodology, and application of living systems theory to organizational behavior. They include two books on human resource management, a monograph on collective bargaining, and articles in *Harvard Business Review*, *Journal of Applied Psychology*, *Personnel Psychology*, *California Management Review*, *Social Behavior and Personality*, *Behavioral Science*, *Systems Research*, *Negotiation Journal*, *Human Resource Management*, *Industrial Relations Journal*, *Industrial Relations*, *British Journal of Industrial Relations*, and *Industrial and Labor Relations Review*.